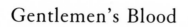

Gentlemen's Blood

Gentlemen's Blood

A HISTORY OF DUELING
FROM SWORDS AT DAWN
TO PISTOLS AT DUSK

BARBARA HOLLAND

BLOOMSBURY

Published by Bloomsbury, New York and London
Distributed to the trade by Holtzbrinck Publishers

Portions of this book originally appeared in a different form in *Smithsonian*.

Library of Congress Cataloging-in-Publication Data

Holland, Barbara.
Gentlemen's Blood: a history of dueling from swords at dawn
to pistols at dusk / Barbara Holland
    p. cm
Includes bibliographical references.
ISBN 1-58234-366-7
    1. Dueling—History. I.Title

CR4575.H65 2003
394'.8'09—dc21

2003050026

First U.S. Edition 2003

1 3 5 7 9 10 8 6 4 2

Typeset by Palimpsest Book Production Limited,
Polmont, Stirlingshire, Scotland
Printed in the United States of America
by RR Donnelley & Sons, Harrisonburg, Virginia

CONTENTS

Illustrations at Chapter Title Pages

I. "Tournament where Henri II received a fatal wound, 30th June 1559," engraving by Jacques Tortorel. Courtesy The Bridgeman Art Library.

II. Duel between the chevalier d'Eon and Monsieur de Saint Georges at Carlton House, London, engraving by Thomas Rowlandson. Courtesy Roger Viollet/Getty Images.

III. Tweedledum and Tweedledee, illustration by John Tenniel for *Through the Looking-Glass* by Lewis Carroll. Courtesy W.W.Norton & Company, Inc., New York.

IV. "A Serious Duel," *Harper's New Monthly Magazine*, March 1887. Courtesy Cornell University Library, Making of America Digital Collection.

V. "The Fortunate Duelist." Courtesy Hulton Archive/Getty Images.

VI. "The Duel between Burr and Hamilton." Courtesy Culver Pictures.

VII. Stephen Decatur, 1779–1820, steel engraving after painting by Alonzo Chappel. Courtesy Library of Congress.

VIII. "Sunday Amusements at New Orleans – Duel at the

Le Tournoy ou le Roy Henry ii. fut blessé a mort le dernier de Juin. 1559.

I. THE FORMATIVE YEARS

I F, IN A bar, someone offends you, and you wheel and knock him off his barstool, and he snatches up a chair and comes after you, this is simply a fight, or brawl, and the bouncer will break it up and throw you both out. But if, as is still the custom in punctilious places, you invite the villain out to the parking lot ("I had to ask him outside," you report later, ruefully but pridefully), and some of your friends and some of his come along to hold your coats and see fair play, and you fight there, this is a duel. A duel with challenge and acceptance, meeting grounds and seconds. A duel in its final degraded, vestigial form, fought with fists instead of rapiers, but hard to kill off, deeply ingrained in social life, with a thousand years of history.

Every parent of sons knows that human males, like the sons of

1

many another mammal, have a strong, intractable, evolutionarily useful urge to hurt each other. When not actually hurting each other, they pretend to kill each other. Small boys, even long before television violence was invented, have always cocked their fingers into pistols, pointed them at friends, and shouted, "Bang! Bang! You're dead!"

In wartime, this instinct is celebrated and rewarded with honors and parades; in peacetime, we try to socialize it into sports and business ventures. Men who don't wrestle professionally or play football are urged to prove their mastery over other men by piling up competitive sums of money and displaying them, peacockwise, with expensive cars, houses, and trophy wives. This works pretty well, all things considered. In most civilized countries now, a respectable man cannot claim a right to fight another man physically, possibly to the death, in defense of his honor. But the urge lurks. It's been around for a long time.

In various places and at various times, the Church opposed the duel because men were setting their own justice above the justice of the Lord, and the courts opposed it because men were setting their own justice above the justice of the law, but neither had much effect on the custom. In cases that came to court at all, juries refused to convict, and when they did, sentences were trivial or nonexistent.

Depending on your viewpoint, the long epidemic of dueling was a judiciary supplement, a useful outlet for social tensions, or simply a bloody celebration of manly bad temper. It does seem to have been a useful safety valve for overheated testosterone, and some experts claim that in cultures where wife-beating is socially acceptable, men fight less among themselves, having satisfied the urge at home.

Bloody spectator sports involving people or animals, or both, seem to help too.

There was much to like about the duel. It was a regulated way for one man to prevail over another when he felt the need to do so, and an improvement over the informal ambush, or sending out henchmen to break the enemy's skull by night on the highway. It had rules enforced by peer pressure that respectable men respected. Its gratifications were more immediate than the gratifications of successful lawsuits, which in early times could take years or decades to settle. In a single dramatic meeting, the duel settled questions of political and regional loyalty, land ownership and boundaries, job preferment, legislation, gambling debts, honesty, newspaper editorials, gossip, female chastity, genealogy, and personal courage.

Sometimes, as in the romantic tales, duels were even fought for the love of a fair maiden, both parties taking it for granted that said maiden would prefer the victor, which, perversely, she often didn't. But the basic bread-and-butter duel was fought to cleanse one's honor after an insult, real or fancied. This may even have improved the general level of civility, since death is a stiff price to pay for the privilege of calling your neighbor a poltroon.

Duels were the only court available for retrieving your reputation with your peers. The level-headed Samuel Johnson, responding to a question of Boswell's, defended the duel, saying, "Now, Sir, it is never unlawful to fight in self-defence. He, then, who fights a duel, does not fight from passion against his antagonist, but out of self-defence; to avert the stigma of the world, and to prevent himself from being driven out of society." At another time he said, "Indeed, we may observe what strained arguments are used to reconcile war with the Christian religion. But, in my opinion, it is exceedingly clear that duelling, having better reasons for its barbarous violence, is more justifiable than war in which thousands go forth without any personal quarrel, and massacre each other."

On a different occasion, Boswell observed that the victim was just as likely to get killed as the villain, and the great Doctor "fairly owned that he could not explain the rationality of duelling." (It's odd that so few people ever grappled with this point. From all the noble talk about honor, you'd assume that the defender, the insulted man, always walked away victorious and never got foully slain by a man adding injury to insult.)

Boswell was rather obsessed with the subject; he'd narrowly avoided half a dozen encounters himself and worried about his courage. Or perhaps it was premonition. Later his oldest son, Sir Alexander Boswell, a writer like his father, wrote a song that appeared anonymously in the Glasgow *Sentinel*. "The New Whig Song," it was called, and it spoke scurrilously about one James Stuart, Esq., with accusations of cowardice. Stuart knew someone at the paper who told him who the author was; Stuart and Boswell met in Fifeshire at twelve paces. Young Boswell had told people he was going to fire into the air, since he had indeed insulted Stuart, or perhaps shoot at his toe. Maybe he did. Stuart hit him in the spine. He died. Stuart was tried for murder, but the jury acquitted him without leaving the box: What else could he have done, after a published insult?

Insults varied: You might make an offensive remark about a man's hat, or his horse, or the shape of his nose, and he might send you a politely worded demand for an explanation, and you might send back a politely worded apology, he'd accept it, and that would be the end of the matter. (Unless he was from Gascony, in which case he might kill you if you just *looked* at his hat, or his horse.) Other insults, like "coward" and "liar," called for bloodshed, not apologies. This challenge would leave no option, stating that if the offender failed to meet you, he himself was the cowardly, craven scum unfit to associate with gentlemen and you planned to shout it from the housetops. The offender had to accept or change his name and leave the country. Then the seconds hunkered down to arrange the details.

For the most part now, a man who feels insulted must resort to the law and prove damage, to be vindicated by pale dry money instead of wet red blood: Blood, a gentleman's blood, even a few drops of it dotting the loser's arm, had a redemptive power no bank deposit can match. As my grandmother used to say, "Let it bleed a little, that's nature's way of cleaning it." Blood is magical. The word "blessing," or "bless," has bloody roots; the *Oxford English Dictionary* says, "Bless: To make 'sacred' or 'holy' with blood; to consecrate by some sacrificial rite . . ."

In peacetime now, a man who longs for the adrenaline rush of risk, instead of insulting his colleagues must resort to such artificial constructs as bungee jumping from bridges and the Sydney-to-Hobart sailboat race. Men may dash their brains out on the road below, or drown, but they haven't conquered another man. The confrontational glory is gone, and that was the whole point.

Jules Janin wrote, "A duel makes of every one of us a strong and independent power . . . it grasps the sword of justice, which the laws have dropped, punishing what no code can chastise – contempt and insult. Those who have opposed dueling are either fools or cowards . . . It is to dueling alone that we owe the remnants of our civilization." This was not some bellicose medieval knight but a successful, witty, urbane Frenchman writing in Paris in the respectable mid-1800s.

Dueling echoes down into the modern American National Rifle Association, with its insistence on the Second Amendment rights. The legacy runs deep: As Doctor Johnson said, self-defense can be understood to mean defense of honor as well as body. The right to bear arms implies the right to carry them with you, as the gentry of yore wore swords at all times. In my state, among others, any man may drive around legally with a loaded handgun on the passenger's seat, in case some scoundrel insults his car, the modern embodiment of a gentleman's honor, by cutting in front of him. Probably he won't shoot the offending driver, but knowing that he could is wonderfully cheering.

An armed man feels better about himself, taller and braver. Not necessarily above the public law, but ready to supplement it with the private one. Imagine John Wayne striding down the dusty Western street armed only with a sheriff's warrant to face the desperado.

Handguns are specifically designed for killing people, not deer or rabbits, and killing people is against the law, but then, in most times and places, dueling was also illegal, and the duelist showed off his courage and burnished his sacred honor by risking prison as well as his life. In Dumas's *Three Musketeers*, young d'Artagnan's father gives him some parting advice as he sets off: "Never tolerate the slightest affront from anyone except the cardinal or the king . . .

Fight duels at the drop of a hat, especially since duels are forbidden: that means it takes twice as much courage to fight one."

In the twenty-first century, nearly half of all Americans keep guns handy, in case legal recourse is unavailable or uninterested. Even a man with a closet full of deadly powerful handguns knows he's unlikely to use one on another person, but just having them, owning them, carrying them with him, upholds his dear right to take the law into his hands if need be. To retaliate. To avenge. To prove himself a man. As the great economist Adam Smith put it in 1776 in *The Wealth of Nations*, "a coward, a man incapable either of defending or of revenging himself, wants one of the most essential parts of the character of a man."

The duel has long been dear to men's hearts.

In Hollywood, Barney Silva, co-owner of a chain of Los Angeles restaurants, experienced irreconcilable differences with jazz musician Jack Sorin over a lady named Dorothy Simon. Resolving to do the thing up right, the two men marked off ten paces in Silva's living room, wheeled, and fired at each other. Both died. It was 1959.

The French prefer a more formal touch. The Paris papers trumpeted, "Duel in Neuilly: G. Differre touches R. Ribiere twice." *Le Monde* gave the story three full columns. After all, the men were important government figures. Gaston Deferre, mayor of Marseilles, former presidential candidate, and minority deputy, had twice called the majority deputy, R. Ribiere, "*abruti*" – brutalized, stupid, an idiot. The president of the National Assembly tried to make peace between them, but they insisted on fighting it out.

While the offended Ribiere was choosing the weapons, he was reminded that duels were illegal, and replied, "Honor is above the law." Traditionalists, and no doubt anxious not to kill each other, they fought with swords.

They took along two witnesses and a doctor. Ribiere eluded the police on his way to the field of honor; Deferre had himself smuggled there in the trunk of his car. They fought outside the city walls, in the overgrown garden of a derelict house, both in white shirts with their collars open and their sleeves rolled up. At the second touch of Deferre's sword on Ribiere's arm, blood was drawn and, as the papers put it, "the insult had been washed away" and "each was satisfied." The wronged man lost, but apparently that didn't matter; the ritual had cleansed the stain. Both were technically subject to anywhere from six days to five years in prison, but the public prosecutor ignored the matter.

It was April 22, 1967.

A Peruvian congressman challenged the Peruvian vice president to a pistol duel, to be fought on Conchon beach south of Lima. The vice president, he said, had called him a coward because he'd criticized some sharp remarks the president's wife had made about political parties. No important duels had been fought there since 1957, when two-term President Fernando Belaúnde fought a saber duel with a political rival who'd insulted him; they wounded each other slightly. The wire services were unable to find out whether duels are illegal in Peru.

It was September 2002.

*   *   *

8

The word "duel" is from the Latin *duellum, duo* plus *bellum*, or a war between two. Historians agree that its roots lie in the medieval trial by combat, which itself goes back a long way and rested happily on the notion that the winner would be not the stronger man, but the virtuous man. David beat Goliath, didn't he? Right would triumph. God would see to it. And if the stronger usually did win, why then, whence came his strength if not from God? Tacitus, the first-century Roman historian, mentions this divine oversight, and the fourth-century theologian St. Augustine says, "During the combat, God awaits, the heavens open, and He defends the party who he sees is right."

In the year 501, Gundebald, king of the Burgundians, made the trial official, "it being just that every man should be ready to defend with his sword the truth which he attests, and to submit himself to the judgment of heaven." Under royal supervision, two litigants, or proxies if the litigants were clergymen or women or otherwise disabled, faced each other and took an oath not to use any charms or magic potions. Then one of them flung down a glove and the other picked it up as a sign of acceptance, spawning the phrase "flinging down the gauntlet." They fought.

Nobles fought on horseback and riffraff on foot; at first, everyone used swords, but then the nobles, jealous of their prerogatives, decreed that the lower orders could only bash each other with sticks. Any man who could keep up the fight from sunrise till star shine was innocent and the loser was guilty. A loser might beg for mercy and the winner virtuously decline to cut off his head, but this didn't help much, since by losing he'd declared his guilt and got hanged instead.

This justice system spread through Europe and, along with it, the custom of hiring proxies. A whole profession of proxy fighters rose up to do battle for anyone who could afford them; naturally the richer man could afford the best fighter. The principals in the fight were kept out of sight of the actual fighting, with ropes around their necks, and the man whose proxy lost was notified of his guilt and hanged on the spot.

In 713, Luitbrand, king of the Lombards, an unusually modern-minded monarch, said, "We are not convinced of the justice of what is called the judgment of God, since we have found that many innocent persons have perished in defending a good cause; but this custom is of such antiquity among the Lombards that we cannot abolish it, notwithstanding its impiety." Nobody listened. Aside from its legal aspects, it was a terrific spectator sport. Huge crowds always gathered.

The Norman Conquest brought trial by combat to England, and there too it became the law of the land. In 1096, one Geofroy Baynard accused the Count d'Eu of conspiring against William II: They fought in front of William and the whole assembled court; the count lost and was castrated and had his eyes poked out. The law lingered on the English books until, in 1817, one Abraham Thornton, accused of murder, insisted on his right to fight. Nobody could be found to fight with him, though, so the case was closed.

Trials by combat were flexible. In Denmark, their justice was held to be so perfectly calibrated that no one needed to hire a proxy and even little old ladies had to defend themselves in person, though efforts were made to level the playing field. If she was defending her case against a man, the man had to stand waist-deep in a pit while she circled around him whacking him with a stone in a leather sling and he flailed back at her with a club. If he missed her three times, she was innocent, with her honor restored.

In France, a splendid duel was fought in 1400 between a suspected murderer and his accuser, a dog. The Chevalier Maquer killed Aubrey de Montdidier in the Forest of Bondy, near Paris, and buried the body. The only witness was Montdidier's greyhound. The dog went back to town to a friend of his master's and led the friend to the spot, where he whined and scratched the ground. The body was recovered and reburied, and the greyhound moved in with the friend. Shortly thereafter, it met up with Maquer and attacked him viciously; three men had to pull it off him. The dog was an otherwise gentle and amiable sort, but it kept on flying at Maquer whenever it saw him.

This was reported to the king, who decided it was definitely an accusation and arranged for the single-combat trial. The fight took place on the Ile de France in Paris, Maquer with a lance, the greyhound with its natural weapons. The dog sprang on the man with amazing ferocity and clamped its teeth around his throat and couldn't be shaken off. Maquer screamed that he'd confess if they'd pull off the dog.

This, in contemporary eyes, proved the justice of combat trials pretty conclusively, and Maquer was hanged and strangled on the gibbet at Montfaucon.

The duel's mother was trial by combat and its father was chivalry, with jousting knights in shining armor. These were a traditional feature of public entertainment by the twelfth century, contests of strength and skill like the Olympic Games but rather more

11

dangerous. In grand ceremonies with cheering crowds, two knights would face each other on horseback to settle some question of honor or landholdings or a lady or whatever. Since these weren't judicial combats, the loser, unhorsed, could beg for mercy and not get hanged for it, but the winner got to stab him in the throat if he were so minded or to carry away, to the cheers of the multitude, his sword, shield, lance, and anything else portable, including his honor and dignity. In addition, if the winner killed his adversary, he could do anything he wanted, however repulsive, with the corpse.

Official fights like these were an upper-class sport. The lower orders simply met each other on the footpath and merrily bashed away, as in the tales of Robin Hood, who turned into an aristocrat later but was still an ordinary fellow in his early twelfth-century tales: He met up with Friar Tuck or Little John, and they whacked at each other until one of them fell into the creek, then they both laughed and became the best of friends. Men of all ranks and conditions hit each other as a kind of basic social activity, a male-bonding gesture, like treating each other to a drink or throwing a ball in a park. The higher orders, being higher, needed formal sanction to distinguish their fights from those of the rabble.

The English King Edward III challenged the French King Philippe in 1340 and then, later, his successor. In 1383, Richard II challenged Charles VI of France. These matches never actually got fought, but they sent a gallant message to the nobility at large, a surprisingly large body of sporting types, and chivalric duels blossomed all over.

In *Morte d'Arthur*, Sir Thomas Malory's 1485 account of King

Arthur's Round Table lads, knights scoured the countryside ostensibly to right wrongs and rescue maidens but basically just spoiling for a fight. Much high-minded talk accompanied the sword clashing, but it was a gory pastime just the same. Malory writes, "Sir Palomides and Sir Goneyeres entered the field, jousted, and broke their spears. Then they both drew their swords; with his first stroke Sir Palomides knocked his opponent to the ground, and with his second stroke beheaded him. Then Sir Polomides went to supper."

Malory doesn't tell us whether he carried the severed head with him to supper and plonked it down on the table, but he was entitled to. Severed heads were a prominent feature of European life right up through the French Revolution and frequently displayed in public places, as a warning, until they rotted and fell off their poles. (It's unclear why Europeans exploring America were so surprised at the Indian custom of taking scalps, since scalps are surely tidier and more portable than the head entire.)

The tournament differed from the chivalric grudge match in that the tournament combatants weren't mad at each other. They were just showing off. There were more people involved in tournaments, and the festivities, forerunner of our tailgate parties, were more elaborate, with pennants fluttering in the breeze and general gaiety and fair ladies" gloves and scarves flying from their knights" helmets and pennants rippling from lances. These war games were royally licensed sport and entertainment, but they were dangerous just the same, and quite a few men died of wounds. At a tournament celebrating a peace treaty in 1559, Henri II of France was tilting with the captain of his guards, took a hit to the temple from the count's lance, and died soon after, which dampened public enthusiasm for the custom and started its decline on the Continent.

The notion of who was and who wasn't gentry solidified. Nobody not certified as nobility was allowed to fight, or at least not fight another knight or the lineup of knights at a tourney. It was an exclusive club. England was a bit more lax, but on the Continent entrants had to prove that their families had been noble back at least four generations on both the mother's and the father's side. Nobody could fight who had insulted the Church or the monarch, or violated women, or killed any innocent people, not even his own vassals that he could have killed if he wanted to. No perjurers, forgers, adulterers, or abductors were allowed into the club, nor anyone who'd advised the killing of the king or invaded a neighbor's land and burned his crops. Most particularly, nobody who'd ever worked for a living, especially one who "debaseth his dignity by buying and selling" instead of living off the rents from his lands, his wife's dowry, or military plunder, could foul a noble adversary's sword with his lowly blood. Like most rules, then as now, these could be broken if you had money enough to buy your way in.

Whatever country you were in, tournaments and trials by combat and the grudge matches of chivalry were all under the eye of the king, licensed by the king, and regulated by the king. If the two of you wanted to fight, you applied to the king to grant you a field and set a time and date. Often the king attended in person; sometimes he picked a supervisor. The master of the field enforced order: Spectators were forbidden to disturb the fight, or "to move or make signs with their feet or hands or to speak or cough, or to blow their noses or spit, on pain of having a hand cut off." The combatants were patted down for hidden weapons or magic charms and talismans, and inspected for "words of enchantment . . . written on the naked flesh the night before." (It was also cheating to mutter secret magic words before entering the field.)

Then the heralds cried, "Let the valiant fighters go!" and they fell to until one of them died or collapsed. The winner could kill the loser, or drag him away, or humiliate the poor man even further by nobly sparing his life. At any time, the king could stop the fight by throwing down his scepter and calling it a draw, with both sides retaining their honor.

The purely judicial trial by combat grew rarer after the fifteenth century. Queen Elizabeth did preside over one in 1571, with two Kentish lords undertaking to settle a land dispute, but she stopped it before anyone got hurt. In Ireland in 1583, the Lords Justices and Privy Council ordered Conor MacCormac O'Connor and Teige MacGillapatrick O'Connor to settle their mutual accusations of treason by force of arms. 'Twas a grand fight, in the inner court of Dublin Castle with a crowd of dignitaries, and Teige O'Connor killed Conor O'Connor and cut off his head.

The terminal trial by combat, though, and the last official chivalric duel, was the Jarnac-Chataigneraye upset, in France in 1547. It was a landmark event in other ways too, breaking royalty's control over civilian battles and throwing the field wide open to the private duel of honor.

It grew out of a skirmish between rival factions at court and rival royal mistresses and other complicated factors, and the aftermath was so fiercely partisan that the historical waters got thoroughly muddled. Everyone has a different take.

According to the most coherent version, the Compte de la Chataigneraye told the then king, François I, that the Compte Guy Charbord de Jarnac lived so lavishly because he was supported by his mother-in-law, with whom he was having an affair. (Other histories call her his stepmother, which seems more likely; in French, *belle-mère* serves for both.) The king went and told Jarnac what he'd said. Jarnac said Chataigneraye was lying. Chataigneraye said not only was it true, but also that Jarnac himself had often bragged about it.

Jarnac appealed to François for a field and a chance to settle the matter in combat. François agreed, then changed his mind. Then he died and was succeeded by Henri II – the same Henri who was later killed in the tournament accident. (Some authorities claim it was actually Henri who spread the tattle about Jarnac, and Chataigneraye was only fighting as his proxy.)

Shouldering his royal duties, Henri agreed to the fight and appointed it for July 10, 1547, at St.-Germain-en-Laye, with the king and his whole court and assorted admirals and marshals and other dignitaries attending. (Some say Jarnac wasn't the one who appealed for a field but on the contrary made endless delays and prevarications, calling for outlandish and expensive weapons, with different breeds of horses involved, and generally dragging his feet.)

On the appointed day, Jarnac had been ill with a fever and was still feeling shaky, but determined. Chataigneraye, a war hero and considered the finest swordsman in France, was the odds-on favorite. Cocky and confident, he'd given detailed orders for an elaborate victory banquet before he came to the field. After the usual ceremonies, they fell on each other.

Chataigneraye started out with the advantage, but Jarnac swooped down and sliced through the hamstring of his left leg – both men were wearing only half-armor, down to the knees. Chataigneraye staggered and couldn't return the blow. Then Jarnac whirled around and cut the hamstring of the other leg, and Chataigneraye crashed to the ground bleeding copiously. (This tactic found its way into the language, and *un coup de Jarnac* still means a low blow and a dirty trick. It was legal, actually, but not very sporting.)

Jarnac ran up to him and said that he'd spare his life "if he would restore him his honor, and acknowledge his offense to God and the King." Chataigneraye refused to answer. Jarnac knelt in front of the king and said now that his honor was restored, he would make the king a present of the fallen man's life, that he be pardoned and the whole thing forgotten without dishonor on either side.

The king made no answer. Chataigneraye was a special favorite of his, but he sat mute.

Jarnac went back and asked the fallen man again to confess to his lie, but Chataigneraye raised himself up on one knee and took a swipe at him with his sword. Jarnac said that if he did that again, he'd have to kill him; Chataigneraye, shamed by defeat, said to go ahead and kill him.

Again Jarnac asked the king to accept the wounded man's life. Again the king said nothing at all. Again Jarnac went back to Chataigneraye, calling him "old friend and companion," and begged him to be reasonable. Mulishly he turned his head away. Jarnac took away his sword and dagger and laid them at the king's feet, and for a third time begged him to interpose for the man's life.

Others, apparently shocked, joined in, and finally the king relented and sent some surgeons out to patch up the bleeding warrior, but "he would not suffer his wounds to be dressed, being wearied of life because of his disgrace, and so died in a little time." Jarnac refused the triumphal ceremonies he'd earned, saying that he'd only wanted to restore his honor. (And, of course, his stepmother's – or mother-in-law's.) Lackeys ate Chataigneraye's victory feast.

Some contemporaries said balderdash, Jarnac wasn't anywhere near so noble, he was just grandstanding, and besides, he'd used his delays to take fencing lessons from Captain Caise, an Italian. Italians were known for cunning and treachery, and the captain had taught him that sneaky hamstring stroke. Others said that Chataigneraye was insolent and arrogant, and God punished him for hubris. Still others said he'd refused to pray in the opening rituals and refused a priest when he was dying, so God punished him for impiety.

Nobody, however, believed it was a fair trial. Nobody believed that God had punished Chataigneraye for spreading gossip about Jarnac. Nobody thought his death proved guilt.

One thing they all agreed on was that the king came out of it worst of all. He was supposed to be in charge, the royal referee, dispenser of justice, court of final appeal, and what did he do? Nothing. Just sat there. Refused to stop the fight. Let his good friend Chataigneraye bleed to death. Jarnac's stroke was called "the defeat of royalty."

It was suddenly clear that the king had nothing to do with it one way or the other. Who needed him? Who said he had to give permission and grant an official field? There were other places. Landowners began to mark off their own fields and rent them out to combatants and build bleachers for the audiences. There were plenty of grudges to fill them.

Duels went private.

II. THE IDEA OF HONOR

K NIGHTS AND CHIVALRY faded out. The old orders of
knighthood and chevaliers stayed firmly in place, as pres-
tigious men's clubs tend to do, but the original point of the knight
had been as a fighting unit, a kind of mounted tank, impregnable
in heavy metal, on a big strong horse, lumbering and clanking onto
the field of battle peering through a slit in his helmet and poking
his lance at enemies similarly encumbered. The idea was to push
the enemy off his horse, since once unhorsed he lay helpless as an
overturned turtle, ripe to be captured and held for ransom.

Henry V's nimble archers at Agincourt beat them easily. Joan of
Arc was particularly outspoken on the subject; she said her heavenly
messengers had told her that artillery was the wave of the future
and knights in armor just slowed everything down.

Gradually they hung up their lances and breastplates to rust in a shed. By the time Cervantes published *Don Quixote* in 1605, the foolish knight-errant was an affectionate joke from the past. Knights turned into gentlemen.

Gentlemen, being unemployed by definition, needed an emotional outlet, a bit of excitement, and some way to measure themselves against their peers now that tournaments were gone. Besides, as the feudal powers of the landowners shriveled under stronger centralized monarchies, a gentleman needed to shore up his status and prove he still mattered, he was still privileged, he still carried a sword. He stopped jousting for glory and started dueling for honor.

John Selden, in 1610, wrote that "truth, honor, freedome and curtesie being as incidents to perfit chivalry upon the lye given, fame impeached, body wronged, or curtesie taxed, a custom hath bin among the French, English, Burguignons, Italians, Almans and the Northern people ... to seek revenge of their wrongs on the body of their accuser and that by private combat *seul a seul*, without judicial lists appointed them." Duels swept Europe.

In France alone, in just the twenty-one years of Henri IV's reign, 1589 to 1610, perhaps ten thousand gentlemen died for their honor. Populations were smaller then, and the aristocracy smaller still, and honor must have made a serious dent in their numbers; the Chevalier d'Andrieux had killed seventy-two gentlemen in duels before his thirtieth birthday. Henri himself was proud of his spirited nobles, but his minister persuaded him to outlaw duels as disrespect to the king, punishable by death. Since everyone went right on dueling, the king had to keep issuing pardons; some seven thousand of them, or almost one a day. The theater was flourishing all over Europe, and scarcely a drama was complete without its duel. Shakespeare lavished them on comedies as well. In France, of the first half of the seventeenth century, Voltaire wrote that "practically every person was inspired by the passion for dueling," including the clergy, and this "gothic barbarism" became "a part of the national character." (Maybe this was sour grapes. He himself in 1726 challenged the powerful Chevalier Rohan-Chabot, who scorned to meet him and had him thrown in the Bastille instead. Voltaire was furious.)

Only little Iceland escaped the great bloodletting, because long, long ago, according to tradition, two great and beloved poets, Gunnlang and Rafn, fought for the hand of Helga of the Golden Hair and killed each other. A mourning national assembly gathered and, stricken with grief, agreed there should be no more dueling forever, and there wasn't, a curiously peaceful note in the land of the pillaging Norsemen.

In Spain, the noble and restless were kept busy with far-away wars and colonies, while the homebodies made do with bullfighting, originally designed as a kind of honorable duel between gentleman and bull. (It was also said that Spaniards much preferred having their enemies assassinated instead of fighting them. Less risky.)

Everywhere else the clash of steel made the welkin ring. Honor was at stake. Honor seems to have migrated out of Italy originally, attached to a code of behavior called *scienza cavalleresca*. Italians considered it the motive force behind civilization: Drinking and wenching aside, gentlemen behaved according to the code of their caste, and were seen to do so, and so set an example for a well-regulated citizenry. Italians saw the gentleman's code as a wall of order against chaos and his courtly duels as a civil hedge against barbarity. Without rules, all Europe might be like the Highlands of Scotland, where clans lived in a constant state of disorganized war, ambushing each other in groups, laying waste the neighborhood, killing as many as they could reach, and then carrying off the womenfolk and anything else portable, always for perfectly sound ancestral reasons. This took up most of a gentleman's time and made civil life impossible.

Blood was inevitable, but the duel would at least confine it to a couple of men and their seconds, constrained by regulations.

The Italians drew up the earliest dueling codes to protect and enforce honor; *Flos duellatorum* came out in 1410 and young gentlemen all over Europe studied its delicate ethical matters and the subtle new swordplay more suited to personal encounters than the slash-and-whack of battle. In 1550, Girolamo Muzio's *Il duello* succeeded it and was even more popular. Italians opened fencing schools, attended by eager young gentlemen from all over, and sent fencing masters to the rest of Europe. By 1480, Germany had opened dueling schools called *Fechtschulen* that enjoyed the special protection of the emperor himself and established a tradition beloved by the military and university students well into the twentieth century – some say the twenty-first.

The notion of a gentleman defending his personal honor, the notion that obsessed the Western world for centuries and spilled many gallons of the bluest blood, now seems as remote as the urge to throw virgins down volcanoes. Nobody now cherishes his personal honor or inspects that of others. Short of indictable felonies, nobody cares. We wouldn't know how to measure it; the concept has vanished. Military valor still lends some luster, though Vietnam cast a shadow on it, and large amounts of money command universal respect, but the word "honor" survives only in a few state documents yellowing under glass. Jefferson was fond of it.

Whatever honor was, only gentlemen had it. Only gentlemen needed to defend it, which made their lives more perilous than those of the lesser beings, who could shrug and laugh off an insult. If a lesser being sent a challenge to a gentleman, the gentleman also could shrug and laugh it off, or send some lackeys to beat the insolent fellow with cudgels.

"Gentleman" has today become a rather idle compliment rarely invoked. It even carries overtones of the sissy, quite the opposite of its old role. Now any upstart lad can spend a couple of days mastering gentlemanly requirements: use the accepted forms of address, hold the door open for a lady, remember to say "please" and "thank you" in social if not in business situations. Use your napkin, not the tablecloth. Don't bully the waiter. Don't wipe your nose on your sleeve. Once he's learned the rules, he's accepted as a gentleman with no questions asked, but in former times he'd be a scoundrel of the worst order. Aping his betters. Flying false colors.

Manners had nothing to do with it. You could be as rude, surly, and bad-tempered as you liked, beat your wife, rape your servants, strew illegitimate children far and wide, drink and gamble till the cows came home, and let your bills pile up for decades till your tailor and vintner starved, but you were always a gentleman because you were born one, and so was your son. It came down through your family by way of inherited estates and ancient medieval fiefdoms and service to your king. Its privileges were many; its responsibilities were bloody.

You could be created an instant gentleman by the monarch, either quietly, for private favors done or money lent, or loudly, for valor in battle. Pumping up his troops before Agincourt, Shakespeare's Henry V said,

> We few, we happy few, we band of brothers;
> For he today that sheds his blood with me
> Shall be my brother; be he ne'er so vile
> This day shall gentle his condition.

Once gentled, he developed an honor. If someone said he was no gentleman, it required a challenge. He could lose respect by cowardice, but he lost gentleman's rank only by committing one of the offenses outlined in the code: perjury, burning his neighbor's crops, opening a shop. Once he'd lost rank, if he sent a gentleman a challenge, the gentleman wouldn't bother to answer. This was the ultimate insult.

Gentlemen were careful not to enter into duels with non-gentlemen because, if they lost or got killed, it stained the family honor backward and forward for generations.

In 1613, Lord Bruce and the earl of Dorset quarreled over a woman. In the course of their antagonism, Bruce allegedly slapped the earl several times. The face was always sacred, as in the Oriental concept of losing face. A glove thrown in the face or simply flicked in the face's general direction was unforgivable, and even a finger snap in the face was incendiary. A slap was a challenge. Friends separated them, but Bruce promptly went off to France to learn to fence. Then they appointed a meeting place in Antwerp, safely out of England. (James I was fiercely against dueling, "a vaine that bleeds both incessantly and inwardly.")

Because their intentions were frankly murderous, they agreed to fight without seconds, with only their unarmed doctors as witnesses, lest the seconds join in and get butchered too, as seconds often did.

They wounded each other severely but, bleeding, pressed on until Dorset twice ran Bruce clear through his body. "Oh! I am slain," cried Bruce. Dorset pushed him down and asked if he wanted to plead for his life, but Bruce nobly scorned to.

Impressed, Dorset withheld the final stroke and let Bruce's doctor come attend to him. Then Dorset rested awhile in the arms of his own doctor. As he was gathering his strength, he wrote later, "I escaped a great danger, for my Lord's surgeon, when nobody dreamt of it, came full at me with my Lord's sword; and had not mine, with my sword, interposed himself, I had been slain by those base hands, although my Lord Bruce, weltering in his blood, and past all expectation of life, conformable to all his former carriage, which was undoubtedly noble, cried out: 'Rascal, hold thy hand!'"

A true gentleman, that Bruce. Dorset has killed him, but, dying, he cries out against being avenged by a doctor's base hands. A doctor, a person who sells his services for money, was socially no better than a butcher who sells a leg of mutton. The noble earl of Dorset, unlike his opponent, would have died ignobly. His grandchildren would be embarrassed to mention him. (There might be a whispered echo of this in the American South in uncomfortably recent years: For a black man to kill a white man was an outrage as well as a crime and could lead to hideous retributions to expunge the desecration. A white man who killed a black one was a murderer, of course, but not a monster; he might even have given the deceased a bit of a boost socially. Nobody tried to lynch him.)

If a gentleman issued or accepted a challenge in proper form and fought like a gentleman, with a gentleman, then to be vanquished was no defeat. Certainly it was nobler than suffering the insult or refusing the fight. And to be killed in a duel by your equal was, if not exactly a pleasure, at least honorable. Your grandchildren could tell of it proudly.

Courage, not manners, was the hallmark of a gentleman. As the duel epidemic spread, courage came to mean a thin skin and an unruly temper, the thinner and more unruly, the more gentlemanly. A gentleman was proud of his temper and indulged and cherished it. There may have been, off in remote country estates, phlegmatic gentlemen landowners, waistcoats bulging with good claret and venison, who chuckled at insults, waved them away, and opened another bottle, but in the cities, the armies, and the universities, prickliness was a point of pride, as proud youths in tough neighborhoods are quick to avenge being "dissed." An easygoing temperament meant your blood was slow, and cold, and lowly.

In *The Three Musketeers*, the noble Aramis studies in the seminary for ten years to fulfill his dream of becoming an abbé, but a jealous officer insults him, and he quits the seminary and goes off to take fencing lessons daily for a year. Then he finds the officer, calls him out, and strikes him dead. "I am a gentleman born – my blood is warm," he explains.

In *The Tempest*, Prospero threatens Ferdinand, son and heir to the king of Naples, and Ferdinand promptly draws his sword. Miranda cries, "O dear father, / Make not too rash a trial of him, for / He's gentle, and not fearful." By gentle, she doesn't mean he's kind to dogs and small children. She means he's well-bred, and therefore bad tempered, armed and dangerous. Not to be trifled with.

As its first definition of "gentle," the *Oxford English Dictionary*, both feet stubbornly planted in the past, gives "well-born, belonging to a family of position; originally used synonymously with *noble*, but afterwards distinguished from it, either as a wider term, or as designating a lower degree of rank. Also, in heraldic use: Having the rank or status of 'gentleman,' the distinguishing mark of which is the right to bear arms."

Gentlemen bore arms. In the Scottish Highlands, where nobody would think of leaving the house without a sword, or perhaps even sitting down to dinner without one, true gentlemen distinguished themselves from their lowlier neighbors by a feather in the bonnet as well – as in "a feather in his cap" – but elsewhere only gentlemen were entitled to the sword. Swords were the badge of a man who needed no help "beyond that of his heart, his sword, and his valor." The French called it *"la noblesse de l'épée."*

In his 1897 play, Rostand, writing nostalgically, like Dumas, about the glorious seventeenth century, gives us Cyrano de Bergerac, hot-tempered Gascon, poet, wit, and insatiable duelist. Cyrano crows,

> I carry my adornments on my soul.
> I do not dress up like a popinjay,
> But inwardly, I keep my daintiness.
> I do not bear with me, by any chance,
> An insult not yet washed away – a conscience
> Yellow with unpurged bile – an honor frayed
> To rags, a set of scruples badly worn.
> I go caparisoned in gems unseen,
> Trailing white plumes of freedom, garlanded
> With my good name – no figure of a man,
> But a soul clothed in shining armor, hung
> With deeds for decorations, twirling – thus –
> A bristling wit, and swinging at my side
> Courage, and on the stones of this old town
> Making the sharp truth ring, like golden spurs!

It sounds grand, and no doubt that's the way gentlemen liked to think of honor: an interior treasure, subject only to its owner's exalted standards. In practice, though, it seems to have been heavily squeezed by social pressures and what the gentleman next door might think, with the morbid self-consciousness of a teenager convinced that the whole school is staring at his pimple. Perhaps nobody had insulted you, but if your friend, or your father or brother, had fought in a duel and you hadn't, perhaps everyone was secretly sneering at you for a craven. Best to go forth and take offense at something. Win your spurs.

The once lofty concept of gentility as an obligation to king, country, or community – noblesse oblige – had shrunk to the purely personal, and the clan of the noblesse was tight-knit and unforgiving. It circled the wagons against the encroachments of the rising bourgeoisie and punished its members for violating the code. Refusing a duel would open a crack in the gentry's façade, through which any fishmonger might peer and see not a separate godlike race but mortals merely.

In Malta, home of the fierce and aristocratic Knights of St. John, if you refused a duel offered by a worthy opponent, you were subject to life in prison.

Norway was more lenient, and the coward only lost all his legal standing as a citizen. In Sweden, under an ancient law, anyone who "told another that he was inferior to any other man, or had not the heart of a man, and the other replied, 'I am as good as yourself,' then a meeting was to follow." If the aggressor showed up but the injured man didn't, then the injured was disenfranchised completely and could never again give legal testimony or even make a will. If the injured party showed up and the aggressor didn't, he was to call out for him loudly three times and then make a mark on the ground denouncing the missing man as infamous. If they both turned up and fought, and the injured party got killed, then the aggressor paid a penalty, but if the aggressor died, it served him right.

Then a great rash of dueling broke out in the Swedish army, and Gustaf Adolph, king from 1611 till 1632, was dismayed by the number of expensively trained officers he was losing. He declared dueling a capital crime, and to show he meant it, he told two of his senior officers on the eve of a duel that he was going to cut off the survivor's head. Swedish duels declined.

In Russia, on the other hand, at the late date of 1894, the czar ordered that army officers must fight not just when they felt themselves insulted, but when anybody else felt they were. If dear old friends were chatting and one of them made jest of the other, maybe calling him "fatty" or "cheapskate," and a bystander overheard it and reported it to the Court of Honor, the dear friends were ordered to go out and shoot at each other. The possibilities for mischief from bystanders were rich.

All of this honor applied only to a worthy opponent, but how to recognize him? How would we know, today, from a lineup of washed, decently dressed males, which was the gentleman? You'd think there might have been cases of mistaken identity, of accepting a challenge from someone baseborn, but nobody mentions it. Apparently everyone recognized a gentleman easily, with or without sword at side. It just stood out all over him. Dumas assures us that no "man of quality" could possibly disguise himself as a peasant, because his "fine limbs" and noble bearing identified him a mile away, like a ballerina pretending to be a cow.

It's not clear how long it took to develop those limbs and bearing after being knighted, but probably a few generations, since the fifth Viscount X would rather look down on a mere second Viscount Y, though doubtless the second's limbs were already finer than his grandfather's. With the rise of the bourgeoisie, a successful merchant might buy an estate that carried a title along with its woods and fields, but after this lowly mercantile transaction it took many generations and prudent marriages to erase the stain and refine the limbs.

Read enough chronicles of the times and you almost believe it, the tall, slim, elegant gentry prancing in the foreground and, shambling across the background shadows, a stooped, misshapen multitude of the Other, with dangling arms like hams. In 1651, in France, an edict was issued blaming the epidemic of duels on "persons of ignoble birth" who incited their betters to duel each other, and deaths from such duels were "the more detestable since they originate from abject sources." When such "low-born citizens" are convicted of provoking noble bloodshed, they "shall be forthwith, and without any remission, hanged and strangled; all their goods and chattels, etc., confiscated." (Official justice was hard on the widow and orphan.)

The lower orders were different beings entirely, subject to different laws. In the military, the Other Ranks were punished for fighting among themselves, while the officers – often the younger sons of landowners – were expected, even required, to fight each other in defense of their own and their regiments" honor. While in most times and places civilian dueling was at least nominally illegal, military matters were privileged. What's an officer for, if not for fighting? In peacetime, whom to fight but each other? As Henri IV explained to the pope in 1609, it came from "the heat and courage which is common among those of this nation who during this happy time of peace ... find themselves without employment."

In England, under the Mutiny Act of 1797, an officer who suffered an affront, or even the secondhand rumor of an affront, and didn't challenge the offender got cashiered and booted out of the service in disgrace. Even his best friends never spoke to him again.

The gulf between upper and lower was so complete you couldn't call it a class distinction; it was more like two separate but mutually useful species occupying the same ground. The class warfare took place inside the gentlemanly caste: Who was braver, whose ancestors more illustrious, whose military victories more bloody, whose mistress more virtuous? Who had money enough to pay his bills without borrowing from the loathly merchant classes? Whose estates were vaster and more productive, and who had more rabbits?

Lord Byron, the poet's great-uncle, fell to arguing over dinner at the Star and Garter with a neighbor of his from Nottingham, a Mr. Chaworth. Byron said the game on his lands flourished because he took no care of it, while Chaworth said he kept an eye on his and was strict about poachers. Byron offered to bet a hundred pounds that he had more rabbits on a manor or manors of his than Chaworth had on any of his. The discussion got hotter, and presently a waiter showed them into an empty room lit only by a single candle. In the sword fight that followed, both were badly wounded, and Chaworth died.

In his defense, Byron declared that Chaworth had treated him "in a slighting and contemptuous manner," claiming he had more rabbits on five acres of his manor than his Lordship had on all his estates. The House of Lords found him guilty only of manslaughter, always a minor matter, fined him, and discharged him.

The protection of honor was hard, dangerous work, but a gentleman had to do it.

III. STARTING A FIGHT

I F YOU VALUED peace, you didn't call a German a coward or a Frenchman a liar, or hint to a Spanish grandee that his aunt or his sister wasn't chaste. In Italy, you didn't sneer at a gentleman's ancestors. In Russia, you stayed out of literature and the cavalry. In England and America, it would have been prudent to swear off politics and card games; in Ireland, best to keep away from horse races, or even from Ireland entirely. Avoid crowds, as at the theater, with their risk of jostling. It would also be wise to eat dinner alone, or only with ladies, since the gentry, having no pressing appointments, sat long at table and ordered more bottles of wine, and waxed contentious.

It was safer to stay on your country estates, away from the friction of the cities, the army, and the universities, but it was deadly dull.

Few duels were fought for the love of ladies; this was after the days of troubadours and courtly love. These were manly times, and most duels were fought for manlier reasons. If you fought over a lady, it was usually because she was your property or responsibility, and an affront to her was an insult to you. In Smollett's eighteenth-century *Humphrey Clinker*, the sensitive Matthew Bramble fights a duel with an officer of the horse guards for "turning aside to the park wall on a necessary occasion, when he was passing with a lady under his protection." Since pissing on walls is still common today even in sophisticated Paris, protecting a lady from the sight in bygone days must have been time-consuming.

Manliest of all was simple truculence. In Merry England, after the Restoration, mettlesome young bucks crowded into the theaters or ballrooms looking for someone to push or insult, to provoke a meeting in Covent Garden or Lincoln's Inn Fields. You could get killed that way, but this was what made it worth doing.

In France, the Comte de Bouteville prowled around looking for famous swordsmen and accosting them, saying, "I understand, sir, that you are a brave man; I should like to allow you to prove it. What are your weapons?" Once, with no quarrel of any kind, he called a man out of church on Easter Sunday to make him prove his courage. The man came out. He had no choice. Thus do small boys on the playground dare each other to jump or eat a beetle, and they jump and eat beetles rather than die of shame.

Once you'd fought your quota of duels and established your reputation for courage, you could afford to be more selective. Saint-Foix, for instance, a writer who managed to pen spirited condemnations of duels while fighting them happily and often, told an officer of the Guard that he smelled like a goat. When the officer challenged him, he replied, "Put up your sword, you fool. If you kill me you will not smell any better, and if I kill you, you will soon smell much worse." He'd paid for his quip and his arrogance in advance. Those still on their way up had to accept.

These scraps were rather like the chivalric duels, fought solely to prevail. They paid off socially, and women flocked to the goriest gallants who had fought the most fights for the least reason. Naturally some were more famous for this than others. Vallon Lagarde was so celebrated for his encounters that Bazanez, jealous, sent him a feathered hat as a challenge, with a note saying to wear it in peril of his life. Lagarde of course clapped it on his head and swaggered forth. They met, exchanged the usual formalities, and on the field of honor Lagarde whacked Bazanez over the head. Bazanez's head was unusually thick and deflected the blow. Lagarde lunged again with his sword, crying "This is for the hat!" and again, "This is for the feathers!" and then again and again for the tassels.

Bazanez was bleeding hard but he rallied, felled Lagarde, and stabbed him fourteen times in the neck and chest, saying, "I am giving you a scarf to wear with the hat!" While he was stabbing away, Lagarde bit off part of his chin and then fractured his skull with the pommel of his sword. At this point both men fainted from loss of blood and were carried away, but against the odds they rallied and lived to pick more fights.

It was a badge of manhood, a rite of passage. One M. Mennon asked M. Disancour for his niece's hand in marriage, but the worthy uncle replied, "My friend, it is not time yet to marry. I will tell you what you must do if you will be a brave man. You must first kill in single combat two or three men; then marry and engender two or three children, and the world will have neither gained nor lost by you."

The word "duelletomane" was coined for those who simply couldn't stop themselves. This is not the civilizing influence the Italians had in mind when they designed the system.

In the seventeenth century, the principal fighting word was "liar." In 1606, in *A Discourse of Civill Life*, Ludowick Bruskett wrote, "It is reputed so great a shame to be accounted a lyer, that any other injury is cancelled by giving the lie, and he that receiveth it standeth so charged in his honour and reputation, that he cannot disburden himself of that imputation, but by the striking of him that hath given it, or by challenging him the combat." That is, if a man called you a poltroon and you retorted by calling him a liar, your insult trumped his, the ball was in his court, and he had to challenge you. In his poem "The Lie," Sir Walter Raleigh wrote, "to give the lie / Deserves no less than stabbing."

In modern America, the concept of lying seems almost as archaic as honor. Lying under oath in a court of law is punishable if you get caught at it, but lying in business or politics or social life is so much a part of the game of getting ahead that nobody bothers to mention it. Nobody over playground age would use the word "liar"; it's old-fashioned. Lies have nicer names now: hype, spin, cover-up, whitewash, fabrication, libel, public relations, waffling, disinformation, misspeaking oneself.

In the seventeenth century, though perhaps people were no more day-to-day honest than we are, "liar" was a fighting word. It didn't need to mean what it means today, a spoken or written falsehood. "Giving the lie" included any implication that a man's public and private life were in disagreement, or his professed and actual opinions, or his appearance and reality. Disagree with a man's statement and you were, in effect, calling him a liar. It was a dangerously subtle concept, but it had staying power and governed the life of gentlemen everywhere clear through the nineteenth century.

Imputations of lying came in elaborate categories. It was, as the clown Touchstone explains in *As You Like It*, all written down: "we quarrel in print, by the book." He mentions having a quarrel, almost ending in a duel, "upon the seventh cause." Asked to explain the causes, he says, "I did dislike the cut of a certain courtier's beard; he sent me word, if I said his beard was not cut well, he was in the mind it was; this is called the Retort Courteous. If I sent him word again, it was not well cut, he would send me word he cut it to please himself; this is called the Quip Modest. If again it was not well cut, he disabled my judgement; this is called the Reply Churlish. If again it was not well cut, he would answer I spake not true; this is called the Reproof Valiant. If again it was not well cut, he would say, I lie; this is called the Countercheck Quarrelsome. And so to the Lie Circumstantial and the Lie Direct." All may be passed off without a fight except the seventh, the Lie Direct.

Some hair splitters reckoned as many as thirty-two categories of accusation and response. Proper gentlemen didn't have much else to do with their time; itchy with idleness, they jockeyed for position. To those of us schooled by Hollywood, this classification of insults and answers lacks glamour, and it was a rare actual duel that would make a good romantic movie. One of them does qualify, though, with the essential ingredients laid on.

Toward the end of the reign of Louis XV, a young man named Du Vighan created a stir in court circles, mostly for his looks, though he was no slouch of a swordsman too. It's said that hackney coach drivers let him ride around free, just because he was such an ornament to anyone's coach. Though he was only what was called of "middling" birth, the king was so impressed by his physical charms that he issued him letters of nobility. The ladies at court called him "Le Charmant," and he must have made use of his opportunities with them because the archbishop of Paris said he was "the serpent of the terrestrial paradise."

He fell in love with a beautiful princess, Mlle. De Soissons, and she returned his affections so enthusiastically that her aunt put her away in a convent at Montmartre. He resolved to rescue her. His letter and a rope ladder were found in her room. Her family persuaded a relative, Baron d'Ugeon, to challenge him; he accepted, and they fought. In the duel, he was badly injured, slashed twice in his right side. He made his way to the convent, bleeding, and somehow scaled its outer wall to find his princess, reopening his wounds as he scrambled up. Her prudent family, when they heard he'd survived, had had her locked away in solitary confinement, so our hero spent the night inside the cloister walls, presumably lying on a cold stone floor. By morning, he'd bled to death.

The princess was brokenhearted. In the movie version, she should pick up his sword still caked with the baron's blood, kiss it, and impale herself on it, to die with her arms around his beautiful corpse. Or, at the very least, she should take the veil and spend the rest of her days telling her beads. In fact, she dried her tears and married the prince of Cobourg, who may have been a better choice. Le Charmant sounds like dubious husband material.

The requirements for starting a fight and the gentleman's subsequent conduct were subject to serious study, and the code of honor was revised and rewritten and adapted for various times and countries. The one most often quoted now was officialized in Ireland in 1777, after pistols became more common than swords, but it distills the essence of its predecessors.

I. The first offense requires the first apology, though the retort may have been more offensive than the insult. Example: A tells B he is impertinent, etc. B retorts that he lies; yet A must make the first apology, because he gave the first offense, and (after one fire) B may explain away the retort by subsequent apology.

This rule applies only after the fight is actually agreed on. Beforehand, if a man tells you you're wearing a silly hat, and you challenge him, he may send back saying "sorry," and no harm done. Or he may go on to insult your shirt, shoes, and sister, and then the rules apply.

II. But if the parties would rather fight on, then, after two shots each (but in no case before) B may explain first and A apologize afterwards.

N.B. *The above rules apply to all cases of offences in retort not of a stronger class than the example.*

III. If a doubt exists who gave the first offence, the aggressor must either beg pardon in express terms, exchange two shots previous to apology, or three shots followed by explanation, or fire on till a severe hit be received by one party or the other.

IV. When the lie direct is the first offence, the aggressor must either beg pardon in express terms, exchange two shots followed by explanation, or fire on till a severe hit be received by one party or the other.

V. As a blow is strictly prohibited under any circumstances among gentlemen, no verbal apology can be received for such an insult. The alternatives, therefore, are: the offender handing a cane to the injured party to be used on his back, at the same time begging pardon; firing until one or both are disabled; or exchanging three shots and then begging pardon without the proffer of the cane.

N.B. *If swords are used, the parties engage until one is well blooded, disabled, or disarmed, or until, after receiving a wound and blood being drawn, the aggressor begs pardon.*

It seems unlikely that a man would be so rash as to slap another, or reach over and pull his nose, which was worse, and then so repent himself as to offer the other a cane and his back to be beaten, presumably in public, leaving his reputation in rags. Probably "firing until one or both are disabled" or slashing until one is "well blooded, disabled, or disarmed," or dead, were the options of choice, but at least the code offered an escape for the hapless drunk stripling, horrified by what he'd done in his cups.

VI. If A gives B the lie and B retorts by a blow (being the two greatest offences), no reconciliation can take place till after two discharges each or a severe hit, after which B may beg A's pardon for the blow, and then A may explain simply for the lie, because a blow is never allowable, and the offence of the lie, therefore, merges in it. (See preceding rule.)
N.B. *Challenges for undivulged causes may be conciliated on the ground after one shot. An explanation or the slightest hit should be sufficient in such cases, because no personal offence transpired.*
VII. But no apology can be received in any case after the parties have actually taken their ground without exchange of shots.
VIII. In the above case no challenger is obliged to divulge his cause of challenge (if private) unless required by the challenged so to do before their meeting.

This seems a reasonable requirement. It's hard to know what brought this rule onto the books, but it's nice that the challenged, if totally bewildered, has a right to ask what he's doing there in the cold misty dawn being shot at by an angry gentleman for reasons unclear.

IX. All imputations of cheating at play, races, etc., to be considered equivalent to a blow, but may be reconciled after one shot, on admitting their falsehood and begging pardon publicly.

X. Any insult to a lady under a gentleman's care or protection to be considered as by one degree a greater offence than if given to the gentleman personally, and to be regarded accordingly.

XI. Offences originating or accruing from the support of ladies" reputations to be considered as less unjustifiable than others of the same class, and as admitting of slighter apologies by the aggressor. This is to be determined by the circumstances of the case, but always favourably to the lady.

XII. No dumb firing or firing in the air is admissable in any case. The challenger ought not to have challenged without receiving offence, and the challenger ought, if he gave offence, to have made an apology before he came on the ground; therefore children's play must be dishonourable on one side or the other, and is accordingly prohibited.

Firing blanks and firing into the air nevertheless grew commoner as time went by. Sometimes the seconds, by private arrangement, loaded the pistols with blanks. Sometimes a principal, reluctantly called out or, like Alexander Boswell, repentant, would nobly announce his intention of firing into the air, leaving his opponent to decide whether it was more honorable to do likewise, or simply kill him.

XIII. Seconds to be of equal rank in society with the principals they attend, inasmuch as a second may either choose or chance to become a principal and equality is indispensable.

The rules were written in Ireland, where this happened regularly. A couple of English authorities, advising on the choice of seconds, said that you shouldn't choose an infidel, because he'd be so happy to see Christian blood spilled, or an Irishman, because he'd be so happy to see *any* blood spilled. One Englishman, seconding a countryman in a duel near Dublin, complained that his opponent's Irish second came up to him before the fight and challenged him to a fight if his own man were felled, as a kind of play-off. As in parliamentary procedure, to second means to go along with the matter, support it, stand by it, and fight for it if necessary.

In France, in the duel between La Frette and De Chalais, their seconds and thirds fought simultaneously with the principals, and then fourths were added when a messenger sent by the king to stop the fight decided instead to join in, if an opponent could please be provided.

XIV. Challenges are never to be delivered at night, unless the party to be challenged intends leaving the place of offence before morning; for it is desirable to avoid all hot-headed proceedings.

This one was routinely broken. The underemployed upper classes didn't hang around the house all day, and unless you wanted to scour every coffee shop and tavern and race track in town, you looked for them, or your second looked for them,

47

when they were likely to be at home and delivered the challenge, or cartel.

Unless the offense was too gross to wait, the challenge was often preceded by a sort of feeler, a prechallenge note asking for an explanation or apology. Sometimes in ambiguous matters notes would fly back and forth for weeks or months, progressing from the equivalent of "Dear John" to "Dear John Smith" to "Mr. Smith" to "Dear Sir," and finally to "Sir," by which time matters were too late to mend. If the preliminaries produced a satisfactory answer, that was the end of the thing; if not, the challenge followed. Challenges should be cool and rather stately, but firm, and delivered by the trusted second.

The Italian classic, for instance, "Sir: If your courage is equal to your impudence, you will meet me tonight in the wood," left little room for waffling. In America, one Southern gentleman wrote to another, "Sir – The various injuries I have received from you make it necessary for me to call on you for the satisfaction usually offered in similar cases. My friend, Mr. Forsyth, is authorized to make the necessary arrangements on my part. With due respect, I am, Sir, Your humble servant, John Clark."

Andrew Jackson, he of the unruly hair on our twenty-dollar bills, wrote to a lawyer who had suggested he wasn't telling the whole truth, "My character you have injured; and further you have insulted me in the presence of a court and a large audience. I therefore call upon you to give me [satisfaction] ... and I hope you can do without dinner until the business is done; for it is consistent upon the character of a gentleman to make speedy reparation ..."

Here and there some brave soul refused. A Kentucky editor

sent back a note saying, "I have not the least desire to kill you, nor to harm a hair of your head, and I am not conscious of having done anything to entitle you to kill me. I do not want your blood upon my hands, and I do not want my own on anybody's . . . I am not so cowardly as to stand in dread of any imputation on my courage."

Refusing took nerve, since it was often followed by "posting" in a newspaper or other public place, as today in a gentlemen's club a member may be posted for not paying his bar bills, announcing to the world that X was a cowardly poltroon.

In most European countries, the written cartel was dropped in favor of a simple oral announcement stating the problem, the name of the friend who would act as second, and a request to appoint the time and place. The northern countries sneered that in Italy they went on writing more and more flowery and punctilious challenges until actual fighting became secondary to literary composition: all talk and no bloodshed. However, the written cartel continued to serve as a symbolic gesture among notables with no intention of killing each other – the chancellor of Poland and the king of Sweden exchanged cartels, and Charles IX of Sweden challenged Christian IV of Denmark, who declined. When he was prince of Wales, George II of England challenged the king of Prussia. Nobody got hurt.

As duelists grew more impatient, what the rule calls "hot-headed proceedings" grew commoner, and the insult, the challenge, and the fight often followed hard on each other's heels. These impromptu battles were properly known as "encounters" rather than duels, but they counted as duels on your résumé.

XV. The challenged has the right to choose his own weapons unless the challenger gives his honour he is no swordsman, after which, however, he cannot decline any second species of weapon proposed by the challenged.

In Europe, the challenging party got to pick the weapons; in Britain, the challenged. Picking the weapons gave you quite an advantage. It was courteous, if the fight would be with swords, for a gentleman to send his sword around to his opponent to be measured and matched.

XVI. The challenged chooses his ground, the challenger chooses his distance, the seconds fix the time and the terms of firing.

XVII. The seconds load in the presence of each other, unless they give their mutual honours that they have charged smooth and single, which shall be held sufficient.

XVIII. Firing may be regulated, first, by signal; secondly by word of command; or, thirdly at pleasure, as may be agreeable to the parties. In the latter case, the parties may fire at their reasonable leisure, but second presents and rests are strictly prohibited.

XIX. In all cases a misfire is equivalent to a shot, and a snap or a non-cock is to be considered a misfire.

The irrepressible Andrew Jackson broke this one pretty thoroughly in the Dickinson duel, shocking purists. He must have known better by that time; some say he fought more than a hundred duels, most of them about his dear wife, Rachel, who'd married him rather prematurely before her divorce went through. Only about fourteen fights got into the records, but one source credits him with eighteen fatalities. As usual, no impartial authority was keeping score.

Jackson's mother had told him, when he was a child, never to take anyone to court for insult or defamation, because "the law affords no remedy for such outrage that can satisfy a gentleman. Fight." (She was descended from the battling Scot Robert the Bruce.) While he was president, he opined that "unless some mode is adopted to frown down by society the slanderer, who is worse than a murderer, all attempts to put down dueling will be in vain."

The Dickinson squabble started out over a horse race and degenerated from there; Jackson said Dickinson had taken Rachel's "sacred name" into his "polluted mouth," and death was the only answer. They squared off, and Jackson let Dickinson fire first. The bullet struck him in the chest, where it shattered two ribs and settled in to stay, festering along with some previous bullets for the next thirty-nine years. He folded his left arm over his chest, and Dickinson, who was a famous shot, cried, "Great God! Have I missed him?" and stepped back a pace, breaking rule XXVI. The seconds ordered him to return to stand on his mark.

Blood was running down into Jackson's shoes, but he raised the pistol and took aim as well as he could, considering his weak eyes. (It was against the rules to wear glasses.) The hammer stuck at half cock. Against rule XIX, he drew it back, recocked, and fired. Dickinson fell, the bullet having passed clear through him, and died shortly thereafter. "I should have hit him," quoth our bloodied seventh president, "if he had shot me through the brain."

(Some say Jackson cheated in subtler ways too. He was over six feet tall and never weighed more than a hundred and forty pounds, but sometimes showed up for a duel in a great billowing overcoat, making it hard for his opponent to see where the slender target lurked in its folds.)

XX. Seconds are bound to attempt a reconciliation before the meeting takes place, or after sufficient firing or hits as specified.

In 1817, in *The Young Man of Honour's Vade Mecum*, Abraham Bosquett wrote, "There is not one cause in fifty where discreet seconds might not settle the difference and reconcile the parties before they came into the field." He means this in theory only – he doesn't say it happened often, especially in places and situations where the seconds, and sometimes thirds, were just as eager for action as the principals. Seconds, originally used as witnesses and protection against ambush, were supposed to be part of the solution – since they weren't going to fight, they could negotiate terms without looking cowardly – but they were often happy to be part of the problem instead. See also rules XII and XXIV.

XXI. Any wound sufficient to agitate the nerves and necessarily make the hand shake must end the business for that day.

Presumably the hand shaking from sheer terror didn't count.

XXII. If the cause of the meeting be of such a nature that no apology or explanation can or will be received, the challenged takes his ground and calls on the challenger to proceed as he chooses. In such cases firing at pleasure is the usual practice, but may be varied by agreement.

XXIII. In slight cases the second hands his principal but one pistol, but in gross cases two, holding another case ready charged in reserve.

XXIV. When the seconds disagree and resolve to exchange shots themselves, it must be at the same time and at right angles to the principals. If with swords, side by side, with five paces" interval.

XXV. No party can be allowed to bend his knee or cover his side with his left hand, but may present at any level from the hip to the eye.

XXVI. None can either advance or retreat if the ground is measured. If no ground be measured, either party may advance at his pleasure, even to the touch of muzzles, but neither can advance on his adversary after the fire, unless the adversary steps forward on him.

N.B. *The seconds on both sides stand responsible for this last rule being strictly observed, bad cases having occurred from neglecting it.*

N.B. *All matters and doubts not herein mentioned will be explained and cleared up by application to the Committee, who meet alternately at Clonmel and Galway at the quarter sessions for that purpose.*

It all sounds rather like instructions for a chess match, or the minuet. It doesn't mention how it feels to have bullets dug out of your flesh or to watch a slash wound pumping your blood onto the grass. What gentleman would stoop to consider such trivia when his honor was at stake? He might, in a purely practical spirit, spend the evening before the duel updating his will and writing instructive letters to his wife and sons, but he was, by definition, a stranger to fear. In various times and places nearly a third of all duels resulted in death or serious injury, and many of the wounded died later most unpleasantly, but the Code Duello scorns to mention it.

Rather more human was the author, who signs himself only as "A Traveller," of the 1836 manual *The Art of Duelling*. He thinks of his reader as a nervous man, in need of soothing. After discussing the usual matters of weapons choice, target practice, and seconds, he warns the reader not to spend the evening before the duel in morbid thoughts: "A man should not allow the idea of becoming a target to make him uneasy; but, treating the matter jocosely, he must summon up all his energy and declare war against nervous apprehension." He should invite some friends in for dinner, and banter merrily with them, and open a bottle of port, or perhaps play a few hands of cards. If, when he retires, he finds he can't sleep, he should read for a while, perhaps "one of Sir Walter's novels, if a lover of the romantic; or Byron's *Childe Harold*, if he delights in the sublime; and read until he drops asleep, leaving word with a trusty servant to call him at five, and provide a cup of strong coffee to be taken immediately on rising." Apparently a family man himself, A Traveller cautions against waking the wife and children, who might make a fuss.

Then, on a less cheerful note, he reminds our gallant to alert his physician, "who will provide himself with all the necessary apparatus for tying up wounds or arteries, and extracting balls." That said, he takes his reader gently back to the coffee, with a biscuit, and then to wash his face, "bathing his eyes well with cold water." Next, off to the dueling grounds, making sure his pistol case is with him and in good order and taking a hired chaise rather than his own carriage, to avoid inconvenience from the law.

If, on the way, he feels a bit queasy, he should stop somewhere for a glass of soda water "flavoured with a small wine-glass of brandy, which I can strongly recommend as a most grateful stimulant and corrective." A person's natural instinct might be to get blazing, roaring drunk the night before and greet the morning with a few more stiff ones, but obviously this would have a bad effect on his marksmanship, though the hangover might improve his courage by weakening his will to live.

At the appointed place he should arrive before his adversary, "dismount, and walk about, coolly puffing his cigar, leaving his second to forward the arrangements and mark out the ground, observing himself, however, that all is correctly done . . ." A Traveller doesn't exhort his man to *be* cool, only to seem cool, even when alone in his bedroom reading himself to sleep. It probably helped.

Then, when the signal is given to begin hostilities, "he should step up quietly and firmly, as though he were going to shake hands with an old friend, instead of to shoot one." After detailed instructions as to the proper position and method of firing, A Traveller admits the possible outcome. Wounded, his reader "must not be alarmed or confused, but quietly submit the part to the examination of his surgeon ... summoning up all his resolution, treat the matter coolly; and, if he dies, go off with as good a grace as possible."

Not everyone summoned grace. Guy de Maupassant, who knew a thing or two about duels, wrote a short story late in the nineteenth century about an unfortunate man who had troubles with grace. The Vicomte Gantran-Joseph de Signoles slaps a man for staring at a lady under his escort and then, waiting for the inevitable, falls apart. His seconds encourage him: pistols at twenty paces, considered quite livable for civilians, and fire until one is seriously wounded. The seconds go away and leave him. He can't eat lunch. His mouth is dry. He orders a bottle of rum and drinks that instead. Night falls.

His seconds come back to report that all is in order and arrange the final details about the doctor, the loading of the guns, and other important matters, but our hero has trouble paying attention. They leave, and he sits down to write his will. He fidgets. He rereads several treatises on dueling. He takes out his pistol case and holds one, standing in firing position, getting used to the idea. His hand is shaking.

"He looked at the end of the barrel, at that little deep black hole which spits death, and he thought about dishonor, about the whispers in the clubs, about the laughter in the drawing-rooms, about the women's contempt, about the allusions in the papers, about the insults cowards would throw in his face."

Lifting the hammer, he sees a cartridge cap. The pistol has been left loaded by accident.

If he behaves badly in the morning, he will be exiled from society. The way out is obvious. He shoots himself. The title of the story is "A Coward."

IV. TWILIGHT OF THE BLADE

T HE OLD ORIGINAL war sword was so massive it sometimes required both hands. It had been designed – and worked splendidly if you were strong enough – for knocking an armored knight off his horse, but it was useless at close quarters except as a bludgeon. The duel of honor refined it.

From the mid-sixteenth century through the seventeenth, the rapier was the blade of choice. It was sharp-edged but used primarily for thrusting, not cutting, and it was a formidable piece, often nearly four feet long, topped by an elaborate hand guard, and weighed two and a half pounds. Wearing it advertised how tall as well as how brave you were: Four feet of steel hanging from your waist, and you swaggering around with it, made a statement.

Elizabethan London passed an ordinance against strolling the streets with more than a three-foot blade; if you came into the city with something longer, the gatekeepers were under orders to break off the extra inches. Even so, that's a lot of blade, and it was often used in combination with a dagger for close work.

In 1599, a gentleman named George Silver published an attack on this newfangled monster, developed, he says, as a purely civilian weapon with no distinguished military history. It was, in effect, a costume accessory, ineffective for serious fighting. Once your opponent is past your point, he complained, it is too difficult to clear your weapon and bring the point to bear again; the length of the blade drags in the hand, and it tends to favor the thrust, which can be turned aside easily, over the cut that takes manly strength to avoid.

Not everyone agreed. Long after the rapier had evolved into lighter, shorter versions, some still swore by it. Late in the nineteenth century, Captain Sir Richard Burton, in *The Sentiment of the Sword*, wrote of it with passion: "Amongst all weapons the rapier alone has its inner meanings, its arcana, its mysteries. See how it interprets a man's ideas and obeys every turn of his thoughts! At once the blade that threatens and the shield that guards, it is now agile, supple, and intelligent; then slow, sturdy, and persevering; here, light and airy, prudent and supple; there, blind and unreflecting, angry and vindictive; I am almost tempted to call it, after sailor fashion, 'she.'"

He was far behind the times. By the mid-eighteenth century, the rapier had given way to the small sword or court sword, light and agile, with an edge designed mostly just to keep your opponent from grabbing it. If he did, you sliced off his fingers and lunged on into his lights and liver. The foil was a further refinement of the small sword, with a thin, flexible blade, good for defensive action and body attacks.

The nineteenth century brought in the unedged dueling sword, or *épée de terrain*, with which you could deliver a crippling thrust in the arm or leg that disabled your enemy without getting you jailed for murder. The épée had a stiff blade with a triangular cross section and large bell guard, and was fine for counterattacks.

Curved sabers operated contrariwise, with an edge that dealt out slash wounds and interesting scars, and the point rather an afterthought. Descended from the naval and cavalry swords, they continued popular in Germany and among the military. Their light, flat blades were good for offensive attacks, and their proponents felt that smiting was manlier than skewering: It took less skill but more muscle.

Manliness and danger were the heart of the matter, and Italy was beginning to fall sadly behind. Back in her glory days, death was a regular visitor at the dueling grounds. In 1606, the brilliant and moody painter Caravaggio was so upset over losing a tennis match that he challenged, fought, and killed his partner, who perhaps had missed an easy lob. Then there was the Italian duelist who killed his opponent and was challenged, one by one, by three of the dead man's friends. He killed them all. And the stalwart Neapolitan who fought twenty duels over whether Dante was a greater poet than Ariosto, although ultimately he was forced to admit he hadn't read either.

Those were the days. Now the rest of Europe was sneering that Italians were using weapons with neither point nor edge – perhaps even button-tipped foils – and counting a victory after a couple of touches. It was even rumored that less than three percent of their duels were fatal, a pitiful showing compared to a quarter of them in Ireland.

Some stalwarts saw all the lighter weapons as decadent and a sad comedown from knightlier days. Even a lady could lift them. La Maupin, for instance. She was by no means a lady, being a principal singer at the Opéra, but she was a woman, and one of her lovers had been a famous fencing master who gave her lessons. She was so hot-tempered and so skillful with the blade that some people didn't believe she was a woman at all.

One evening at a ball, she insulted a lady, and the lady's gentlemen friends demanded that she leave the room. She said she would, but only if the indignant gentlemen would come outside and fight. They did and, according to the generally accepted story, she killed them all, fair and square, and then smoothed down her dress and went back to the ball. These accounts don't say just how many of them she skewered, but certainly several. In an era when masculine pride was so firmly tied to swordplay, this must have been annoying.

In an earlier and possibly more likely account, we learn that she was tall, athletic, and strikingly beautiful, with white skin, blue eyes, and auburn hair as well as a lovely contralto voice. She often dressed as a man and enjoyed the attentions of women as well as men. By this version, she didn't insult the lady at the ball; on the contrary, dressed as a dashing cavalier, she was dancing and flirting with her, and kissed her in the middle of the dance floor. Three of the lady's suitors objected, and she replied, "At your service, gentlemen," the standard offer of an instant duel. All four of them went out into the dark gardens to fight it out, and only La Maupin returned. As to whether the three gentlemen were dead or only bleeding, nobody says.

La Maupin as swaggering cross-dresser seems reasonable, since if, as the modern account maintains, she was wearing this ball gown that she smoothed down before she went back to the dance, how was she carrying a sword? In her teeth?

In any case, Louis XIV pardoned her, and she went off to Brussels to become mistress of the elector of Bavaria. She took her sword with her.

A sword was more than a weapon; it was the visible representation of the essential self. On it depended one's life and, more important, one's honor. Men wrote poetry about their swords. Sons revered the swords of their fathers. A gentleman might take an oath on his sword and pledge its service in fealty to his liege. A sword that had tasted battle would be displayed in state over the mantel. It embodied the spirit and good name of the family. It was a personage, in a way no mere gun could hope to become.

Naturally the making of swords developed into a fine art. Swordsmiths were the kings among artisans and guarded their secrets like sorcerers; indeed, they let it be known that more than mere worldly skill was involved. The Archangel Michael himself was their guardian spirit.

In the west, Spain's Toledo was the mecca of the craft, and Toledo's swords were regarded with reverence everywhere, from the courtly samurai to the Arabs with their curved scimitars. They were good; in a fight, a genuine Toledo blade might almost be considered an unfair advantage. The secrets lay in the choice of raw materials, their proportions, and the simultaneous forging of soft steel and hard steel with a high carbon content, at 1,454 degrees Fahrenheit for precisely the right length of time; in early days the smiths calculated the minutes by rote recitations of prayers and psalms. (Quietly, of course, lest a bystander learn too much.) Then came the cooling with water or oil to achieve the perfect tempering, and the finishing. A perfectionist might turn out only two or three masterpieces a year.

Solingen in Germany and Nîmes in France both produced respectable blades, but Toledo had mystic significance. Blades from lesser places pretended to be from Toledo. Renowned smiths signed their blades; lesser smiths forged their signatures. An inexperienced buyer could pay dearly for his gullibility.

Ultimately, of course, the owner's skill mattered more than the blade's tempering, and fencing lessons were an essential part of a gentleman's education. As a sport and a pastime, fencing improved the grace and posture and contributed to Dumas's "noble bearing" that so distinguished the elite from the mob. Burton considered swordplay an extension of one's very soul. He wrote, "They [his listeners] began to understand that mind or brain force enters, as well as muscle, into the use of the sword; that character displays itself even more than in the 'bumps' of the phrenologists, or the lines of the physiognomist; and that every assault between experts ... is a trial of skill and temper; of energy and judgment, of nerve, and especially of what is known as *coup d'oeil* and the 'tact of the sword.'"

Fencing was an art form, maybe the only one acceptable to the truculent, being the art of two men pretending to kill each other. It was also necessary. Fencing lessons could save your life. More than a few men who'd neglected their education were forced by a challenge to take immediate cram courses.

In the popular imagination, swordplay now seems a less serious matter than bullets. We think of it as Hollywood swashbuckling, or as a ballet, or an Olympic sport with contestants in face masks and padded vests. In their heyday, though, swords in the hands of truly angry men could do business as gory as any gangland shoot-out.

When the stakes were high, when the cause ran deeper than a fancied insult, when the inheritance of a lucrative property hung on the outcome, or when the principals had been simmering in grievance for years, or decades, swords were quite sufficient for their task.

James Douglas Hamilton, fourth duke of Hamilton, and Charles Mohun, fourth Baron Mohun, were both born on April 11, Hamilton in 1658, Mohun in 1677, five months before his father died of lingering wounds from a duel. Both were soldiers, hell-raisers, and ambitious politicians; both ran themselves deeply into debt supporting the lavish lifestyle demanded of a peer. Both married nieces of the second and third earls of Macclesfield, excessively prosperous nobles who both died childless. Hamilton was a Scot and a Tory, heir to estates in Scotland; Mohun was an Englishman and a Whig, heir to estates in Cornwall and Devon.

Hamilton, in his portrait as a young man, has a long, curly wig, an arrogant expression, full, curly lips, and the beginnings of a double chin. Mohun, in his portrait as a young man, has an even longer, curlier wig, a petulant look, and fat, soft jowls. Hamilton wears armor, probably not his usual clothing; portrait painters of the time often kept some metallic dress around because the gentry liked to be seen in it, a reminder of their valiant ancestry. He looks more dashing than Mohun, who wears a velvet jacket over a foppish waistcoat, but both have an unmistakable air of disappointed entitlement, of men to whom the world owes a great deal more than they have so far received.

Gloomy Cromwell was gone, the Stuarts were back, and politics was a seesawing balance between the Tories, loyal to the monarchy and the Church of England, and the Whigs, who favored limiting the monarchy and tolerating various religions. Under Charles II, the court was great fun, wild and raunchy, and thence repaired the young Hamilton, who threw himself into the spirit of the times, to the horror of his pious and tightfisted parents. He fathered at least three illegitimate children, got wounded in a duel with Lord Mordaunt, and ran up immense bills. Charles made him master of the wardrobe and sent him to Versailles to charm Louis XIV. Then Charles died, but his successor, James II, was just as fond of him and gave him a regiment of cavalry.

James was a Catholic, and when he had a legitimate son the Protestants panicked, threw him out, and sent for his son-in-law, William of Orange, who was unexciting but Protestant. Hamilton stayed loyal to James, and his fortunes plummeted. He even spent some time in the Tower.

Hamilton was out, young Baron Mohun was in. He'd grown up obscurely in Cornwall, never even going to university, and the high point of his youth was his first duel, fought when he was fifteen and quite drunk, with the young Lord Kennedy, also drunk.

In London, he found himself in the Tower, shortly after Hamilton left it, due to a nasty incident involving an actress, two rival lovers, and a murder. He wasn't high on the food chain, but he was entitled just the same to be tried in the House of Lords, which rarely convicted its own. He celebrated his acquittal with a duel in which he killed a captain in the Coldstream Guards.

Back when he was fourteen, he'd married a niece of the childless earl of Macclesfield, but after her first baby died he stowed her away in remotest Cornwall under the care of his uncle, who seduced her. Later she had a daughter that Mohun said wasn't his, and after that she disappears from the story.

Duke Hamilton, whose first wife had died in childbirth, married Macclesfield's other niece.

It was Mohun, though, who'd managed to make friends with the childless earl, and after much haggling in the courts it was Mohun who inherited the richly profitable Macclesfield estate of Gawsworth. The income from its rents, they say, would feed and clothe ten thousand people.

Mohun suddenly had money and lots of it, the golden road to influence, money for clothes and carriages and hospitality, with immense dinners and rivers of claret poured into useful people. He got made a brigadier general, though he never did any soldiering, being busy drinking and whoring. With all that claret, he grew quite porky.

Meanwhile Hamilton suffered from gout and poverty, with creditors banging on the door of the house he couldn't afford;

the aristocracy demanded a certain standard of living, whether or not you could pay the rent. His mother flatly refused to die or even to raise his allowance. She was stingy and didn't like him much.

In 1702, Hamilton took his claims against Mohun over Gawsworth to court, launching a legal battle in Chancery that would trail on for ten years, giving both principals plenty of time to seethe.

Queen Anne took over when King William died. Last of the Stuarts, she was a depressing monarch who'd had over a dozen pregnancies but no living child to inherit the throne, leaving the succession open to either the German Georges or the son of the exiled King James, living in France and calling himself James III.

Anne didn't care for Whigs like Mohun. Now Hamilton was in, Mohun was out. As a Scottish peer, Hamilton went to the newly unified British Parliament, and he and Mohun faced each other across the aisle in the House of Lords. He got made a privy councillor, master of the ordnance, and ambassador to France, and received the Order of the Garter, highest honor in the realm. He had his portrait painted wearing it and looking better pleased with life than in the earlier portrait. Expected to go to France, he hung around London enjoying his new importance.

Mohun sold the regiment and devoted his energies to the lawsuit. Hamilton's lawyers based their claims on how stingy his mother-in-law had been with her daughter's fortune and calculated that Mohun owed Hamilton, as her husband, some forty-four thousand pounds, twelve shillings, and sevenpence. (This included the value of some long-deceased horses, of which one named Squirrell had been worth fifty pounds and poor Skewball only four.) Mohun stalled.

The litigants met in the Court of Chancery to sort it out. Mohun called an elderly estate employee as witness for the finances of the estate, and sharp words were exchanged over whether the old man was trustworthy or perhaps wandering in his wits, or even lying. Both peers felt themselves insulted.

Said Mohun later to his best friend, General Maccartney, "His Grace has, before a Master in Chancery, treated my witnesses so very ill, that I cannot help thinking it as meant to myself."

Maccartney was not a man to try to patch things up. He was even rowdier than Mohun. A comrade-in-arms wrote that he "has already squandered all his own and his lady's fortune, and I fear his children's also, and has in one year by his gaming and rioting run his own regiment into debt, and is so much himself in debt that he can now neither go to England or Scotland." Drunk one night, he tried to rape his landlady, and when she resisted, he "swore . . . he wou'd make her unfit for the use of any other man, and so with his fingers has tore her in those parts past the skill of the ablest surgeons to cure."

The lord chief justice let him off with a fine, but Queen Anne heard about it and had him dismissed from his command, leaving him in debt and unemployed, sponging off Mohun. Mohun was his sole means of support. Mohun's fortunes were dear to his heart.

The next day Maccartney called on Hamilton several times and on his fourth visit finally found him at home. He presented Mohun's compliments.

Hamilton had every reason to dodge a duel. The queen hated duels; he would lose his new positions. He was fifty-four and his gout was a misery; Mohun might be fat, but he was younger and an experienced swordsman. However, for reasons unknown, he agreed to a meeting. With Maccartney in charge, they met at the Rose in Covent Garden to arrange the matter.

Afterward Mohun, Maccartney, and assorted friends dined at the Queen's Arms till past midnight. Hamilton spent the evening alone, writing to his five-year-old son and heir with instructions about paying off his debts.

Very early the next morning, he sent for a young relative, Colonel John Hamilton. It was November, and cold. He told his master of the horse that he was going out to "vindicate his honor," and the carriage clattered away toward the west. Mohun and Maccartney hired a hackney coach.

At the appointed spot, the principals waved away everyone but their seconds. The driver of the hackney coach felt there was more afoot than a morning stroll and appealed at a nearby inn, where the innkeeper grabbed some stout truncheons and collared a passing laborer to come help stop the fight.

Hamilton greeted Mohun, saying, "My lord, have I come time enough?"

Maccartney answered for his friend, "Time enough." They crossed a shallow ditch and joined the others.

Hamilton said to Maccartney, "Let the event of this be what it will, you are the occasion for it."

Maccartney snapped back, "I had a commission for it."

Mohun promised that the seconds would take no part in the

fight, but Maccartney, who was calling the shots, said no, "We will take our shares."

Hamilton said, "Here's my friend, he will take his share in my dance."

The four men threw off their coats and drew their swords. A groom who'd been exercising some horses nearby had the best view. It was no graceful ballet of parry-and-thrust; they simply stormed into each other hacking and stabbing.

Maccartney attacked Colonel John. The colonel managed to beat down his sword, which gashed his foot, and then disarmed him and turned to the raging peers.

Hamilton had leaped on Mohun and slashed him deeply in the left side, then plunged his sword clear into his right side and out through his back. Thrown backward, Mohun struck out wildly and sliced into Hamilton's calf and then his arm, but the older man kept pressing on. Mohun raised his sword up high and plunged it eight inches into Hamilton's chest. Still the duke flailed at him, and Mohun, backing up, stumbled in the ditch just as Hamilton, with the last blind strength of rage, impaled him like a loaf of bread, into the groin and out through his buttock, opening an artery on the way.

The groom heard Mohun cry, "I am killed!" and saw him fall into the ditch and lie still in his blood, following the family tradition established by his father.

Hamilton was staggering and pouring blood; Mohun had cut an artery in his arm. The seconds ran up, and Colonel John asked Hamilton how he was. Hamilton, still clutching his bloody sword, said, "I am wounded," collapsed against a tree, and presently died.

The innkeeper and his helpers came panting up and disarmed the seconds, who slunk away by separate paths. The butchered bodies were taken home. It was said that Lady Mohun was furious because her husband's corpse was laid on a valuable bedspread and quite spoiled it.

London grieved. Hamilton had been popular. Jonathan Swift said he was "a frank, honest, and good-natured man," and Mohun was a dog.

Maccartney escaped to Holland. At the inquest, Colonel John claimed that after Mohun fell, it was Maccartney who skewered Hamilton to his death. No other witnesses had noticed this, but it was widely believed, thanks to the general's wicked reputation, and a contemporary drawing shows him doing the deed.

Colonel John stood trial, got off with manslaughter, and walked out free.

Maccartney lurked abroad until Queen Anne died and George I took over. He'd somehow ingratiated himself with that German potentate – who was no rose himself; doubtless they had hobbies in common – and went on to a glittering series of honors and high positions that he plundered with both hands, piling up a fine fortune. He was a sore blow to the old trial-by-combat faith in a God who aided the good and punished the wicked.

The widows of the duke and the baron continued to sue each other over the Gawsworth estate for the rest of their lives.

The sword had been quite sufficient for its gory tasks, but over the course of the eighteenth century the dueling pistol began to replace it, a switch that romantics like Burton lamented as "an ugly exchange of dull lead for polished steel." During the transition, people sometimes used both at once. In 1690, in Ireland, the high sheriff of Country Down had an argument with a neighbor over dinner, and they fought with sword and pistol: One was run through with a sword and the other was shot. Both died. Sometimes, if the pistols misfired, the combatants threw them away and whipped out their reliable swords.

Slashing and killing a man with a sword offered visceral pleasures not found in guns. It was a physical experience. You held the sword in your hand and felt the flesh of your enemy give way under its point. As Lewis Carroll gleefully put it,

> One, two! One, two! And through and through
> The vorpal blade went snicker-snack!
> He left it dead, and with its head
> He went galumphing back.

Your arm quivered to the crunch of bone and cartilage, and knew the spongy resistance of lung or bowel. His blood, probably mixed with yours, splashed your shoes. His face was close; you could see his eyes.

Another advantage of sword over pistol was that the damage done was directly related to the gravity of the occasion. In a casual matter, you could swoop in with the upward-cutting *manchette* blow that disabled his sword arm, ending the encounter and leaving him with nothing but a bruised elbow. Swords did what they were told to do. You could defend yourself with a sword and parry a thrust; the only way to parry a gun is to shoot the man who's shooting it.

A sword was always a sword, but pistols often misbehaved or misfired. The skillful swordsman could inflict as much or as little damage as he wanted, but pistol duels were fraught with accident and surprise. You could kill an old friend who'd laughed at the wrong moment, instead of merely flicking a drop of blood from his arm and then taking him out for a drink. Or you could hit the wrong target, which never happened with swords: In one duel in France, both parties fired simultaneously and simultaneously killed each other's seconds.

When you'd killed a man with your personal sword and not by some proxy impersonal bullet, your soul had killed his. When the victor claimed the sword of the fallen as his right and broke it over his knee, killing him in effigy, generations quivered. When Lee handed his sword to Grant at Appomattox, strong men wept. Some say Grant wept.

With guns, the satisfaction was remote. You stood well separated by the agreed-on paces. Shoot your man and he crumples and falls, his weapon drops from his hand, but as far as your own hand knows he might have been struck by lightning. You didn't press the bullet into his chest; it flew there by itself, mechanically. You were distanced from the action, like the pilot of a high-altitude bomber.

Guns were good at death, loud and sudden, but swords held out the bright dream of power, power over a man on his back, begging for mercy, and you with the tip of your blade at his throat. And considered as pure potency, as a sort of *über*-penis, surely the three-foot sword was more satisfying than the nine-inch pistol.

Edged blades left visible scars, those shiny white weals in the flesh that wrote the permanent record of courage: "Then will he strip his sleeve and show his scars / And say, these wounds I had on Crispin's Day." Old bullet wounds were usually invisible under clothes, since few lived to walk around with a bullet's mark on the face, but a visible sword scar was a badge for the scarred one – he had fought – and gave the man who inflicted it the pleasure of knowing he'd left his mark, plain for the world to see.

The sixteenth-century Danish astronomer Tycho Brahe, later the first to study a supernova, fought a duel with a fellow student to determine who was the better mathematician. Brahe got his nose slashed off. Not completely off, but most of it, and ever after he had to wear a flesh-tinted metal replacement kept glued to his face with some sticky jelly from a tin he carried with him. I suppose sometimes it fell off in his lap, or his soup. Apparently he didn't wear his badge of courage proudly; they say it made him cranky and unsociable, and his colleagues complained about his attitude.

As medicine grew more scientific and doctors began attending duels, if a man lost his nose his quick-witted physician could snatch it up, unbutton, and piss on it to disinfect it and rinse off bits of dirt and leaves, then whip out needle and thread and sew it back on the gentleman's face. Sometimes, they say, this actually worked, but your doctor had to be quick off the mark. Later, they tried primitive skin grafting, and apparently that too worked occasionally.

Burton tells a tale, perhaps apocryphal, of two men, one dashingly handsome, one ugly, who fought, and the ugly one slashed off the nose of the handsome. It fell on the ground, and as the once-admired dandy scrambled to retrieve it, the ill-favored one stomped it into a pulp in the dirt.

In gunfighting, a man hit in the nose didn't need to worry about cosmetics.

In the sword fight, your skill was everything – life, death, and all the wounds in between. With pistols, you were downgraded from combatants to targets, passing the advantage from the skillful to the slim. You stood edgewise to each other, hoping your profile was less bulky than your front. One chronicler wrote, "The celebrated Bully Egan . . . fought another duel with Curran, and when on the ground complained of the disadvantage in which he stood, Curran being like a blade of grass, and he as broad as a haystack. Curran declared that he scorned to take any unfair advantage. 'Let my size be chalked upon your body,' he said, 'and any shots of mine which hit outside the chalk shall not count.'"

For hundreds of years, gentlemen had worn swords, not just on military or formal occasions but as a regular item of dress, like shoes, and a badge of social as well as physical power. A gentleman had a weapon on hand at all times, ready to use even at the dinner table. After around 1770, fewer civilians clanked around thus encumbered.

Fashion changed. Swords went out of style. The brace of dueling pistols took over, which may have prevented some of the more impulsive encounters, since the mahogany pistol case stayed at home or in your luggage and had to be sent for, though at least one bellicose Irishman carried his with him at all times, *semper paratus*, and around popular dueling grounds like the Palais Royal, cafés kept a stock of swords and pistols on hand for the impatient.

In Germany, the saber never did go out of vogue, nor its decorative scar on the manly cheekbone, and the French clung to their swords longer than the English – high-minded Frenchmen, especially the military, considered guns uncouth. Russians and Americans, on the other hand, with no aristocratic swordly traditions, embraced the everyman's pistol.

The Japanese, consummate gunsmiths, after some enthusiastic blazing that peaked in the late sixteenth century, gradually ceased fire and rolled the years backward to the traditional grace of swords. Restricted to the samurai, the Japanese duel was fought to avenge insults to the samurai, not the person, whose honor was insignificant compared to the honor of the group. Even today, in Japan, the art of the swordsmith has a mystical aura.

And emotionally, the sword is still with us all. Saint George didn't slay the dragon with bullets, nor could King Arthur's singing Excalibur have sliced a niche in mythology as a pistol, and when the Almighty wants to loose his fateful lightning, he does so with a terrible swift sword. Decades after the pistol took over, a man willing to defend his honor was still called a "man of the sword." It just has a nicer ring to it. "Man of the gun" sounds downright rowdy.

Swords still turn up at military funerals, marking the honor and courage of the deceased. Mussolini, preparing for war, enticed an army with promises of comic-opera fezzes and sashes and swords.

And in a galaxy far, far away, packed with postmodern spacecraft and exotic equipment for vaporizing enemies, in the climactic man-to-man showdown Luke Skywalker and Darth Vader fight with swords. Magic swords, of course, but swords, not guns.

Deep in our hearts we still feel that honor requires a sword. However, in the practical world of the dueling ground, the prosaic pistol gradually took over.

THE FORTUNATE DUELIST

V . BLAZING AWAY

PISTOLS WERE DEMOCRATIC. Anyone could own them. Anyone not blind or palsied could learn to shoot them. Burton insists that a good swordsman must start his lessons by age ten or twelve and practice daily with a fencing master; with pistols, you needed only the eighteenth-century equivalent of a beer can on a fence post. You needn't be rich, or athletic, or experienced, or gentry. Doctors, lawyers, politicians, and newspaper editors joined in. Dueling spread downward into the middle classes and outward into the colonies.

With pistols, even women could manage a duel without first having an educational affair, like La Maupin, with a fencing master. Most women's duels were prevented or aborted; in one, a thoughtful second stashed the loaded pistols in a mud puddle, wetting the powder so the guns misfired. Other scraps caused only modest injuries, and most of the women involved weren't to be taken seriously anyway. Women had no honor to defend except their reputation for chastity, and that was a man's business. A man's good name was at stake in their chastity, and a man defended it. Women who had to defend their own honor tended to be actresses or singers, or worse.

All the accounts are written by men, who cite these squabbles as evidence of women's silliness, spitefulness, jealousy, bad marksmanship, and poor sportsmanship.

In one that amused tout Paris, it seems the Duc de Richelieu, famous duelist and ladies" man, had arranged a rendezvous with each of two amours, the Comtesse de Polignac and the Marquise de Nesle, in one afternoon. He'd meant them to arrive two hours apart, but he left the matter to his secretary, who bungled it and scheduled both women for the same hour. They ran into each other. In a rage of jealousy, they agreed to meet with pistols in the Bois de Boulogne.

The duc himself attended and left a delighted account of it: "The two ladies, dressed in riding habit, gave a preliminary curtsy and then exchanged pistol shots. People came running up when they saw Madame de Nesle fall to the ground, with blood flowing over her bosom. But on examination, it was found that the blood was coming from a scratch on her shoulder, the bullet having only grazed Madame de Nesle's skin . . ." When onlookers asked her "if the lover in question was worth fighting for, 'Yes, yes,' said the wounded lady, 'he is worthy of having even finer blood shed for him . . . He is the most charming nobleman at court, and I am prepared to shed all my blood for him, down to the last drop.'"

That's the charming nobleman's own version. In a different account, when the ladies met, the comtesse said, "Fire first, and mind you don't miss me; don't you think I'm going to try to miss you!" The marquise fired and missed. The comtesse fired and shot away a piece of the marquise's ear, not bad shooting for a comtesse. This version doesn't mention shedding any last drop of blood. Perhaps the duc added it for literary reasons.

In America, in 1817, an amused newspaper in Georgia reported a more pragmatic encounter: "Last week a point of honor was decided between two ladies near the South Carolina line, the cause of the quarrel being the usual one – love. The object of the rival affections of these fair champions was present on the field as the mutual arbiter in the dreadful combat, and he had the grief of beholding one of the suitors for his favor fall dangerously wounded before his eyes. The whole business was managed with all the decorum and inflexibility usually practiced on such occasions, and the conqueror was immediately married to the innocent second, conformably to the previous conditions of the duel."

Americans are results oriented; we like a practical return on our investments. The record doesn't show whether the loser died of her dangerous wounds, or if the newlyweds lived happily ever after.

Other women fought over masculine matters like precedence and insults but never really put their backs into it. There are no recorded fatalities. Women were respectable objects for duels, but as players they were always a bit of a joke, like a monkey riding a bicycle.

As the duel spread into new territory and the pistol opened it to new players, the old notion of a gentleman defending his honor got more complicated. Some of the new duelists were obviously not gentlemen in the traditional sense. Many of them worked for a living. Many were Americans, who by European definition couldn't possibly be gentlemen. If only certified gentry had an honor at all, what did these people think they were defending?

The idea of honor fragmented until it was hard to tell from workaday credibility. Editors fought duels to defend their editorial opinions. Doctors fought duels to determine whose medical procedures were right and whose were wrong. Judges fought duels to prove that their decisions were justified. The upwardly mobile middle class fought duels to look more aristocratic.

After the American Revolution, notions of democracy took tentative hold all over, and elections were more frequent, more hotly contested, and more interesting to the general public, sparking many a challenge among partisans. In a monarchy, everyone in court circles fights for position and favor, and sometimes interior factions do battle, but at least the fights were limited by upper-class interests; in a democracy, everyone's got a horse in the race.

In Ireland in particular, politics and duels became inseparable. The friends and families of rival candidates fought each other and, once elected, legislators regularly challenged each other in Parliament and then trooped out back to settle the matter properly, under strict protocol. Politicians everywhere fought to prove they were men of conviction who ought to be elected and then fought politicians of other parties to prove their parties were best; they wrote nasty things about each other in newspapers and defended their words with bullets.

Alexander Hamilton, explaining why he'd accepted the duel with Aaron Burr, wrote, "The ability to be in future useful, whether in resisting mischief or effecting good . . . would probably be inseparable from a conformity with public prejudice in this particular." A pompous way of saying that the country wouldn't pay any attention to a sniveling coward who'd refused a duel. He was willing to die rather than lose his political influence, and he did.

Democratized, the duel lost some of its traditional punctilio. The rules made official in Ireland in 1777 were specific to gunfighting, but some people hardly bothered to follow them. Some people took creative liberties with the ancient rite.

In 1808, M. de Grandpree and M. le Pique quarreled over an actress who was supposed to be the former's mistress but got caught in a compromising position with the latter. Because, they said, they had "elevated minds," they agreed to fight an elevated duel. From a field next to the Tuileries, they rose up in a pair of hot-air balloons, each with a second and a supply of blunderbusses, since pistols wouldn't have been up to the job. A great crowd gathered to watch what they thought was a balloon race.

The wind stood fair from the north-northwest. The balloonists managed to stay within roughly eighty yards of each other, and when they'd risen to about twenty-five hundred feet, M. le Pique fired and missed. M. de Grandpree fired back, apparently not at his opponent but at the more obvious target, his balloon. It dropped like a stone and smashed the duelist and his second to pieces on the housetops.

Triumphant, the victor soared majestically off into the sky, descending unhurt some twenty miles away.

For the more traditional, the standard dueling pistols were usually about .50 caliber, handsomely engraved and housed in their own velvet-lined mahogany box with their own cleaning rods and accessories. Though they never took on the glamorous shine of a fine sword, they were a distinguished feature of any gentleman's haberdashery and handed down from father to son, preferably with stories attached.

Rifling in the barrel, the grooves that spun the ball for greater range, was used in muskets but considered pretty unsporting in dueling pistols. Lord Cardigan, in 1840, was frowned on socially because his guns used both rifling and a hair trigger when he wounded Captain Tuckett, who was using the good old basic model.

Up until the 1830s, hair triggers enjoyed a vogue; they needed only the most tentative touch. A man who, through nerves or inexperience, touched too soon would shoot a tree, or his own foot, depending on whether he used a falling or a rising aim. For the less ham-handed, the hair trigger was faster and more accurate, but after various accidents – occasionally seconds or bystanders were felled – it lapsed into disrepute.

Accuracy improved as gunsmiths worked overtime to supply the dueling trade. In America, Alexander McClung, known as

"The Black Knight of the South," set a new record in 1834 by fatally shooting his man in the mouth with his first shot from a percussion pistol at over a hundred feet. (It was in his blood, of course. Those transplanted Scots were dangerous.)

The more usual distance was twelve paces, a pace being generally considered as sixty inches, adding up to twenty yards.

In *The Art of Duelling*, A Traveler gets down to specifics. The gentleman, he says, should "stand with the right and left shoulder in a line with the object he wishes to hit; his head bent to the right and his eyes fixed on the object. His feet should be almost close together; his left arm hanging down and his right holding the pistol with the muzzle pointing to the ground close at his feet; he should keep his shoulders well back and his stomach drawn in, then stamping his feet twice or thrice on the ground to feel he stands firmly, let him raise his right arm steadily, bending it at the elbow, and drawing the pistol into a line with the object, bring that part of the arm between the shoulder and the elbow close to the side – throw the muscles strongly and let it cover the breast as much as possible."

He should choose a target on his target, such as a coat button, focus on it, and "bring the head straight, keeping the eyes turned as much to the right as possible and the pistol directed steadily towards the small object that has been noticed; be cool, collected, and firm, and think of nothing but placing the ball on the proper spot; when the word is given, pull the trigger carefully and endeavour to avoid moving a muscle in the arm or hand – move only the forefinger, and that with just sufficient force to discharge the pistol."

Most important, I suppose, was trying not to watch the man twenty yards away, who has read the same book, going through exactly the same motions, drawing in his stomach, stamping his feet, and focusing hard on *your* second coat button.

The combatants could stand on their marks and wait for the word "Fire!" or a dropped handkerchief, or they might stand back to back, as they do in so many old engravings, walk away from each other, and then, at the signal, wheel and fire. This didn't encourage careful marksmanship, but maybe that was the point: They could fire, miss, and forget about it.

The Irish chronicler Daniel O'Connell describes a row in which one man has knocked another down and satisfaction is demanded: "Then they fought, fired a shot each, came home safe and arm-in-arm together, got tipsy in company with each other, went together to the ball and danced till morning." Perhaps a more wholesome resolution than brooding about the matter for years, or generations. In Chekhov's story "The Duel," neither man is wounded; they shake hands and both have been personally transformed by the encounter into better, kinder, and more virtuous men.

There were always those who questioned the morality of dueling, but for those who didn't, shooting at someone had a simplicity, a stark clarity, that seemed to settle matters more firmly and much faster than argument and recrimination. The smell of gunpowder, like the blood in a sword fight, cleared the air.

The English had fetched the idea of the duel to Ireland, and the Irish national temperament pounced on it like a duck on a june bug, at least according to the English, who wrote many scolding articles about the bestial and uncontrolled citizens of the emerald isle and how they themselves, the English, had "corrected many of our own unstable and more excitable habits," a statement not borne out by statistics. Actually, dueling had a shorter life in Ireland than in other western European countries, only about three hundred years, but while it flourished it flourished with gusto and a high fatality rate. One Thomas Macnamara of County Clare fought thirty duels before his twenty-fourth birthday.

The choice of weapons was settled before each duel, and many a citizen used guns or swords with equal aplomb, but a man who had never studied fencing, facing a master swordsman, had the option of choosing pistols. Guns quickly gained the ascendancy: In the first half of the eighteenth century, over half the Irish duels were fought with swords, fifteen percent with swords and pistols, and just over a quarter with pistols alone; in the second half of the century, over three-quarters used pistols alone.

Trying to establish what the fighting was about, James Kelly in *"This Damn'd Thing Called Honour"* catalogs the causes of the Irish duels actually recorded between 1716 and 1790. He finds that insults accounted for ninety-three, politics and elections seventy-two, women twenty-one, "legal matters" fourteen, drinking eleven, "playhouse" ten, gambling and jostling four each, religion two, and one listed as a "feud." The bulk of the rest were vaguely attributed to "a quarrel" or "some words." Of course most of them never got into the records at all. Participants didn't usually report them to the record keepers, though with people of any importance the newspapers found out anyway.

Frowned on by law and Church, dueling was never well documented. For details of actual fights, we're usually dependent on the accounts of the seconds, if they survived, who were by definition close friends of the principals and may have suppressed or burnished the facts. Mortality rates are hard to come by too, since you might stagger victorious from the field, recorded as surviving, and die weeks or months later from your wounds.

Without basic sterilization, doctors excavating your flesh for a pistol ball were far more likely to kill you than if they'd left the thing alone. If you were hit in the arm or leg, the doctor sawed off the offended limb and you died of gangrene. A torso shot could cause the bowels to discharge copiously and involuntarily; in one recorded Canadian case, at this point the victor and both the seconds fled the island and left the poor man to wallow bleeding in the mess.

In a sampling of three hundred and six Irish duels fought in the nineteen years between 1771 and 1790, mostly with pistols, Kelly reports sixty-five instant deaths, sixteen mortal wounds, ninety-four with one man injured and twenty-four with both. Out of the sampling, only ninety-eight, or less than a third, ended bloodlessly. Another study concludes that in England the death rate was one in fourteen, and in Ireland one in four.

Being always more tribal than feudal, Ireland was more egalitarian than western Europe. Brewers, merchants, foot soldiers, and goldsmiths fought as enthusiastically as lords, with equally gentle treatment from juries in the cases that went to court; when a landowner's duel found its way to court, it was impossible to get up a jury at all, since the citizens were all his relatives, his tenants, or his employees. The usual verdict, when a trial was held, was "manslaughter in self-defense," which meant innocent, and if the rules of the duello had been followed, the judge might simply declare that the defendant had conducted himself in a manner "becoming a man of honour."

The tribal structure lent itself to hereditary duels, in which men fought because their fathers had fought, like the Hatfields and McCoys of Appalachia. "Duels" was often a courtesy title for mayhem. At the other end from these blind, inherited brawls was the cold, premeditated duel: If you were sure of your aim and had a disputed legacy to lands or titles, you could go find your rival, insult him, and, in the ensuing duel, take him out of the running. This worked with elections as well: Killing the other candidate was faster than stumping for votes. One man who owed another enormous sums of money challenged his creditor to a duel, hoping to kill him and cancel the debt. He went on to fight twelve more duels, mostly over his debts, and was ultimately hanged for assassinating another famous duelist.

In the army, fights could be about anything or nothing, and since the combatants were better trained and more persistent than civilians, more of them died. The Irish army officers were inter-woven with the society; they came from all the noble families and formed a combustible mix of royalist Catholics and Cromwellian Protestants, spiced with outlanders from Scotland and continental Europe. When they were temporarily laid off from actual warfare, fights were easy to pick, and often more than the usual two people got into them. One fracas, in 1667, pitted Lord Brabazon, Captain Fitzgerald, and Ensign Slaughter against Captain Savage, Lieutenant Bridges, and Ensign Lloyd. (A duel in which Slaughter and Savage faced each other should have sparked at least one sermon or play, but apparently nobody noticed.) Slaughter was killed and everyone else was wounded, and Brabazon, as the ranking participant, got a royal pardon. The record doesn't say what it was all about. Perhaps nothing.

The Irish carried their tempers with them when they left the country. The Irish peers in Parliament had to defend their country's honor against rude jokes by English peers. In 1666, in the House of Lords, the duke of Buckingham told Lord Ossory, the duke of Ormond's son, that anyone who opposed a bill against importing Irish cattle into England must have "an Irish interest or an Irish understanding." This, as Samuel Pepys observed at the time, was a mortal insult: When the English called you Irish, it wasn't a compliment.

Ossory challenged Buckingham, who cleverly showed up at the wrong field, then accused Ossory of not showing up and ratted on him to the House of Lords, which, exasperated, sentenced them both to three days in the Tower. (We think of prisoners in the Tower as languishing for decades gnawing on rats and waiting to get murdered by wicked uncles, but apparently it had comfortable quarters for brief visits from unruly noblemen.) Ossory, a prickly type, was undeterred and went on to fight again.

And the English went on insulting the Irish. The earl of Orrery, who was condemned to go live in Ireland, wrote home calling the natives "bears and tygers" and drunk too. One Samuel Madden wrote that in Ireland it was legally safer to kill a man than to steal a sheep or a cow.

After 1750, cheered by economic recovery and prosperity, more Irishmen took up dueling as a kind of national sport, and bakers, hairdressers, engravers, and clockmakers got into the records.

Newspapers wrote exciting accounts of important duels and their readers were riveted. Almost no cases were prosecuted.

At the same time, as sputtering but simple pistols replaced the wicked but complicated sword, the death rate, formerly around seventy percent, dropped slightly. Encouraged, the populace took up arms in every coffeehouse and tavern. In Dublin, Lucas's coffeehouse, next to Dublin Castle, was the center of excitement, and few customers came in searching for a peaceful cup of coffee. They fought in the yard out back, which was so cramped that even the clumsiest marksman found his mark.

Honor was prickly and combustible. A gentleman's letter published in the *Freeman's Journal* said that he would far rather see his son dead than find out he'd declined a challenge. "My honour," proclaimed the lord chancellor of Lifford, "is dearer to me than my life." Irish Attorney General John Scott wrote, "There are cases where it may be, and when it is prudent for a man to fight a duel – cases of persevering malignity, cases of injured honour, cases of a wounded spirit, and a wounded spirit who can bear?"

Honor was insidious. One man was dishonored by a thrown snowball; he fought and killed the thrower. A man who'd been passed over for a promotion or failed to secure a job for a relative considered himself dishonored, and might challenge the high official in charge. The high official would have to take him on, a job-related risk. If the official had been debating whether or not to give the man the job he wanted, the possibility of a challenge might help him decide.

Military men were still more likely to get hurt than civilians; in Dublin, two lawyers fought and between them fired forty shots without scoring a hit. Perhaps they were just dreadfully bad shots, or perhaps, not being used to bloodshed, they were squeamish about it. Few officers would have either problem.

The army was ambivalent about dueling, outlawing it in theory and cheering it in practice. In 1772, Captain Garstin and Major Birch of the Seventeenth Dragoons had an argument, collected their seconds, and met. At the order to fire, Garstin "burst into a flood of tears," aimed his pistol at the ground, and told Birch to "do with him whatever he pleased, but that he would not fire upon him." Disgusted, Birch reported him to the authorities and the poor man was court-martialed for cowardice. He got off on a technicality, but he was soundly scolded by everyone from the lord lieutenant on down. What happened to him afterward doesn't bear thinking about.

The Irish in the military took their tempers all over the world. In 1803, in London, Lieutenant-Colonel Montgomery of the Ninth Foot and Captain Macnamara of the Royal Navy were riding in Hyde Park, each followed by his dog. One source says that both dogs were Newfoundlands, which seems unlikely, but whatever their breed they were Irish at heart and got into a fight. The colonel jumped off his horse to separate them. "Whose dog is that?" he growled. "I will knock him down!"

"Have you the impudence to say you will knock my dog down?" cried the captain. "You must first knock me down!"

They met to fight near Primrose Hill, where the captain took a shot clear through the body but survived and hit the colonel in the chest. The colonel died. The captain was tried for murder and spoke from a stretcher in his own defense, still prostrated from his wound. "It is impossible," he wound up, "to define in terms the proper feelings of a gentleman, but their existence has supported this country for many ages, and she might perish if they were lost."

The honor of an officer and a gentleman was essential to national defense, and sometimes the price of his honor, and his dog's, was death. The jury was so patriotically moved that, although the judge told them to convict for manslaughter, they found him not guilty of anything.

The far-flung armies of the British Empire carried their traditions with them, and when their colonies were peaceful and battles few, bored and armed, they challenged each other. A senior officer who suffered an affront without challenging would lose the respect of his juniors and his reputation with his superiors. A fine disregard for physical danger and pain was considered the very essence of an officer's character, and a duel was the way to prove it.

Irish politics was almost as contentious as military life, though fewer politicians died of it, being less accustomed to guns. The country was divided between the Protestant nationalists and the supporters of the British government – Patriot versus Castle. Neither side could stand up in Parliament and speak without enraging the other. The speaker of the House of Commons complained that if challenges and duels resulted every time an MP offered an opinion, "there would be an end to all parliamentary freedom of speech."

Politics was even bloodier at the local level. Lord Townshend, the former lord lieutenant of Ireland, said that "among the qualifications for public station, the gladiatorial is one of the most essential."

The relatives of people standing for election fought each other, or the writers of letters to the editor, or people who didn't vote for their relatives.

Local officials were of no use in preventing duels, being busy with their own. John Scott, attorney general and chief justice of the Common Pleas, fought four duels with the earl of Clonmel, and another chief justice fought three country gentlemen, wounding them all. Dublin alderman Benjamin Geale fought the sheriff. In a by-election in County Kerry, Sir Barry Denny, the sitting MP, had promised to stay out of it but then showed up anyway to stump for one of the candidates. The other candidate, John Crosbie, accused him of breaking his word. Denny challenged him, and Crosbie, who'd never before had a pistol in his hand, killed him instantly with his first shot.

Demythologizers are at work trying to tell us that things weren't all that bad. They insist that few Irishmen of the time were actually principals in more than five duels in their whole lives, and one claims that perhaps even a majority of Irish gentlemen never once fired a pistol in anger at another. Others disagree. Modern sensitivity might feel that even a mere five duels in a lifetime would be plenty.

In the nineteenth century, an Irishman, himself a noted duelist, wrote, "A duel was indeed considered a necessary part of a young man's education, but by no means a ground for future animosity with his opponent. When men had a glowing ambition to excel in all manner of feats and exercises they naturally conceived that manslaughter, in an *honest* way (that is, not knowing *which* would be slaughtered), was the most chivalrous and gentlemanly of all their accomplishments. No young fellow could finish his education till he had exchanged shots with some of his acquaintances. The two first questions always asked as to a young man's respectability and qualifications, particularly when he proposed for a lady wife, were 'What family is he of?' and 'Did he ever blaze?'"

VI. BIRTH OF A NATION

T HEY MOVED TO the New World, the Irish, the English, the
Scots, the Germans; the French settled in the South and in
Canada, the Spanish in the Southwest. They brought their assorted
customs with them.

Snobbishly, many in the Old World disowned their emigrants
and refused to ask what happened to them later. My edition of the
Encyclopaedia Britannica, an heirloom from the 1950s, devotes four
large pages of small print to duels in Britain and western Europe.
America appears only in a clause at the very end: "The military
duels of the European continent and the so-called American duel,
where the lot decides which of the two parties shall end his life,
are singular survivals."

Britannica, court of final authority, officially believed that this unique American custom continued far into the twentieth century, even unto the time of its writing: The combatants draw straws and the loser shoots himself. Certainly it would have speeded up and simplified the procedure, doing away with seconds, witnesses, doctors, dueling grounds, legal complications, and even the need for more than one pistol, besides letting Aaron Burr off the hook in that Hamilton matter, but no American source has ever heard of it.

Britannica was not alone. Apparently Europe knew it for a fact. It sounds like a joke that made the rounds, poking fun at the ignorant, graceless transatlantic hicks, until everyone believed it and scholarly historians took it for gospel.

In 1894, late in the duel's day, Bronson Howard wrote, "The Italian firmly believes – which belief he shares with the Frenchman – that when two Americans wish to fight a duel, they load one pistol, draw lots for it, and the winner shoots himself. Why this should be supposed to be the American way of duelling I cannot imagine. If there is any such thing as an 'American' duel, it is what is familiarly known as 'shooting on sight.' The challenger sends word to his enemy that he will shoot him the next time he sees him, and thereupon the latter arms himself, and takes his walks abroad with much caution, until the two meet, when both begin a brisk fusillade with their revolvers, and one of them is usually killed, together with from four to six of the bystanders. This sort of duel would never do for a sparsely-populated country like Italy; and as for the other and falsely called 'American duel,' it lacks everything that could recommend it to the lover of athletic sports."

Mr. Howard seems to have anticipated – or maybe inspired – Hollywood.

American duels were actually brought over unchanged from the Old Country, and by 1719 Massachusetts found it necessary to pass an antidueling law. It had no more effect than European laws on the subject; ten years later our first recorded fatal duel was fought in plain sight on Boston Common, by two gentlemen with swords who'd quarreled over cards in a tavern, just like those real gentlemen fighting real duels back home.

In Colonial times, the military, armed and dangerous as always, provided much of the excitement. A diary from Georgia offers a glimpse: "Thursday, June 12, 1740. This Day began with the melancholy News of more Duelling at the Camp in the South, and the fatal Consequences of it. Ensign Tolson, of Capt. Norbury's Company, having a Quarrel with Mr. Eyles, a Surgeon in the Army, they fought; and the latter was killed on the spot; a Man of very good skill in his Profession, and well esteemed; Not many Days after Peter Grant, lately of this Town, and a Freeholder, afterwards made Naval Officer at Frederica by the General, and since changing to be a Cadet in the Army; having a Quarrel with one Mr. Shenton, a Cadet likewise; which Mr. Shenton endeavored (as far as he well could) to avoid deciding by the Sword; but the other admitting of no Terms of Reconciliation, they fought, and the Aggressor dropt dead."

As a nation, America hit the ground running: Button Gwinnett's signature on the Declaration of Independence was barely dry before he challenged General Lachlan McIntosh, who'd defeated him in the election for governor of Georgia. They fired pistols at twelve paces and Gwinnett was killed. (All right, some sources say McIntosh challenged Gwinnett. It's anyone's call.)

In 1831, after his American sojourn, Alexis de Tocqueville did concede that duels were fought in America, but they were quite, quite different from proper duels. Points of gentlemanly honor, he wrote, were unknown – what American would fight to defend his honor? "In America, one only fights to kill; one fights because one sees no hope of getting one's adversary condemned to death. There are very few duels, but they almost always end fatally." None of this was true, but it suited our overseas cousins to believe it. If they'd heard that Americans routinely cooked and ate their defeated adversaries, they would have believed that too.

Tocqueville was looking for our honor under the wrong rock.

The great American pontificator Henry Adams wrote, "Politics . . . had always been the systematic organization of hatreds."

Modern political persons consider their party affiliations as attachments to their personal selves and subject to adjustment, but in our early years a man's political opinions were inseparable from the self, from personal character and reputation, and as central to his honor as a seventeenth-century Frenchman's courage was to his. He called his opinions "principles," and he was willing, almost eager, to die or to kill for them.

Joanne B. Freeman, in *Affairs of Honor*, writes that the dueling politicos "were men of public duty and private ambition who identified so closely with their public roles that they often could not distinguish between their identity as gentlemen and their status as political leaders. Longtime political opponents almost expected duels, for there was no way that constant opposition to a man's political career could leave his personal identity unaffected."

Later the political party system solidified and took some of the pressure off the individual: Principles and opinions were laid down by the party and built into the platform, so the man himself couldn't be exclusively blamed or praised for them. In the beginning, though, every man felt the eyes of posterity watching him every minute.

Schoolteachers, history texts, and modern politicians speak with awe of our Founding Fathers as if they were a team, an inspired collective voice guided by the Lord. They weren't. Each interpreted the Almighty's suggestions in his own way. Fine-tuning the infant republic, they found a thousand points of disagreement, and they didn't just disagree with a man's opinion, they hated the man himself for it and all his friends and relations too.

Every faction considered all other factions a threat to the republic and a personal insult. Men in public life called each other, not just the traditional "liar," "poltroon," "coward," and "puppy," but also "fornicator," "madman," and "bastard"; they accused each other of incest, treason, and consorting with the devil. Legislative debate at all levels often led straight to whatever secluded local spot had been set aside to soak up the blood of satisfaction.

It was political suicide to suffer an affront without challenging, or to decline a challenge. Such things had a way of getting around, by means of dinner parties, pseudonymous newspaper articles, or the custom, popular into the 1890s, of posting in taverns and on street corners notices that called the coward a coward; these often appeared in newspapers under the heading "A Card." Obeying the code of honor showcased a man's integrity and marked him as leadership material. It was a wise career move. One James Jackson, at the tender age of twenty-three, killed the lieutenant governor of Georgia for his "overbearing" manners and went on to become governor himself, as well as congressman and senator.

Judges, governors, legislators, and rival candidates for office blazed away at each other. Even as today wars and dramatic announcements can be timed to coincide with or avoid elections, long-standing political grievances could be timed to explode at the right moment. Duels were fought before elections, to showcase the candidate's courage, and after elections, when the losers challenged the winners.

While he was our second president, John Adams insulted James Monroe, later our fifth president, and Monroe consulted with Madison, later our fourth president. Monroe was aching to take a shot at Adams but said, "I cannot I presume, as he is an old man & the Presidt." Madison agreed – even the founders felt that killing a sitting president because he'd hurt your feelings would be politically unpopular – and suggested he write still another furious paper instead, so he did. Adams insulted a lot of people, but he didn't fight duels. When Alexander Hamilton challenged him he wouldn't even answer, so Hamilton had to post him in print.

From 1795 until 1800, Federalists dueled with Republicans. After Jefferson's election, Republicans who liked DeWitt Clinton battled Republicans who preferred Aaron Burr, Jefferson's vice president. Burr man John Swartwout said Senator Clinton was "governed by unworthy motives" and they fired five rounds; Clinton won. Later the Republicans went back to shooting Federalists.

Every factional leader had his own tame newspaper to praise him and insult his rivals editorially. In New York, William Coleman had the *New-York Evening Post,* Clinton the *American Citizen,* and Burr the *Morning Chronicle.* If you couldn't find a sympathetic paper, you launched your own. After duels, the seconds published in their papers detailed accounts of their own man's gallantry and the other man's swinish behavior.

Congressional duels had a regional flavor. The Federalists, like Hamilton of New York, were largely Northerners, who naturally considered themselves cool and reasonable, and the Republicans, like Monroe of Virginia, were largely Southerners, who considered themselves more spirited and aristocratic. The Northerners liked to tell each other they were too civilized for such barbaric customs, but when taunted in Congress by the other side, they had little recourse but to fight, or at least demand an explanation and then try to negotiate out of the bloodshed.

Ideally, after a public insult, the insulted party sent a preliminary note by a second, asking for a retraction or apology, either by letter or at a meeting with seconds. This was the old-fashioned equivalent of that first phone call from a lawyer, saying you'd insulted his client and would soon be hearing from him further. It could be worded gently and answered in kind to end the matter: as former Treasury Secretary Hamilton correctly wrote to future President Monroe, "Mr. Hamilton requests an interview with Mr. Monroe at any hour tomorrow forenoon which may be convenient to him. Particular reasons will induce him to bring with him a friend to be present at what may pass. Mr. Monroe, if he pleases, may have another."

If you were determined on vengeance, the preliminary note

could be phrased as so rude a demand that no proper man would humiliate himself with an apology. New York senator DeWitt Clinton cried out as he faced his opponent, "I am compelled to shoot at one whom I do not wish to hurt, but I will sign no paper – I will not dishonor myself."

The temptation to insult one's fellow legislators was irresistible, but it carried a price: Insults had to be answered. As James Madison the Virginian said, "No man ought to reproach another with cowardice, who is not ready to give proof of his own courage." Be ready to fight, or else be very, very polite.

Just the same, blatant ferocity was considered bad manners and politically damaging. The duel should be less an excuse for assassination than a manly show of courage, and it was correct to shoot your opponent not through the heart but in the leg.

The ultimate insults were public canings and nose pullings, which implied that the victim was not only a scoundrel but also socially inferior. Sad to say, some of our early lawmakers bought large, stout hickory sticks and carried them to work. Republican Brockholst Livingston insulted Federalist James Jones. Jones beat him with his stick on the floor of Congress and then went for the grand slam by grabbing and twisting his nose. In the resulting duel, Jones was killed. Afterward Livingston was said to be "conscious of having done nothing but what he was compeled to do & at the same time sorry for the Necessity."

However punctilious the arrangements, if you were seriously angry the choice of weapons and distance could shrink the odds on survival. On Bloody Island, a favorite dueling spot near St. Louis,

Congressman Spencer Pettis, who was running for reelection, and army postmaster Major Thomas Biddle, who had called Pettis "a bowl of skimmed milk," killed each other at the brutal distance of five feet. At Bladensburg, Maryland, the semiofficial federal dueling ground, Congressman Jonathan Cilley of Maine and Congressman William Graves of Kentucky had a falling-out over a newspaper article and chose rifles at eighty paces. Graves survived.

Then there was the once-famous Burr-Hamilton duel. Nowadays few Americans remember anything about it, perhaps because the issues involved seem murky, which they were. People in New Jersey remember only that it happened in Weehawken, since New Jersey cherishes its scant history. It remains the one American duel out of thousands that gets a mention in history textbooks, so that any students paying attention think it must have been a shocking and isolated incident. They wonder why Burr wasn't hanged. Actually, he was tried – for treason – and acquitted, but that was years later and involved some land he'd bought in the West and whether he planned to secede with it. Shooting Hamilton, though widely deplored, was fairly routine.

The schoolbooks themselves sound rather embarrassed and seem to be mumbling; they can't ignore it, lest some busybody ask whatever happened to Hamilton, but it's unpatriotic to suggest that our early statesmen shot at each other. It sets a bad example for the young. Our virtues shift tectonically underfoot; previously unmentionable practices like incest and sodomy are now discussed at interminable length, while our once-dignified dueling is too shameful to mention.

At the time, though, it was the talk of the town.

Aaron Burr and Alexander Hamilton were born within a year of each other; both had horses shot out from under them fighting in the Revolution, both were New York lawyers, and both were a size smaller than average, which doesn't improve any man's temper.

Burr was born in New Jersey, grandson of Jonathan Edwards, whose hellfire-and-brimstone sermons rattle the opening chapter in American literature textbooks. Burr's parents died when he was young, but a kindly uncle raised him and, when the boy was thirteen, sent him to Princeton, where he studied Greek and Latin and theology. Abandoning religion, he took up law instead, then joined the Continental Army and served in the Quebec, Westchester, and Manhattan campaigns and froze at Valley Forge.

As an officer Burr was rather a handful, with a tendency to strike out on his own in defiance of orders whenever he thought he had a better idea. After a particularly bad idea in the Battle of Monmouth, he had a nervous breakdown and left the army.

He was known as a successful ladies" man, so his friends were surprised when he took up with Theodosia Prevost, a married woman ten years older than he was with five children and a nasty scar on her face. He'd been seriously depressed and traveled to various spas looking for a cure, and Mrs. Prevost cheered him up. She wasn't rich or influential, any more than she was young or pretty, but she was cheerful. After her husband died, Burr got admitted to the New York bar and married her, and enjoyed a fine social and professional success. With various schemes and investments he got quite rich, and he was an excellent lawyer, not much burdened with ideals: He defined the law as "whatever is boldly asserted and plausibly maintained."

After he got a man off on murder charges, the man couldn't pay his fee and gave him, instead, a handsome cased pair of dueling pistols. He practiced with them, as his enemies pointed out later. Polishing your swordsmanship had been a most gentlemanly pastime, but pistol practice was so unsporting it was almost cheating.

The Burrs were apparently a loving and faithful pair, and he was greatly upset when she died. They had a daughter, Theodosia, of whom more later.

Hamilton's beginnings were less fortunate. He was, as his enemies put it, a bastard. His mother, a fun-loving lass, was married at fifteen to a stuffy middle-aged planter on St. Croix in the Caribbean, and when she couldn't take it anymore she left him. She was living with her mother on St. Kitts when the dashing young Scot James Hamilton showed up, and they moved in together. Presently Alexander was born, and later a second son, James Jr. Hamilton Sr. was careless and lazy and failed at everything he tried. He soon disappeared, leaving the young family behind.

Alexander was an industrious student under a Presbyterian minister in St. Croix, but his mother, depressed by it all, died when he was eleven, and he was put to work as a merchant's clerk. Then his old teacher took up a collection and raised enough money to send him to school on the mainland. After a year's cramming, he went to King's College in New York. On top of his studies, he flung himself into politics, writing fierce anti-England articles and making speeches defending the Boston Tea Party.

In 1776, he joined right up as captain of an artillery company. He was a more tractable soldier than Burr. Washington made him his secretary and aide-de-camp. Considering means to help finance the war, he got interested in the idea of a national bank and drew up a plan to organize the government around money. Then he went back to active warfare in time to fight at Yorktown and see the end of the war.

He passed the bar and, like Burr, took up law in New York.

Sometimes he and Burr worked on cases together, though his fans insist that he was quite different from Burr and much more high-minded. He also had the good luck to fall in love with Betsy Schuyler, of the rich and politically powerful Schuylers, and charm her father, General Philip Schuyler.

Burr and Hamilton threw themselves into the piranha tank of the infant government. Burr was a Jeffersonian Republican; Hamilton, Washington's secretary of the treasury, gathered his followers into what came to be called the Federalists. Both parties quarreled among themselves almost as often as they did with each other.

The Jeffersonians believed in a community of small farmers, but Hamilton felt that cash, not land, was the wave of the future and the backbone of the country, and he designed structures for taxes and revenues and financing and public credit and investments and the war debt. He was seriously interested in money, which is why he's on our ten-dollar bills.

In 1792, a committee of congressmen went to his office and accused him of handing over quantities of treasury funds to a man named Reynolds, who was currently in jail, so Reynolds could play the stock market. Hamilton freely admitted giving Reynolds money but said there was nothing wrong with it, since it wasn't public money, it was his own, and he was just paying off Reynolds for the affair he'd been having, and was still having, with Mrs. Reynolds. He went public with the whole story and seemed to feel that made everything all right. (Whether or not Mrs. Hamilton and the children were surprised to hear of the affair, we don't know.) Later there were allegations about some shady foreign loans. Jefferson tried to get him thrown out of office for "maladministration," but Hamilton beat him to the punch and resigned.

Burr beat Schuyler, Hamilton's father-in-law, in the New York senatorial race. Then, with help from Hamilton, Schuyler turned around and beat Burr. Discouraged, Burr applied for a brigadier's commission in the army, but he didn't get it. He was sure Hamilton had turned Washington against him.

We have no way of knowing whether Burr was simply paranoid about it, or whether Hamilton really did spend a lot of his energies spreading ugly stories about Burr. Certainly Burr believed it, and the evidence did pile up.

Burr rallied and ran for president against Jefferson. They tied. The election went to the House, where Hamilton worked hard to throw the vote to Jefferson, in spite of their political differences, rather than let Burr have it. After thirty-six ballots, he succeeded.

Under the peculiar rule of the time, this made Burr Jefferson's vice president. It was a more interesting job then than it is now, and everyone agreed that he was very good indeed as presiding officer of the Senate. Somehow, though, there were always nasty, vague, anonymous stories circulating around him like invisible snakes. Hamilton's Federalists seemed to be lurking in his closet and under his bed, in the Senate cloakroom and the White House hallways, whispering.

Like Hamilton, he'd expected to be president eventually. It was a reasonable hope for anyone who'd been in at the birthing. Now it began to look as if he couldn't even hold onto the second-place spot. It was charged that Burr, back during the photo-finish election, had tried to forge a deal with the Federalists to give him enough of their votes to make him president. Never mind that the Federalists' leader had used all his clout to elect Jefferson – Burr was branded a traitor. His political future was shipwrecked.

He appealed to Jefferson, already locked in for a second term. As he retired, or retreated, from the vice presidency, he asked to be sent as ambassador to France. "My enemies," he begged, "are using your name to destroy me; and something is necessary from you to prevent it, and deprive them of that weapon – some mark of favor from you which will declare to the world that I retire with your confidence."

It would have been a simple matter and scotched the rumors, but Jefferson did nothing to restore his vice president's reputation. He'd always distrusted Hamilton and once wrote warning John Adams against his tricks and subtleties. (Adams didn't need warning; he'd called Hamilton proud spirited, conceited, debauched, and hypocritical, "devoid of every moral principle" and dedicated to "his fornications, his adulteries, and his incests.")

On the other hand, Jefferson didn't like Burr any better than he liked Hamilton. The election had been a tie, after all. These things rankle.

Back in New York, Burr geared up to run for governor, but

he found that Hamilton's tongue had been busy there too. A man named Charles Cooper had published a letter mentioning some nasty things Hamilton said about Burr. Burr sent the letter to Hamilton and asked for an acknowledgment or denial. Hamilton spent two days working over his reply, a masterpiece of waffling.

Cooper's letter, wrote Hamilton, says, "'I could detail to you a *still more despicable* opinion which General Hamilton has expressed of Mr. Burr.' ... To endeavor to discover the meaning of this declaration," Hamilton continues, "I was obliged to seek in the antecedent part of this letter for the opinion to which it referred, as having been already disclosed. I found it in these words: 'General Hamilton and Judge Kent have declared, in *substance*, that they looked upon Mr. Burr to be a *dangerous man*, and one *who ought not to be trusted with the reins of government*.' The language of Cooper plainly implies that he considered this opinion of you, which he attributes to me, as a *despicable* one; but he affirms that I have expressed some other, *more despicable*, without, however, mentioning to whom, when, or where."

The letter goes on at considerable length, musing on the correct usage of "despicable" and explaining that the allegation is far too vague to warrant an explanation, and besides, it is against his principles "to consent to be interrogated as to the justness of the inferences which may be drawn by others from whatever I may have said of a political opponent, in the course of fifteen years competition." Even for a lawyer, it's a work of art.

Burr wrote back, more briefly, saying that doesn't quite clear things up; whether or not Cooper used the word correctly, he plainly means something nasty. "Your letter has furnished me with new reasons for requiring a definite reply." He sent it by his friend William Van Ness.

Hamilton decided this was so rude that it was time to call in his own friend Nathaniel Pendleton, and he wrote to Burr saying his writing style was "too peremptory" and he still wasn't going to explain the charges.

Van Ness and Pendleton conferred. Pendleton suggested that Van Ness tell Burr to write to Hamilton asking if he remembered saying anything to anyone about Burr's private life. Then, on Hamilton's behalf, he wrote saying that anything he might have said in the conversation Dr. Cooper spoke of would have been "wholly on political topics, and did not attribute to Col. Burr any instance of dishonourable conduct, nor relate to his private character."

Apparently Burr had been picking up more whispers. He and Hamilton had friends in common in the close-knit political-legal community. Van Ness wrote back saying it wasn't good enough to explain one particular conversation; something more general was called for. In its absence, he was obliged to ask for a personal interview with Hamilton.

Pendleton wrote back for Hamilton, calling this "an inquisition into his most confidential conversations" and saying that he "cannot consent to be questioned generally as to any rumours which may be afloat derogatory to the character of Colonel Burr." And he says he'll be waiting at home between eight and ten o'clock tomorrow morning.

Van Ness wrote back, pointing out that "secret whispers

traducing his fame, and impeaching his honor, are, at least, equally injurious with slanders publicly uttered."

It sounds as if rumors spicier than the vice president's political opinions were making the rounds in New York.

Van Ness goes on to say that Burr "felt the utmost reluctance to proceed to extremities, while any other hope remained," but apparently "satisfactory redress, earnestly desired, cannot be obtained."

This was, in the language of the code, a formal challenge.

Hamilton was apparently alarmed and wrote again saying he was perfectly willing to explain "any and every object of a specific nature; but not to answer a general and abstract inquiry." (Burr had been in Washington and had no way of knowing exactly what words Hamilton said and to whom on what occasion, as Hamilton well knew.) Besides, he added, he was busy with Circuit Court and far too honorable a lawyer to keep his clients waiting while he fought a duel. Maybe later.

Van Ness waved this aside. The seconds met and decided on a meeting at Weehawken on the following Wednesday at seven A.M.

Hamilton had reason to be squeamish about Weehawken.

Two and a half years before, his eldest son, Philip, who was just twenty and recently graduated from Columbia, got into a scrape at the theater. In the adjoining box sat a rising young lawyer and politician named Eacker. Eacker had made a speech saying that Alexander Hamilton wouldn't mind overthrowing President Jefferson by force. During intermission, Philip and a friend of his crowded into Eacker's box and made rude comments about the speech. (Kindly historians say he was defending his father's honor, but it sounds as if the boys might have been rather drunk.) Eacker moved away toward the lobby, saying, "It is too abominable to be publicly insulted by a pair of damned rascals."

Philip and friend followed him, determined to quarrel, and cried out, "Whom do you call 'damned rascals'?" (At least, that's what Don C. Seitz, in *Famous American Duels*, says they said, and perhaps in 1801 people were more scrupulous about grammar.) The three wound up in a nearby tavern, where the boys kept up their clamor until Eacker said, "Gentlemen, you had better make less noise. I shall expect to hear from you."

"That you shall!" they cried.

Eacker met Philip's friend first, at Weehawken, and after four shots apiece and no damage, they shook hands and parted. Then it was Philip's turn. He refused to apologize for his rowdiness. Eacker refused to retract the "rascals." At Weehawken, his first shot hit home while Philip's hair trigger went off too soon, firing into the air.

A college classmate of Philip's recounted the rest for the *New York Historical Magazine*. When the news flashed through town, he hurried from the theater to the Hamiltons" house, where he was admitted to Philip's room. "On a bed without curtains lay poor Phil, pale and languid, his rolling, distorted eyeballs darting forth flashes of delirium. On one side of him, on the same bed, lay his agonized father; on the other, his distracted mother; around him were numerous relatives and friends, weeping and fixed in sorrow. Blanched with astonishment and affright was the countenance which, a few minutes before, was illumined by the smile of merriment."

Philip Hamilton died painfully the next morning.

Scholars are baffled as to why, exactly, his father showed up at the same spot in Weehawken at seven A.M., July 11, 1804. Burr was a better shot. Hamilton was at fault. He could have simply explained and apologized, early in the game, instead of sending all those lawyerly evasions.

In a long justification written just before the battle, he freely admits he'd made "extremely severe" attacks on Burr's political and private life but insists that he couldn't apologize.

Some suggest he was suicidal, eager to end it all without the stigma of doing it to himself. Others say he so hated Burr that he hoped to be killed, just because it would ruin the other man's career. Some wonder why Burr ever bothered to challenge him over such a vague statement as Cooper's; perhaps the vice president was just naturally murderous, or insane?

It seems likely that Hamilton and Burr both knew something the scholars don't. They knew what it was that Hamilton had been saying, off the record, at dinner parties after the ladies had left the room, about Burr's "private" character.

Cooper didn't put the "more despicable" allegation in print because it was unprintable.

Hamilton didn't apologize because it was beyond apology.

Burr challenged him because it was beyond forgiveness.

Which brings us back to Theodosia, the Burrs' beloved only child. By all accounts she was both beautiful and brilliant. After her mother died, Burr transferred all his love to her and personally supervised her education – Latin, Greek, French, German, harp, piano, dancing, skating, riding – far beyond the usual for girls at the time. He molded her into his perfect companion. They were inseparable. She managed his household while still not much more than a child, and visitors said she was competent, gracious, charming, and a pleasure to talk to, witty and sensible. He plainly adored her and she adored him; she wrote, "I had rather not live than not to be the daughter of such a man."

On a Burr Web site, one fan has gushed, "The love he lavished upon this daughter lends a sublimity to Burr's character which all the detractors in the world cannot blur." It may be, though, that at least one detractor used this same love to do more than blur. If Hamilton had been suggesting that Burr's relations with Theodosia were more than fatherly, the duel could hardly have been dodged.

The scholars dismiss this notion as just what you'd expect from modern Americans obsessed with sex, but then, the scholars don't know, any more than we do.

The night before the duel, Hamilton sat up late composing his own eulogy. He wrote, "My religious and moral principles are strongly opposed to the practice of duelling: and it would ever give me pain to shed the blood of a fellow-creature in a private combat forbidden by the laws." (This must have been a recent conversion, considering his prickly history. A principal in eleven affairs of honor and an assistant in several more, he'd once, after giving an unpopular defense of the Jay Treaty, walked down the street and issued two challenges within ten minutes. If your religion really prohibits shooting at people, it's rash to keep offering to do so.)

He tells us that since he was too honorable a gentleman to refuse the fight, but too good a Christian to shoot anybody, he has resolved *"to reserve and throw away my first fire, and I have thought even of reserving my second fire, and thus giving a double opportunity to Colonel Burr to pause and reflect."* The italics are Hamilton's. Apparently he's worried about Burr's immortal soul as well as his own; what could be more Christian?

He told everyone that he wouldn't fire at Burr, and most people believe to this day that he didn't. It seems against nature, somehow, to show up for a duel and just stand there waiting to get shot, like a beer can on a fence post, but perhaps he really was as noble as he said he was. What actually happened is open to interpretation.

Pendleton and Van Ness both left us their accounts. Hamilton, Pendleton, and Dr. Hosack were rowed across from New York to Weehawken, where they found Burr and Van Ness busy clearing brush away from the ground. Hats were doffed and polite greetings exchanged. Then "the seconds proceeded to make their arrangements. They measured the distance, ten full paces, and cast lots for the choice of position, and also to determine by whom the word should be given, both of which fell to the second of General Hamilton."

As the challenged party, it was Hamilton's duty to bring the pistols. He borrowed them from his brother-in-law, steel-barreled, brass-mounted .56-caliber flintlocks, sixteen inches long. They were fitted with hair triggers, but the world didn't know that until 1976, when a surviving original was taken apart to be reproduced; the hair-trigger mechanism was cleverly concealed under a lock in the stock.

They'd been used before several times, once by the owner against Aaron Burr in Hoboken, and once by Eacker against young Philip Hamilton when he fell on that very spot; history is fond of these little grace notes. They were used again later. With one of them, in 1820 in Missouri, Captain Samuel Hopkins killed a member of the Spanish nobility on his first fire. It's said the Burr-Hamilton guns killed their man in at least eleven duels. If you had them in the house, I expect you'd tiptoe around them with nervous respect.

The pistols loaded, Pendleton laid out the rules: "The parties being placed at their stations, the second who gives the word shall ask them whether they are ready; being answered in the affirmative, he shall say, 'Present'; after this the parties shall present and fire when they please. If one fires before the other, the opposite second shall say, 'One, two, three, fire,' and he (the principal) shall then fire or lose his fire."

Here the accounts diverge. Pendleton and the Hamiltonians say that Burr fired and hit Hamilton, who refrained from firing but, when he was struck, spun around and his gun went off into the air as his finger involuntarily clutched the trigger.

Van Ness begs to differ: "The pistol of General Hamilton was first discharged, and Colonel Burr fired immediately after. On this point I have the misfortune to disagree with the friend of General Hamilton, and without doubting the sincerity of his opinion, I can safely declare that I was never more firmly convinced of any fact that came under my observation. On the discharge of General Hamilton's pistol ⸮ observed a slight motion in the person of Colonel Burr, which gave me the idea that he was struck. On this point I conversed with Colonel Burr, when he returned, who ascribed the motion of his body to a small stone under his foot, and added the smoke of General Hamilton's pistol obscured his sight."

According to a letter from Burr himself, "When the word 'present' was given, he [Hamilton] took aim at his adversary and fired very promptly. The other [Burr] fired two or three seconds after him and the Gen'l instantly fell, exclaiming, 'I am a dead man.'"

Some authorities now believe that Hamilton, unused to the sensitive hair trigger, fired too soon and wildly. Others believe he simply missed. Many insist that, knowing he was at fault, the honorable gentleman felt he deserved to die and stood with his arms at his sides to meet his fate, though this doesn't fit well with anything else we know about him. Most still subscribe to the general feeling, widespread at the time, that Hamilton was a saintly martyr and probably would have become a noble president, and never fired at Burr, and the vice president was a murderous psychopath.

Many Americans confuse Burr with the assassin John Wilkes Booth.

Theodosia Burr was drowned in a shipwreck in 1812, off the treacherous Outer Banks of North Carolina. Her father was devastated. Various locals have seen her ghost. It seems to be upset about something.

*   *   *

Politically, Southerners have a soft spot for the colorful, for their scamps and rascals and scapegraces, and a genius for producing them. Over and over, they'll reelect the likes of a Huey Long or a Strom Thurmond, just to see what he'll get up to next. For a certain segment of Southern voters, entertainment value – the joy of opening the morning paper – ranks high at the polls. Will he, to make a point, ride a donkey up the steps of the Senate Office Building, hoist the Confederate flag over the statehouse, draw a sword, throw inkwells, throw food? Give an impassioned filibuster on arming schoolteachers or replacing the national eagle with the flamingo? Once in, if he goes on delivering entertainment and outrage, he's senator or governor for life. Agree with him or not, he's a grand old tradition.

John Randolph was the prototype. He was first elected to Congress in 1799; he spent twenty-four years in the House and two years in the Senate. (Being a Randolph never hurt anyone. To this day, in Virginia, a Randolph woman who marries will insert her maiden name in the middle, before her married one, and anyone whose mother was a Randolph will find occasion to bring it up. Thomas Jefferson's mother was a Randolph. It mattered.)

By all accounts John Randolph was one of our more peculiar politicians. Even his home was a plantation named Bizarre. He fought his maiden duel when he was eighteen and a student at William and Mary, where he seriously wounded another student over the pronunciation of a word used in the debating society. Long years later, with his opponent still carrying the bullet in his hip, they met again, and Randolph promptly snapped, "But Robert, it *was* pronounced so!"

He was brilliant, fractious, occasionally charming, more often vicious, and frequently drunk, though perhaps not as frequently as people thought; it was hard to tell. In one of his first pronouncements in Congress, he offered the toast, "Damn George Washington!" Accompanied by his pack of hound dogs and carrying a whip, he strode around the Capitol in riding breeches or flowing robes, voluminous coats, weird hats, and buckskin riding gloves, calling out for more glasses of porter and glaring insolently at his colleagues.

Physically, he was unfortunate, perhaps from mumps or scarlet fever as a child, perhaps from some genetic defect. Thin and undeveloped, from a distance he looked like a boy and, close up, like a wizened old man or a sickly bird, with sallow, wrinkled skin, a drizzle of coarse dark hair, and darting little eyes. His voice was shrill. He had no discernible sex life and, observers claimed, no reason to shave. A doctor's examination after his death confirmed that his manly parts were far from adequate, and of course his colleagues during his life made plenty of rude allusions to them, which can't have helped his naturally bad temper. His replies to their slurs are unprintable and shocked even Congress.

He called Daniel Webster "a vile slanderer," President Adams a "traitor," and Edward Livingston "the most contemptible and degraded of beings, whom no man ought to touch, unless with a pair of tongs." In return, people called him "the half-mad Virginian," "that long-dreaded churl and tyrant," "a planetary plague," "a boy with a mischievous syringe full of dirty water," and "a maniac in his strait jacket, accidentally broken out of his cell."

He challenged Daniel Webster to a duel over a debate on sugar. He called John Eppes a liar and promptly accepted his challenge. Nothing happened. Associates kept negotiating him out of duels. Once, he retracted his words. He told a man that he "wasn't fit to carry guts to a bear." The man demanded an apology or a duel. Randolph smiled and said, all right, he'd take it back, the fellow *was* fit to carry guts to a bear.

A raging snob, he hated democracy, the working classes, Negroes, most people who weren't Virginians, and above all, Kentucky, that unworthy backwoods poor relation of Virginia's, and Kentuckians like Henry Clay.

Clay was Speaker when the disputed election of 1825 was thrown into the House and Clay decided it in favor of John Quincy Adams instead of Jackson. Shortly thereafter, Adams made Clay secretary of state, and quite a lot of people complained that they must have made a deal. Most got over it, but not Randolph. In the words of a contemporary, "The very thought of Clay seemed to inspire his genius for vituperation; his eye would gleam, his meagre and attenuated form would writhe and contort as if under the enchantment of a demon; his long bony fingers would be extended as if pointing at an imaginary Clay, airdrawn as the dagger of Macbeth, as he would writhe the muscles of his beardless face ... pouring out the gall of his soul."

Things came to a boil over a mission to Latin America, supported by Clay and opposed by Randolph on the grounds that it might involve us in dealings with dark-skinned people. In a screeching speech, Randolph accused Clay of crucifying the Constitution and cheating at cards. Clay was indeed an ardent cardplayer, and he took umbrage: "Your unprovoked attack of my character, in the Senate of the U. States, on yesterday, allows me no other alternative than that of demanding personal satisfaction."

Randolph's well-chosen mentor in the matter was his friend Thomas Hart Benton, granduncle of the painter. Benton was probably the Senate's premier expert on duels. Once, back when he was an aide to Andrew Jackson, he'd quarreled with his boss over a rumored insult to his brother. The general threatened publicly to horsewhip him. What happened next was either a duel or a brawl, depending on your definition, at Nashville's City Hotel. Theodore Roosevelt wrote, "The details were so intricate that probably not even the participants themselves knew exactly what had taken place ... At any rate, Jackson was shot and Benton was pitched headlong downstairs, and all the other combatants were more or less damaged." When Jackson was carried off to a doctor, Benton snatched up his sword and triumphantly broke it over his knee.

Elected as the first United States senator from Missouri, he served for thirty years, and he and Jackson were the best of friends again. Sometimes only a fight will clear the air.

Benton couldn't act as a second because he was a blood relative of Mrs. Clay's and the rules on that were strict, but he stood loyally by. A Colonel Tatnall and the ubiquitous James Hamilton served as seconds.

Randolph kept telling them all that, like Alexander Hamilton, he didn't intend to shoot. His reasons were complicated. For one, his own kindheartedness: "I have determined to receive, without returning, Clay's fire; nothing shall induce me to harm a hair of his head; I will not make his wife a widow or his children orphans." This seems out of character, since he'd been longing to harm Clay's hairs ever since the War of 1812, and besides, Kentuckians hardly counted as human. What he may have had in mind was his own social and political future after killing a secretary of state with young children. If he showed up but held his fire, he'd be a hero in the Senate – assuming he survived.

For another, he believed that Clay had no right to demand an answer to something he'd said in a senatorial speech. As Benton wrote in his memoirs, "It was as much as to say, Mr. Clay may fire at me for what has offended him; I will not, by returning the fire, admit his right to do so."

At four in the afternoon of April 8, 1826, the party convened on the bank of the Potomac, near Little Falls Bridge. Randolph had insisted. Benton wrote, "If he fell, Randolph chose Virginia sod as the ground to receive his blood ... There was a statute of Virginia against duelling within her limits, but, as he merely went out to receive a fire without returning it, Randolph deemed that no fighting, and consequently no breach of her statute."

Actually, on his way there, he'd changed his mind about firing, when he was told that Clay would ask for a long, slow one-two-three count, giving him plenty of time to take aim. This must have meant Clay planned to kill him Then he heard this wasn't true and changed his mind back again. He wouldn't fire, he said, unless he could tell from "the devil in Clay's eye" that his opponent had murder in mind.

James Hamilton wrote, "I shall never forget this scene as long as I live. It has been my misfortune to witness several duels, but I never saw one, at least in its sequel, so deeply affecting. The sun was just setting behind the blue hills of Randolph's own Virginia. Here were two of the most extraordinary men our country in its prodigality has produced, about to meet in mortal combat."

Extraordinary indeed: The wizened Randolph had produced from his eccentric closet a long, white, flowing flannel bathrobe to wear for the occasion.

Tatnall loaded Randolph's gun and set the hair trigger. Randolph said he was one of the best shots in Virginia but he'd never fired a hair trigger; he pulled on a heavy buckskin glove which, he said, "will destroy the delicacy of my touch, and the trigger may fly before I know where I am."

What happened next is subject to debate. Because of their unofficial status and the abashed cover-up, duels leave no historical footprint and sometimes seem to float amorphously in the realm of mythology. No disinterested reporters stood by to take notes; few disinterested reporters could have been found, and even fewer disinterested newspapers for them to report to. Partisan seconds, witnesses, friends, and enemies posted different accounts.

Before Clay had received his pistol, Randolph was holding his pointed at the ground, and it went off. For a brief moment it looked as if he'd fired at an unarmed man. "I protested against that hair trigger," he cried to Tatnall. Generously, Clay said it was surely an accident. This must have irritated Randolph, who planned to come off as the generous one himself. It was humiliating. He changed his mind again.

The count was given. Both fired, Randolph as well as Clay, and missed. Randolph's bullet hit a stump, Clay's hit the ground. Benton suggested they call it quits, but both insisted on another fire. Clay's hit the long white bathrobe. Randolph, reverting to his original plan, fired at the sky, loudly announcing, "I do not fire at you, Mr. Clay."

Overwrought chroniclers report that the reconciliation was affecting. One reports, "The moment Mr. Clay saw that Randolph had thrown away his fire, with a gush of sensibility he instantly approached Mr. Randolph, and said, with an emotion I never can forget; 'I trust to God, my dear sir, you are untouched. After what has occurred I would not have harmed you for a thousand worlds.'"

I'm not sure about that. Another reports, less emotionally, that Randolph pointed to the hole in his robe and said, "You owe me a coat, Mr. Clay," and Clay said, "I am glad the debt is no more."

Thomas Hart Benton wrote, "The joy of all was extreme at this happy termination of a most critical affair, and we immediately left with lighter hearts than we brought."

Carl Schurz, in his life of Clay, wrote, "Randolph's pistol had failed to prove that Clay was a 'blackguard' and Clay's pistol had also failed to prove that Randolph was a 'calumniator'; but according to the mysterious process of reasoning which makes the pistol the arbiter of honor, the honor of each was satisfied."

Benton summed it up more briskly: "It was about the first

high-toned duel that I have witnessed, and among the highest-toned that I have ever witnessed."

You could always count on a Randolph for tone.

Stephen Decatur

VII. BLOODY BLADENSBURG

I N A RATHER longer version – the author was apparently paid by the word – the following appeared in *Harper's New Monthly Magazine* in March of 1858.

On the old stage road leading from Washington to Baltimore, a short half mile beyond the District of Columbia, and within a mile of Bladensburg, a few years ago the traveler might have observed the right hand side of the road – just where it crossed a little bridge – a small patch of low, unreclaimed land, thickly overgrown with trees and tangled vines. There may have been ten or fifteen acres of it. It was one of those neglected corners where everything had been so long permitted to have its own way, that even a bold cultivation might pause before it in despair. A rank vegetation had overspread the place in savage exuberance, apparently defying all human efforts to penetrate it ... Altogether, it was as forsaken a little spot, and one little likely to be sought by man, for any purpose whatever, as would probably be encountered in a summer's day journey.

Apart from this wildness, however, there was nothing about the place to attract the attention of the traveler, and unless it had been specially pointed out to him by someone acquainted with its history, he would, in all likelihood, have passed it wholly unobserved. But yet that dark looking jungle, apparently so void of interest, is a locality known all over America. It is the celebrated BLADENSBURG DUELING GROUND.

And it was precisely such a spot as would naturally have been selected for the purposes of the duel. It was just outside the jurisdiction of the District of Columbia, it was easy of approach from the city of Washington, and convenient for escape from the authorities of Maryland. It was hemmed in on three sides by hills, which seemed to stand like sentinels to guard the privacy of the place; while on the fourth, by which the road ran, it was effectually screened from observation by the thick foliage of the trees, and the matted roof of overhanging vines; so that in every respect it seemed peculiarly adapted for the objects to which it had been dedicated. A small brook crosses the turnpike, and wound its way among the elders toward the Potomac. Along the banks of this stream by dint of much patient engineering the cattle had trampled a path into the thicket in search of shade or water.

This narrow cowpath was "the field of honor." Here, in the dim twilight of this wilderness of brambles, not fifty yards from the road, the impetuous spirits from Washington and the States adjacent brought their controversies for adjustment. It was an appeal from the rhetoric of words to the logic of arms. It was the court of last resort, in which knotty points of dispute, abstruse social problems, and questions of veracity, propriety, and right were expounded by the convincing power of gunpowder.

The process of ratiocination was exceedingly luminous and so simple as to be adapted to the commonest capacity. It was based on the theory of some supposed connection between saltpeter and a change of opinion. It assumed that an argument made by a rhetorician might be unintelligible or inconclusive, but that a syllogism propelled by powder, if properly aimed, could hardly fail to carry conviction to the dullest intellect. It believed that the intricate bearings of a subject could be best investigated at ten paces; and that propositions, difficult, and apparently irreconcilable, by a piece of hollow hardware, held parallel to the observer's line of vision, could be rendered perfectly simple and harmonious. Hence the pistol was esteemed the most effective of moral agents; though new views of duty were sometimes revealed through the rifle, and obstinate ideas exploded from the muzzle of the musket. Principals with their friends, seconds with their instruments of relief, were generally the sole witnesses of these desperate proceedings. The ground was measured, the choice decided, the antagonists placed, the word given, and then, by administration of justice somewhat peculiar, if the Honor which had demanded redress for a grievous wrong limped away with the loss of his leg, or if the reputation which had sought to vindicate itself from unmerited aspersion received a ball through its heart, the "satisfaction" was deemed simple and complete.

The ground usually chosen for the combat was that portion of the path which ran along the west margin of the brook, at right angles to the road. It is estimated that upward of twenty duels have been fought at this particular spot. Other portions of the field, and even other fields in the same neighborhood, were sometimes selected, where the parties wished more effectively to baffle pursuit and secure for their meeting greater privacy. But the path above described was emphatically the dueling ground. It was the spot which has given to Bladensburg so much uncoveted notoriety. It was the magniloquent "elsewhere" that casts so formidable a shadow in the wordy controversies of these latter days. What peculiar virtues were there in this particular cowpath, that it should have been accorded such high pre-eminence over all other places, and that it should have been selected by duelists even from the remote States of the Union, it would be a difficult task to determine. The blood of the gallant Decatur undoubtedly gave a melancholy celebrity to the soil, and on that account it may have been esteemed as the most fitting field for a contemplated conflict. With some it may have been supposed that an affair should be attended with greater *eclat* when conducted so near to the dignitaries of the National Government, and under the very eyes of the law makers of the land. Another reason may have been its convenient proximity to Washington City – a locality, from the very nature of its heterogeneous society and the conflicting interests concentrating there, unusually fruitful in scenes of personal difficulty. Certain it is that this neighborhood became the resort of dueling parties soon after the removal of the present seat of government to its present location. As early as 1814 it is recorded that Edward Hopkins, of Maryland, an ensign of infantry, was slain in a duel in this vicinity. Since then, it is said to have been the scene of over fifty hostile meetings. Many of the difficulties were amicably arranged on the arrival of the parties in the field. Others were adjusted after a bloodless exchange of shots. In some the conflict was continued until one or both of the parties were wounded; and in not a few death has resulted from the first shot.

The brook beside the path was known locally as Blood Run. Historians estimate that over a hundred duels were fought there. Nobody knows. Much of the time, nothing got into the records unless one of you died, and the records themselves, such as they are, are elusive.

Stephen Decatur, naval hero, fell at Bladensburg, and as *Harper's* points out, his blood gave "a melancholy celebrity to the soil" and helped make it the traditional pilgrimage for Washington-area combatants.

Unlike the real Alexander Hamilton, the real Decatur seems to have been almost too noble to live, and unlike most military heroes, he was even a sweetheart in civilian life. The usually surly John Quincy Adams wrote, "He was kind, warm-hearted, unassuming, gentle and hospitable, beloved in social life and with a soul totally and utterly devoted to his country." He was even born in a log cabin.

In short, the perfect man of his day.

For those who can't quite remember him, it was Decatur who raised his glass in the deathless toast, "To our country! In her intercourse with foreign nations, may she always be in the right; but our country, right or wrong!" In his various portraits, he's a handsome dog whose shapely legs enhance the form-fitting naval trousers. One historian calls him "the beau ideal of a naval officer."

According to his awed biographer, Alexander Slidell Mackenzie, "The erectness of his figure, adding to the appearance of his height, harmonized with the towering arrangement of his head, which, inclining upwards, gave him a spirited and noble air, and contributed to the graceful stateliness of his carriage. His hair and beard were black and curling, his brow lofty and calm, terminating in dark and well-arched brows; his eyes large; black, and lustrous, habitually soft and gentle in their expression, but of piercing brightness in moments of excitement ... The expression of his countenance, when in repose, was calm, contemplative, and benignant; in conversation, complaisant and persuasive; in scenes of excitement, spirited, stirring, and commanding."

James Barron, who killed him, looks less like a post captain than a Victorian paterfamilias a bit too fond of his port, but no doubt his picture was painted in later life.

Both men came from naval families; both were involved with the Barbary pirates that gave us so much grief in our early years. Under the wicked guidance of the emperor of Morocco, these shark ships patrolled the Mediterranean and extracted ruinous tributes from those passing by or, alternatively, captured their ships and sold the crew. Nobody managed to do much about them until, in 1804, Decatur led seventy-four volunteers into Tripoli harbor and burned the captured American frigate *Philadelphia*. Britain's Lord Nelson called this "the most daring act of the age," and Decatur was made a captain at just twenty-five, the youngest ever in the American navy.

He had the lucky star of the born hero. In the War of 1812, as captain of the frigate *United States*, he defeated the British frigate *Macedonian* and brought her safely back to the United States, where she was refitted and commissioned in the American navy, the only such triumph in the whole war.

Barron's star was less benign. After the Revolution, a vexing question left unsettled was the right of search at sea, under which British ships stopped American ships and scoured them for sailors who, according to the British, might be deserters from the British navy and needed to be hauled back and flogged. In 1807, James Barron was sent out as captain of the American frigate *Chesapeake*, but he'd had to leave in haste and nothing was in order. In fact, she seems to have resembled a fraternity house on Sunday morning, with tackle and spars and crates of supplies littered all over the decks, nothing to fire the cannons with, and a crew that scarcely knew a cannon from a capstan anyway.

This wasn't really Barron's fault. The Norfolk navy yard and the brass in Washington should have known better, considering the tense state of the high seas. Unsurprisingly, Barron met up with the British frigate *Leopard* almost at once.

The *Leopard* hailed the *Chesapeake*, asking her to stop and take on some dispatches for delivery, a common enough practice at sea, but when Barron lay to, the *Leopard* instead sent a boat with a search order for several suspected deserters on board. Barron refused them and tried to get his shambles of a ship in shape to fight.

After the messenger rowed back to the *Leopard*, she opened fire and pounded the *Chesapeake* nonstop. Wounded, Barron begged someone to try to fire something, anything, to look like a response, and a gallant Lieutenant Henry Allen picked up a live coal from the galley stove in his fingers and touched it to a cannon, managing to discharge a single hopeless shot that went through the hull of the *Leopard*, but by that time the *Chesapeake* had three dead, eighteen wounded, twenty-one holes in her hull, her masts in splinters, and her sails in rags. Barron asked to surrender.

Some sources say he surrendered; others say the British captain refused surrender, since this would have put things on a wartime footing, but whatever happened, the British captain sent some armed men on board to pluck up four alleged deserters and then sailed away with them, leaving the crippled *Chesapeake* to wallow slowly back to Hampton Roads.

Poor Barron faced a court of inquiry, prerequisite for a court-martial, on charges of "neglecting, on the probability of an engagement, to clear his ship for action." To those of us who weren't on board at the time, this seems unfair; would clearing away some of the clutter on deck have turned up, maybe under a carton of soup, something to fire the cannons with? Or was the Navy Department so embarrassed by the unreadiness of the *Chesapeake* that it needed Barron to take the fall? Who knows? Anyway, he was suspended from rank and pay for five years, starting in February 1808.

Stephen Decatur sat on the inquiry board.

Hurt and angry, Barron went abroad and stayed there, in Denmark or Belgium or perhaps somewhere else, depending on which account you read, until 1818, long after his suspension expired. By the time he came home, as his enemies pointed out, the War of 1812 was safely over. He applied to be restored to active service.

Stephen Decatur sat on that board too.

Decatur was now the darling of Washington, with a pretty wife and a handsome house on Lafayette Square, within hailing distance of the White House. He was chosen to give the first of many prenuptial parties for President Monroe's daughter Maria. Everyone loved him, or almost everyone; nobody can be a popular national hero and social pet without a few enemies gathering in the shadows. His wife, for one, always believed that the duel was more complicated than it seemed, instigated by a cabal of jealous naval officers rather than just the disappointed Barron.

Along with most of the other officers involved in the inquiry board, Decatur, now commodore, opposed Barron's welcome back.

He said that "he ought not to be received again into the naval service; there was not enough employment for all the officers who had faithfully discharged their duty to their country in the hour of trial; and it would be doing an act of injustice to employ him to the exclusion of any one of them."

His wife may have been right. Troublemakers might well have embroidered Decatur's opinions in reporting them to Barron, as with Hamilton and Burr. In the American upper professional levels, malicious manly gossip had replaced the old European model of affronts and jostling.

If there were no meddlers behind the quarrel, it all seems a bit silly: Barron's grievance was that Decatur, having sat on the first board of inquiry and formed an opinion, shouldn't have sat on the second, which imposed "the cruel and unmerited sentence passed upon me." And, of course, the usual rumors about what Barron said people said Decatur said.

A voluminous correspondence followed. Barron accused Decatur of saying he "could insult me with impunity." Decatur wrote back denying it. Barron accepted his denial, but Decatur wrote back again saying that was the *only* statement he denied. Then Barron wrote a long letter accusing Decatur of "ungenerously traducing my character whenever an occasion occurred" and that "you tauntingly and boastfully observed that you would cheerfully meet me in the field, and hoped I would yet act like a man . . ."

If Decatur was half as nice as John Quincy Adams thought, it's not likely he'd talk like that. It sounds like troublemakers" tattle. After the fight, Barron himself said, "There have been some cruel meddling men engaged in this affair for a long time past."

He concludes his missive by saying his eyes were bad and he wasn't as good a shot as Decatur, but feels himself entitled to choose the time, place, and distance.

By now the exchange of mail had lasted five months. Decatur replied recapping it all and reminding Barron that he, Decatur, had indeed begged to be excused from the court-martial because of his prior experience in the matter, but the secretary of the navy insisted. Further, he'd told Barron's advocate on the court that he'd step aside if Barron wanted, but since Barron didn't ask him to, he didn't.

He doesn't want to fight Barron: "I should be much better pleased to have nothing to do with you. I do not think that fighting duels, under any circumstances, can raise the reputation of any man, and have long since discovered, that it is not even an unerring criterion of personal courage." (He spoke from experience, having been involved in several.)

Unable to resist a snide shot, he adds, "From your manner of proceeding, it appears to me, that you have come to the determination to fight some one, and that you have selected me for that purpose; and I must take leave to observe, that your object would have been better attained, had you made this decision during our late war, when your fighting might have benefited your country, as well as yourself."

Barron writes back at even greater length, page after page of paranoia, until the historian longs for the old simple glove in the face. He accuses Decatur of "a ridiculous, malicious, absurd, improbable falsehood," of "assertions unsustained by the shadow of truth," and says he did, too, apply for active service during the War of 1812.

As for dueling, "I consider it as a barbarous practice which ought to be exploded from civilized society. But, sir, there may be causes of such extraordinary and aggravated assault and injury, received by an individual, as to render an appeal to arms, on his part, absolutely necessary." (By then, most nice people felt about duels rather the way the nicer Southern aristocracy felt about slavery: a perfectly dreadful institution, but there it is and what can you do?)

Decatur replied that he'd really prefer to ignore the letter but can't let its various calumnies slide, and besides, can't Barron simply stop it with the letters and call him out if he's going to do so? Perhaps, he hints, Barron just wants to goad Decatur into giving the challenge, leaving himself to decide on the delicate matters of weapons and distance. After hashing over whether Barron could have come back from Europe to fight in 1812 if he'd tried, he closes, "I have now to inform you, that I shall pay no further attention to any communication you may make to me, other than a direct call to the field."

Barron, incapable of a simple sentence, sends still more grievances, but he does say that "whenever you will consent to meet me on fair and equal grounds, that is, such as two honorable men may consider just and proper, you are at liberty to view this as that call."

Exasperated, Decatur replies that he is "at a loss to know what your intention is. If you intend it as a challenge, I accept it," and says he'll send his friend Commodore Bainbridge.

Bainbridge met with Barron's second, Jesse Elliott, and they agreed on Bladensburg, pistols at eight paces, and that "previously to firing, the parties shall be directed to present, and shall not fire before the word 'one' is given, or after the word 'three.'"

After hosting a last grand memorable party, Decatur sat up late writing his will, and then on March 22 he met Bainbridge and his associate, Samuel Hamilton (Hamiltons do keep turning up in the annals), for breakfast at Beale's Hotel on Capitol Hill before setting out by carriage to Bladensburg.

The ground was paced off, the combatants took their places, and Barron said he hoped that they would be better friends "on meeting in another world." Decatur said, "I have never been your enemy, sir." At the word "two," they both fired.

One source says that Decatur had announced that, having no desire to kill, he would shoot Barron in the hip. Another says it was true about the hip, but that was in a different duel, in Philadelphia. One says Barron was wounded in the thigh; certainly he was wounded, and looked in a fair way to perish, but recovered within a month and went on to a long though undistinguished career in the navy and died at eighty-nine.

Decatur was hit in the stomach. "I am mortally wounded," he told his second, "at least I believe so, and wish that I had fallen in defense of my country."

A patriot to the end. He was carried to his house on Lafayette Square and died twelve hours later.

Washington mourned. Most of the town's population came to his funeral, including the president, the cabinet, half of Congress, and the Supreme Court. The nation's grief found outlet, as it usually did in the nineteenth century, in a torrent of dreadful poetry. Sample:

Our hero dies, and yet his name emblazoned on the naval
  role of fame
Shall live till yonder bright star to seamen dear
Shall cease to brighten the northern sphere
Till winds no more shall rage nor fires roar
And freedom's sun shall rise to set no more.

Dueling stories often leave questions hanging in the mind, such as, Why did Decatur agree to meet Barron? It's true that Barron was unusually persistent, and true that the navy had always been strict about answering challenges, but surely the man had been so thoroughly discredited and surely Decatur's credentials were so well established that an icy aloofness would have served. Why not simply refuse the letters? Hand them back unread? What could Barron do, post him for a coward, the hero of Tripoli, gallant commander of 1812? Decatur's life at the time looks unusually well worth living. Why did he risk it? Who knows?

You'd think that after the death of a man so beloved, the authorities might have cracked down on dueling, but it was eighteen more years until the District of Columbia made it illegal to offer or accept a challenge within its small boundaries; traffic to Bladensburg continued anyway. Virginia's antidueling law had passed back in 1809, New York's not until 1828. The navy didn't forbid it until 1862; they'd always been proud of their spirited lads, and the Code Duello was in every midshipman's handbook.

These restrictive efforts had the usual effect, especially in

Washington, where the average cop on the beat thought twice about marching off with a brace of handcuffed senators.

Most of Bladensburg's visitors were more political than Decatur. Unlike the impulsive Old World quarrels over card games and jostling, political duels tended to be long-festering: sullen, incestuous differences that would suddenly flare to the fighting point over a nothing. Much depends on who said what to whom at the time. Nobody seems quite clear what triggered the Mason-McCarty fight.

General Armistead T. Mason of Virginia was a United States senator, though rather illegally, since he was only twenty-eight in 1816 when he was elected and senators are supposed to be thirty. Colonel John M. McCarty was a cousin of his, but this doesn't signify; they were Virginians, and all the Virginians who mattered were cousins. Mason was a Republican, McCarty was a Federalist.

According to their hometown newspaper, *The Genius of Liberty* of Leesburg, some forty miles northwest of Washington, Mason had introduced a bill to allow the numerous Quakers of his home county, when called up for military service, to pay five hundred dollars to hire proxies, since war was against their religion. Presumably McCarty disapproved. A different source says the first quarrel took place at the Leesburg polls during an election, when Mason questioned McCarty's right to vote, but this seems absurd. McCarty was an adult white male army colonel and, more important locally, a grandson of George Mason of Gunstan Hall. If he couldn't vote, nobody could.

In any case, McCarty sent Mason a challenge in which he

impertinently presumed to set the terms and conditions of the fight. Mason was persuaded to decline the challenge but to add that he would accept one in proper form, properly worded. McCarty ignored this offer and posted Mason as a coward. Mason challenged McCarty. McCarty declined on the grounds that it was Mason who was a coward, since he'd declined to fight the first time.

At this point Mason's friends got together and persuaded him to forget the whole thing, and the matter would have faded away if he hadn't found himself, months later, riding to Richmond in the same stagecoach as Andrew Jackson. Jackson, who loved duels second only to horse racing, urged him to follow through and try again. Jackson was a persuasive man.

Perhaps out of respect for Virginia's new antidueling law he resigned his commission as general of militia. He made his will and wrote to McCarty, "I have resigned my commission for the special and sole purpose of fighting you; and I am now free to accept or send a challenge and to fight a duel. The public mind has become tranquil, and all suspicion of the further prosecution of our quarrel having subsided, we can now terminate it without being arrested by the civil authority, and without exciting alarm among our friends . . . I am extremely anxious to terminate at once and forever this quarrel. My friends _____ and _____ are fully authorized to act for me in every particular. Upon receiving from you a pledge to fight, they are authorized and instructed at once to give the challenge for me, and to make immediately every necessary arrangement for the duel, on any terms you may prescribe."

In a separate letter he gave to his seconds, he added that he would "agree to any terms he may propose, and to any distance –

to three feet, his pretended favorite distance – or to three inches, should his impetuous and rash courage prefer it. To any species of firearms – pistols, muskets, or rifles – agree at once."

Again Mason's seconds went to McCarty with the message; again McCarty refused to accept it, again because Mason was unworthy. The seconds, insulted, started a fight and one of them threatened to post McCarty if he didn't accept. He accepted.

Apparently he accepted in a fatalistic spirit, determined that neither of them should survive. Or else he was joking; political duelers were a humorless lot, but McCarty just might have been teasing. Or he might have been suicidal. His first proposal was that he and Mason should jump together off the dome of the Capitol. This was considered contrary to the Code Duello, so he proposed fighting across a barrel of gunpowder. The seconds understandably objected. Then he suggested a hand-to-hand combat with daggers, which was also disallowed, and finally proposed muskets charged with buckshot, at ten feet. This would be nearly as conclusive as jumping off the Capitol, but Mason had said he could set the terms, so they were accepted, with the adjustment of a single ball instead of buckshot and twelve feet instead of ten.

They met on the Bladensburg grounds in February, 1819, in a ferocious snowstorm, accompanied by many curious local citizens. Did either of them, by this time, have the slightest recollection of what started it all? Was it really about Quakers in the military? A taunt at the polls on election day? Calling each other cowards? Federalism? Some sulky, half-forgotten incident at a family picnic twenty years before?

In spite of the weather, McCarty showed up in a shirt with the sleeves rolled up. Mason wore a voluminous coat. They were set in their places, muzzles almost touching, and fired. Mason was literally blown away. Bizarrely, McCarty, though badly wounded in the arm, survived. One source says Mason missed because, as he raised his musket to fire, it got tangled in the long skirts of his overcoat.

Mason's remains were carried to Leesburg and buried at St. James Episcopal. *The Genius of Liberty* wrote, "A Great Man Has Fallen – On Saturday morning last, about 10 o'clock, Gen. Armistead T. Mason, of this county, fell in a duel with Mr. John M McCarty, near Bladensburg. Various and contradictory are the reports in circulation about this melancholy and mournful catastrophe. We forebear making a statement of the facts as we find them afloat, but shall remain silent until they are developed by those who have it in their power to make a full and correct detail . . ."

An investigation accused McCarty of cheating. The deceased was found with three wounds in his left side and one in his elbow; the rule was for a single ball. However, careful investigators rinsed off the bits of lead and weighed them and, put together, they weighed about what the single ball would have weighed. They decided that the ball had struck the elbow bone and split into three parts, each one crashing separately into the senator, which doesn't speak well for the quality of shot in the nineteenth century.

For reasons unclear, Mason's disappearance was never formally announced to the Senate and he's largely slipped below the gaze of history. Nobody mentions whether his constituents mourned his loss, or the other senators noticed his vacant desk, or the Quakers lamented the loss of their proxy-bill sponsor – if indeed there was such a bill – or even what the problem was in the first place.

When McCarty died, his ghost, apparently repentant, went back to Bladensburg and was often seen wandering around brooding. According to the locals he had plenty of company, including the ghost of Francis Scott Key's son Daniel, age twenty, who died here following an argument with a friend about the relative speed of two steamboats they were watching.

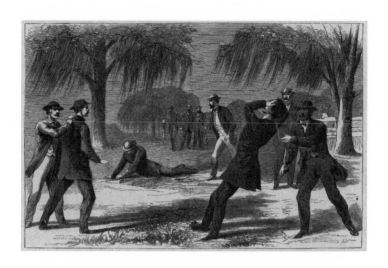

VIII. SOUTHERN SPIRITS

I N 1838, THE same year that duels were outlawed in the nation's
capital, the governor of South Carolina, John Lyde Wilson,
published a sixteen-page pamphlet revising the Code Duello for
American use. For twenty years it was reprinted over and over
and sold like hotcakes.

The South liked its duels. People in cool, damp places like
England are fond of saying that southerners everywhere are quarrelsome. In England, warm, sunny weather is well known to rot
the character and inflame the baser passions; it takes a bone-chilling
island fog to produce reasonable, thoughtful, temperate people.
Perhaps it does; more duels were fought in New Orleans than
in Boston.

More than climate was at work, though. Southerners liked to

think of themselves as spirited and aristocratic, compared to the soulless, cold, money-grubbing merchants of the North, and duels were an aristocratic tradition. Besides, in much of the South, a passion for hunting was passed down from fathers to sons; boys grew up with firearms and kept them handy and well oiled.

In his introduction to "The American Code; or, Rules for the Government of Principals and Seconds in Dueling," Governor Wilson, like all good people, claims to be against dueling. Frivolous dueling, that is. But in some situations, only a duel will do. As precedent, he points to the American Revolution: "If an oppressed nation has a right to appeal to arms in defence of its liberty and the happiness of its people, there can be no argument used in support of such appeal which will not apply with equal force to individuals. How many cases are there that might be enumerated where there is no tribunal to do justice to an oppressed and deeply-wronged individual? If he be subjected to a tame submission to insult and disgrace, where no power can shield him from its effects, then indeed, it would seem that the first law of nature, self-preservation, points out the only remedy for his wrongs."

There's no getting away from it: "The elements themselves war together, and the angels of heaven have met in fierce encounter." When a man finds himself shunned by his friends and "traces all his misfortunes and misery to the slanderous tongue of the calumniator, who, by secret whisper or artful innuendo, had sapped and undermined his reputation, he must be more or less than man to submit in silence." Duels, he says, "will be persisted in as long as a manly independence and a lofty personal pride in all that dignifies and ennobles the human character shall continue to exist."

It would be nice, he admits, if Christian forbearance ruled the world. It would be nice if everyone stopped insulting everyone else. In the meantime, here are the rules.

Wilson puts less emphasis on the subtle degrees of insult than the old code – an insult's an insult, except when it involves a lady and then it's worse. "Insults at the wine table" must be answered for, but if the fellow claims he can't remember a thing about it, he may say so in writing and take back whatever they say he said. "Intoxication is not a full excuse for insult, but it will greatly palliate."

Wilson gives more authority to the seconds in the matter: Tell your second everything about the problem, then leave it entirely in his hands. The Code Duello was drawn up in Ireland, where seconds were notoriously volatile and often even fiercer than the principals; in America, Wilson relies on them to calm people down and, if possible, prevent the fight.

As a second, he says, "You are supposed to be cool and collected, and your friend's feelings are more or less irritated . . . Use every effort to soothe and tranquilize your principal; do not see things in the same aggravated light in which he views them; extenuate the conduct of his adversary whenever you see clearly an opportunity to do so . . . Endeavor to persuade him that there must have been some misunderstanding . . . Check him if he uses opprobrious epithets toward his adversary, and never permit improper or insulting words in the note you carry."

Seconding was not to be undertaken lightly. If you carry your friend's note and the blackguard won't receive it, demand a reason, and if he won't give one, send him a note yourself insisting on an explanation, since now you too have been insulted. If he won't explain, or says that your friend is beneath his notice, it's your duty to challenge him. If he won't meet you, post him for a coward.

When all peacemaking efforts have failed, the two seconds get together to make the arrangements. Wilson claims that perfect equality must reign: "The old notion that the party challenged was authorized to name the time, place, distance, and weapon, has long since exploded, nor would a man of chivalric honor use such a right if he possessed it." This must actually have been fairly recent, or fairly Southern, since Barron worked hard enough to force Decatur to give the challenge so he could make the choices. (Both differ from the Code Duello, which says, "The challenged chooses his ground, the challenger chooses his distance, the seconds fix the time and terms of firing.")

On the appointed day, Wilson says, "The principals are to be respectful in meeting, and neither by look nor expression irritate each other. They are to be wholly passive, being entirely under the guidance of the seconds." The weapons should be smoothbore pistols, not more than nine inches long, with flint and steel, and the seconds as well as the principals have them, "to enforce a fair combat." If the other man fires before the signal, you as a second may shoot at him, and if your friend got hit by the illegal shot, it's your duty to do so.

Like Hamlet, the gentlemen of the Old South may take arms against a sea of troubles, and by opposing end them.

It was appropriate that the new rules came from South Carolina, home to the country's only known dueling club. Its officers were chosen on the basis of the number of men they'd killed or wounded, and of course the president was the man with the most. One day a British naval officer was visiting Charleston to investigate some property of his wife's and chanced to quarrel with the club president, who challenged him. The officer accepted, and the next day eight or ten club members paid him a warning visit: His opponent was an expert, all but invincible, such as might be called a professional duelist, and it would be prudent to find some way to back out of the engagement without dishonor.

His country's reputation at stake, the Englishman retorted, "I am not afraid of any duelist in the world" and, to everyone's dismay, mortally wounded the president at first fire. Expiring, that gentleman called his club members to his bedside and told them the club had been a bad idea and they ought to disband it. The day after he was buried, they formally did so.

Somehow this has a whiff of bad sportsmanship about it, almost of sour grapes, as if it had been a fine idea to meet in honor of killing other people, but when your own ox gets gored, you pack up and go home.

Historians make much of the fact that South Carolina also had an antidueling society, with many prominent citizens among its members, but few people paid any attention at the time.

The Southern novelist William Simms wrote proudly that the Southern duelist "fights to maintain his position in society, to silence insult, to check brutality, prevent encroachment, avenge a wrong of some sort, and in obedience to fierce passions that will not let him sleep under the sense of injury and annoyance." Some, of course, were more easily annoyed than others.

Richmond duelists headed for Belle Isle in the James River. Natchez favored Vidalia, in the Mississippi, because it was convenient for the citizens to row over and watch. Bloody Island served St. Louis. Memphis crossed the river into Arkansas to fight; Arkansans farther south repaired to the mouth of the White River in Mississippi. Midriver, on a paddle-wheel steamer, was a law-free oasis, and James Bowie killed a gambler in a duel over a card game aboard a riverboat.

New Orleans went to the Oaks.

New Orleans treasures its traditions and its tourist trade; nobody has chopped down the Dueling Oaks to make room for an office tower. Indeed, it would take more than ordinary nerve to lay an ax on one of these ancients. However pragmatic you might be, and real-estate developers are known to be pragmatic, it would be hard not to believe in some extra-arboreal spirit here, not necessarily friendly. Revenge from these trees might be fearsome. They know a lot about revenge.

Safely surrounded now by City Park, the oaks grow wider than tall, and twenty people might live comfortably under one, like Robin Hood's gang under the Greenwood Tree. Half a dozen duelists at once might fight in its shelter. The trunks are massive and bulging, no two grown alike, grotesquely molded, trunks such as a prehistoric rhinoceros would have if a rhinoceros were a tree. Too short to tempt lightning, too thick and well anchored for hurricane winds, they squat safely under the weather and endure. Their far-flung branches drip gray curtains of Spanish moss, reaching out and down over their pools of shade until they touch the grass. All among them now joggers go about their grim duties, looking neither left nor right, and tales of dead men trot along beside them.

In their glory days the Oaks lived on the plantation of one Louis Allard, far enough from the city to be out of the eye of the law. In 1892, the New Orleans *Times-Democrat* wrote, "Blood has been shed under the old cathedral aisles of nature. Between 1834 and 1844 scarcely a day passed without duels being fought at the Oaks. Why, it would not be strange if the very violets blossomed red of this soaked grass! The lover for his mistress, the gentleman for his honor, the courtier for his King; what loyalty has not cried out in pistol shot and scratch of steel! Sometimes two or three hundred people hurried from the city to witness these human baitings. On the occasion of one duel the spectators could stand no more, drew their swords, and there was a general melee."

On a single busy Sunday in 1839, ten duels were fought under the Oaks. I suppose parties of strollers dressed in their churchgoing finery wandered among them, sampling the entertainment, mindful of stray bullets, and moving on, like going from booth to booth at a country fair.

In the old cemeteries, proud headstones mark the graves: "Died on the Field of Honor"; "He Fell in a Duel." They admired themselves for their tempers, these Creoles of French and Spanish descent. Bernard de Marigny took his future wife to a ball and wouldn't let any of the other young blades dance with her. Furious, seven of the slighted sent him challenges; he fought and conquered all seven, one after the other.

By 1830, the bloodshed had risen to a flood, and a contemporary journalist observed, "The least breach of etiquette, the most venial sin against politeness, the least suspicion thrown of unfair dealing, even a bit of awkwardness, are causes sufficient for a cartel, which none dares refuse." The exception was a blow. Should a gentleman so far forget himself as to strike another gentleman, he was cast instantly beyond the pale. No duel resulted. He'd forfeited the privileges of killing or dying and become socially invisible.

Across the ocean a hundred years later, the Viennese writer and playwright Arthur Schnitzler looked back on the lost gallantry and mused, "Life was more beautiful and certainly had a more elevated air in those days – among other reasons, precisely because one sometimes had to put one's life on the line for something that in a higher sense or at least in a different sense possibly did not exist . . . For honor, for example, or the virtue of a beloved woman, or the good reputation of a sister, or for some other such triviality . . . That alone, believe me, gave social life a certain dignity or at least a certain style."

At a supper, Bienaime Christe de Lauzon moved his sister's chair too close to the chair of M. Morel's fair companion. Morel called him out onto the balcony, slapped his face with a glove, and, two days later, killed him under the Oaks.

Unsurprisingly, New Orleans was hog heaven for fencing masters. They set up shop in the French Quarter, on Exchange Alley between Royal and Bourbon streets, and formed a separate clique of their own. They were the rock stars of their day. Small boys followed them around town, agog with admiration. The mulatto Bastile Croquere, one of the best, was a great dandy and strolled the streets resplendent in his trademark green broadcloth suit, jingling under his collection of antique cameo jewelry. Like rock stars, though, they weren't considered quite top-drawer, and however you worshiped your fencing master, you wouldn't want your sister to marry him.

She wouldn't have had a peaceful life. The teachers fought extracurricularly, partly from pride in their skill and partly as advertisements for their competing schools. Bonneville fought and killed his rival, the Frenchman Dauphin, and then Reynard fought and killed Bonneville and took over all his pupils. L'Alouette killed Shubra. If he fought half as many duels as they say, Don José Llulla, known as Pepe, may have broken all records for sheer quantity; he was the South's best hand with the saber, just as good with a broadsword, and unbeatable with rapier or smallsword. With a rifle, he could hit any coin you tossed into the air or shoot an egg off his little son's head at thirty paces. With the bowie knife he was simply a genius. He maintained his own graveyard, now St. Vincent de Paul's, and, they say, filled it with his victims, but this is probably not true: At least with the blade, he was so good he easily disarmed his opponent in the first few moves and then called off the fight.

Most famous of all was a Frenchman, Gilbert Rosiere, called Titi, who started out as a lawyer but found fencing more fun. He made a tidy fortune readying young army officers for the Mexican War and was known to have fought seven duels in a single week. In spite of the corpses he left in his wake, he was said to be too tenderhearted to swat a mosquito, and at the theater he wept copiously during the sad parts; if people around him laughed, he met them at the Oaks to teach them better manners.

New Orleans took its theater and opera seriously. Everyone had his favorite soprano, and if she didn't get the part he thought she deserved, there were boos and catcalls and cartels exchanged. If a critic suggested in a review that Saturday's performance wasn't her best, he had half a dozen challenges to answer.

Criticism has always been a dangerous profession. In 1950, Paul Hume, music critic of the *Washington Post*, wrote, "Miss Truman is a unique American phenomenon with a pleasant voice of little size and fair quality . . . There are few moments during her recital when one can relax and feel confident that she will make her goal, which is the end of the song."

The singer's father, a scrappy Missourian, snapped back, "Some day I hope to meet you. When that happens you'll need a new nose, a lot of beefsteak for black eyes, and perhaps a supporter below!" This was inappropriately worded, and Hume was right not to accept the president's challenge: Angry, threatening cartels could always be ignored as unworthy of a gentleman.

Very few New Orleans disagreements were subject to peaceful arbitration. Medicine, currently considered a genteel way to earn a living, was one of the more boisterous jobs there, and differences of opinion on diagnosis and treatment were settled at the Oaks.

In other areas, doctors went to the dueling grounds carrying probes and bandages, not pistols, and turned their backs on the hostilities, so that later they could claim they didn't know there'd been a duel; they hadn't seen a thing, merely rushed in to help since they were passing by. In New Orleans, they met each other to defend their medical honor. Under the Oaks, they shot or slashed at other doctors over the correct management of dysentery and typhoid and the uses of laxatives and cold baths.

The healers of New Orleans were an alarmingly colorful lot, almost as volatile as the fencing masters. One physician, it was rumored, improved his marksmanship on cadavers from the charity ward, strung up as targets.

A Dr. Luzenberg bragged in public about his successful eye surgery on a young Indian woman who, he said, had been born blind. The newspapers were enchanted and wrote reams in praise of his "benevolence and skill," which naturally irritated all the other doctors in town. A committee of them visited the patient and came back crying foul. Not only had she not been blind before, she was actually worse off since Luzenberg worked on her.

Cartels flew back and forth all over town. Half the doctors and their seconds challenged the other half. Luzenberg challenged the same Dr. Hunt who had killed the *Crescent*'s editor. Hunt said he'd been motivated only by a search for medical honesty. Luzenberg's seconds accepted this, so Luzenberg, still fuming, challenged Dr. G. W. Campbell. Campbell refused to meet him, calling him "an individual who has been stigmatized and disgraced." Dr. Lindoe, one of Luzenberg's seconds, insisted; Campbell went further, calling Luzenberg a liar and saying he "cannot expect a gentleman to elevate him to a position of equality."

Dr. Lindoe, as was right and proper, promptly challenged Dr. Campbell. Campbell wouldn't meet him either and told the newspapers that his deportment was "boisterous, rude and discourteous and indecent, and I believe him to have been intoxicated."

This brought the newspaper's editor and the writer of the article into the fray. Things heated up until still another doctor, previously uninvolved, published the following in the papers: "If the contemptible puppy, Charles A. Luzenberg, who has long humbugged the community with false ideas of his courage, but who has always succeeded in shuffling off his responsibility upon third persons, is at all anxious to enjoy the privilege of a shot, he can obtain one by applying to: J. S. McFarlane, Corner Poydras and Circus Streets. N.B. No substitutes admitted." Before McFarlane and Luzenberg got a shot at each other, though, Dr. Campbell reconsidered and offered to meet Luzenberg within twenty-four hours. All was arranged.

Suddenly, after all the drawn-out public hostilities, the municipal authorities sat up and took notice. The day before the duel, Luzenberg and Campbell were arrested and had to post a peace bond of five thousand dollars each. The discussion was over.

Though nobody was killed or even wounded, medical care in New Orleans must have ground to a halt for months.

Sometimes the disputes raged over the prostrate bodies of actual patients. Dr. Samuel Chopin, long the house surgeon at Charity Hospital, finally resigned his post to Dr. John Foster, but old habits die hard and he kept prowling the halls and interfering with the patients. When he and Foster passed each other, they turned aside and pretended not to notice, but whatever Chopin prescribed for a patient, Foster threw out when he came by later. Then Chopin stopped in again and threw out Foster's recommendation.

They were bound to collide, and they did. They met over the bed of a young law student who'd lost a lot of blood at a ball, in an encounter with a medical intern who carried a knife. The student lay weak and fainting, visited at different times by both Foster and Chopin with their conflicting treatments, each doubtless muttering darkly about the other's incompetence. One morning they met at bedside. Foster glared at Chopin. Chopin shouted an insult. They seized each other and grappled fiercely, possibly on top of the patient, until staff members rushed in to separate them.

They met again, more formally, in front of the hospital – presumably the matter was too urgent to wait for a trip to the Oaks – and fired. Chopin fell, shot through the jugular vein. He was lucky in having expert attention only a few steps away, but while he lay recovering, Foster held sway without interference. Unmolested, he ministered to the law student, who presently died. All that excitement can't have helped.

In fairness, Southerners weren't alone in their dueling doctors. In Philadelphia, a Dr. Smith and a Dr. Jeffries had a disagreement. They fired at each other at eight paces, missing. The seconds tried to calm them down, but they insisted on trying again, and this time Smith's right arm was broken. He refused to quit, saying that since he was wounded he might as well die, so they tried a third time, and Smith, using his left hand, hit Jeffries in the thigh. He fainted, but upon recovering consciousness insisted on carrying on. To shorten the procedure the physicians shortened the distance to six feet. Each fired. Both fell, Smith dead on the spot and Jeffries mortally wounded.

A contemporary wrote that Jeffries asked if Smith were dead, and "being assured that he was, he declared his own willingness to die. Before he expired, he said he had been schoolmate with Dr. Smith, and that they had been on terms of great intimacy and friendship for fifteen years; and he bore honourable testimony to his character as a man of science and a gentleman."

Just what fine point of medicine caused these two dear old friends to kill each other has not been established.

Like New Orleans, Savannah prided itself on its battling citizens, and one visitor in the late eighteenth century reported seven duels scheduled for a single day. James Jackson, Revolutionary War hero, leader of the Georgia Jeffersonian party, was king. Savannah historian Thomas Gamble calls him a "truly notable man whose life is an inspiration in sterling patriotism and unselfish devotion to the public weal, one of that exceptional type whose careers and characters should be more impressed upon the receptive minds of the children of to-day."

You wouldn't want their young minds to be *too* impressed. As a role model, Jackson could get the children of today in trouble.

As a twenty-three-year-old major in the Continental Army, he had a falling-out with Georgia's lieutenant governor, George Wells, apparently over Wells's overbearing attitude. Jackson described himself as having a "fiery disposition." Wells was said to be "governed by jealousy, inordinate ambition, and a desire for power and place" – in short, a perfectly normal politician, but he somehow got on the wrong side of Jackson. Whatever it was, they both must have been simply furious, because they agreed to fight without seconds, standing almost muzzle to muzzle, and to keep shooting until one of them fell.

They both fell. Wells died on the spot; Jackson was found later by some friends, crippled and helpless with bullet wounds in both knees. The doctors were eager to amputate but Jackson fended them off, recovered, and finally hobbled back to active duty. He was short, like Burr and Hamilton, with a profile like a parrot and a single pale blue eye, having lost the other in battle, but he soldiered on and made himself so popular that after the British pulled out of Savannah, he was chosen to be the first American soldier marching into the retaken city.

He was elected to the first Congress in 1789 and then ran for reelection against his old commander, "Mad Anthony" Wayne. Wayne's campaign manager was Thomas Gibbons, Savannah's rich and famous lawyer and politico, and Gibbons ran a fine slippery campaign, rounding up many more votes than there were voters. Wayne won.

Jackson lodged a protest in Washington and appeared at the hearing in the House on his own behalf. Wayne, he said, was all right, even though he'd called Jackson a "damned liar." It was his campaign manager who was the problem, a man "whose soul is faction," a man of "abominable corruption," and the election under his guidance "a scene of iniquity." It was a grand speech, and the House cheered and moved to seat Jackson anyway, but the motion tied, twenty-nine to twenty-nine. So Congress simply declared Wayne's seat vacant and called for a new election.

Both men declined to run again. Wayne went off to command George Washington's forces. Jackson was still seething about Gibbons, and Gibbons, who had his own political career to worry about, hadn't forgotten the "abominable corruption" line.

They met and traded three shots each, missing all six times, and then shook hands. Gibbons went on to be several times mayor and alderman of Savannah. Jackson went on to the Senate.

Perhaps he fought a duel with the neatly named General Gunn. Nobody's sure, but it seems likely: Gunn was the sort of Southern politician who carried a loaded whip onto the Senate floor to whack at his colleagues. (It's not clear what a "loaded whip" was, but probably something with a weight in its tail, for extra pain.)

Jackson disapproved of dueling but took his dueling duties seriously, especially over the Yazoo land grant. This had to do with a grab for some two and a half million acres of Georgia public lands, recently cleared of Indians and crying out for development by what he called "the rapacious graspings of a few sharks." To fight it, he resigned from the Senate and went back home to serve in the General Assembly. The deal's defeat brought joy to some and rage to others, and a whole rash of duels broke out. In 1796, as Jackson was leaving the state capitol, he was met by a Robert Watkins and "a posse of his Yazoo friends."

According to a letter of Jackson's, Watkins said, "I consider you the leader of a damned venal set or faction who have disgraced their country." Naturally, "flesh & blood of such texture as mine would not bear it, & the lie and the stick involuntary flew on him; until my little Lucas stick broke, I finely frapped him, but the third blow it broke in my hand & till then he had not struck me; but now at his mercy I received one blow on the head which for a moment stunned me, & I Fell.

"I rose and my blood rose with me – I made at him & was told he had pistols. This made me recollect one I had carried, apprehensive of an attack from John Greene who I had been under the necessity of telling was a damned lyar a night or two before, & I immediately exclaimed, "Tis well, we are on a footing. Clear the way.'"

One of Watkins's friends suggested they do it properly, with seconds, and meet in the morning, but Jackson said he never fought "a base assassin" anywhere but on the spot. "I should have killed him, for I fired as soon as we were open to each other, but my hand was knocked up by one of the party, & as soon as I fired he ran at me with a bayonet at the end of his pistol. We closed and twice I threw him."

All this was on the statehouse steps. Small wonder the electorate finds politics less gripping these days.

Whatever happened to Jackson's pistol, it was gone, and Watkins started to gouge out his eye. Jackson tried to bite off his finger. Watkins grabbed still another bayoneted pistol and stabbed him over and over. "He stabbed me in the left breast which fortunately entered my collar bone and ran me through my shirt and grazed my ribs a second time – a half inch lower in the breast the Doctors pronounced, would have finished my business."

The ambush, he points out, was the more despicable since several weeks before he'd sent a friend to tell Watkins he was ready to meet him properly, wherever and whenever he chose, and never got an answer. Besides, thumbing out your opponent's eye, though widely practiced among the riffraff, was considered unbecoming to a gentleman – doubly so when it was the only eye he had.

They weren't finished with each other. After this unseemly skirmish, Watkins reformed his rowdy ways, and they fought three proper duels; Jackson, at the time governor of Georgia, was badly wounded in one of them. One witness wrote, "Jackson and Watkins conversed with great elegance and entire politieness on different matters, while the seconds were arranging the terms of the combat that within the next minute was expected to put an end to at least one of them." It didn't. When he was finished being governor, Jackson went back to the United States Senate and died in its service in 1806.

Thomas Hart Benton recognized him as a kindred spirit. In his tribute, he called him "as ready with his pistol as his tongue, and involved in many duels on account of his hot opposition to criminal measures. The defeat of the Yazoo Fraud was the most signal act of his legislative life, for which he paid the penalty of his life, dying of wounds received in the last of his many duels, which his undaunted attacks upon that measure brought upon him."

Southerners carried their traditions to Washington. In the messy presidential election of 1824, there were four candidates, John Quincy Adams, Andrew Jackson, Henry Clay, and somebody named Crawford. Since Crawford got more votes than Clay, more people must have heard of him at the time than remember him now.

Everyone in Georgia knew who William H. Crawford was. He'd been a United States senator, minister to France, and secretary of both war and treasury. Inheriting James Jackson's influence, he was Jackson's opposite, a big, calm, scholarly fellow who'd been a schoolteacher, then studied law and went into the legislature. He read Greek and Latin but the voters didn't mind; he was a fine fellow anyway. He would never, like Jackson, call himself "fiery," and temperamentally he wasn't the dueling sort at all, but it came with the job.

His biographer, J. E. D. Shepp, wrote, "In the early history of the State of Georgia the crime of dueling was prevalent among the better class of her citizens; perhaps more so than in any other state. The fatal practice became general when the virtuous and best citizens, Governors, Congressmen and Legislators – on the most trivial excuses and slightest provocations, were shedding each other's blood ... A coward was contemptible, and no man could remain long in the public eye without distinguishing himself for bravery. True, common law declared that homicide in a duel was murder. Yet Georgia was too 'high toned' to enforce the law, which had in practice become obsolete. The trial in the courts of all the Southern states turned entirely on the fairness with which the duel had been conducted, and, if fair, a verdict of acquittal was invariably rendered."

Actually, the law seldom took any notice at all. Why waste time and money?

In the legislature, the pro- and anti-land-grab forces were at each other's throats, sometimes literally. Crawford was staunchly anti. Chief among the pros was General John Clark, who felt he had a particular right to get rich from the land because he'd been the main broom sweeping the Indians off it. For point man against Crawford, he and his friends chose Peter Van Alen, or Van Allen, a sharp-tongued wit and famous duelist imported from New York for the purpose. As Shepp puts it, "Finding his talents and integrity very much in the way of their success, a conspiracy was entered into to kill or drive [Crawford] away."

Van Alen worked obliquely by needling Crawford's dear old friend and former school principal, the one-legged Judge Charles Tait, insulting him relentlessly, then spreading the word that Crawford was a coward, and finally cursing him publicly. Some say Crawford challenged, some say Van Alen, but either way, it was clear that Crawford had to fight or give up politics and go back to teaching school.

The latter option may have looked tempting. The New Yorker was an old hand at the game and Crawford could barely tell one end of a gun from the other. For the occasion, he borrowed an ancient, dusty brace of pistols from a friend and didn't even try them out until the day of the fight, when they both misfired.

The match was set for Fort Charlotte, a well-trampled meeting ground over the line in South Carolina. Rather unsportingly, Van Alen distracted his opponent by making horrible faces at him, which indeed distracted him and his shot went wild. Van Alen's first fire missed too, though just by a whisker. For the second shot, Crawford pulled his hat brim down (nobody had told him that duelists don't wear hats) so he couldn't see his target sticking his tongue out, and fired, apparently blindly. Van Alen, the hired gun, fell wounded and dying.

It was rather like the medieval divine intervention.

Crawford's reputation soared. Clark, though, was madder than ever. The burly general was a man of action, stumping for votes through backwoods Georgia and famous in his hometown for deep drinking, riding his horse into taverns where he smashed up chairs and crockery, galloping down the street firing right and left, and generally pleasing the manlier type of voters. Could such a man, and a general to boot, be defeated by a former schoolteacher?

Their friends got drawn into it. Crawford's friend Judge Tait took the field against Clark's friend Judge John Dooly, with Crawford and Clark as seconds. When Crawford arrived at the dueling grounds, he asked Dooly where Clark was. Dooly said Clark was out in the woods looking for a gum tree for Dooly to put his leg in, to make things more fair.

"Do you suppose," he said, "I can risk my leg of flesh and blood against Tait's wooden one? If I hit his leg, he will have another tomorrow and be pegging about as well as usual; but if he hits mine, I may lose my life by it, but almost certainly my leg, and be compelled like Tait to stump about the balance of my life." With one leg in a tree, presumably a hollow one, "I am as much wood as he is and on equal terms with him."

Crawford said Dooly didn't sound as if he wanted to fight. Dooly said no, he didn't.

"Well, sir," said Crawford, whose win over Van Alen may have gone to his head, "you shall fill a column in the newspapers in no enviable light."

"Mr. Crawford," said the judge, "I assure you I would rather fill two newspapers than one coffin."

The fight was called off. Few people involved were half as sensible as Mr. Dooly.

After assorted insults and contentions, Clark challenged Crawford directly. The two met at the usual place, but just as they were taking their positions a horseman rode up. It was Governor Milledge, in person, come to reason with them. Because the combatants were such crucial figures in Georgia's politics, and the repercussions of the duel would be so wide-ranging, they were urged to submit their differences to a court of honor. Clark grumbled, but it amounted to an order.

The assembled gentlemen of the court of honor said their quarrel was of "not sufficient weight, and ought not to have produced the subsequent heat and animosity," and they should shake hands and forget it.

Clark didn't forget it for a minute. He was extremely handy with a pistol and confident that Crawford's Van Alen upset wasn't likely to happen twice.

Georgia took sides. Fights broke out at country dances. Women slapped each other's faces. Preachers thundered from the pulpit. Everyone was either for Clark or for Crawford.

It didn't take long. Clark heard a rumor that Judge Tait had perhaps slandered him, and he challenged Crawford as Tait's friend. This time they drew up an elaborate agreement of twelve articles covering every aspect of the fight, including a body search for concealed armor and the proviso that either man could declare himself satisfied after being wounded, though Clark told his second he wanted the fight to go on as long as either of them could "stand or sit."

They met on a winter morning in Indian Territory. At first fire, Clark hit and shattered Crawford's left wrist. (Proper duelists kept their left arms behind their bodies. Crawford still had a lot to learn.) Clark said a broken wrist was nothing and wanted to fire again, but Crawford's seconds said he was satisfied and stopped the fight.

Clark was far from satisfied. It was summer before Crawford

was well enough to leave the house, and as soon as he did, Clark challenged him again. "It is high time," he wrote, "that the differences between us should be brought to a final issue, and from the situation in which the affair was left, I presume nothing more is necessary than for you to appoint the time and place. My friend, Mr. Sherrod, will hand you this and receive your answer."

Crawford said no. He said that according to the articles of their last fight, the thing was settled. For Clark, nothing short of murder would settle it, and he tried to drag Crawford back into battle by picking on Tait again. Seeing him riding through Milledgeville, he cantered up to him and said, "Tait, you've used your judgeship to destroy my reputation. For that I'm going to give you the lash." He horsewhipped the hapless one-legged judge all over his head and back and shoulders until Tait's horse bolted, and then spurred his own horse after him, still thrashing.

This was too much even for Georgia, and Clark was fined and made to post a five-thousand-dollar bond for good behavior for five years. Five years might have cooled him down, but a new governor, an old army comrade of his, took over and lifted his restrictions. The field was clear for another fight.

In the nick of time, Crawford was appointed to replace a recently resigned Georgia senator. Off he went to Washington, to rise as previously noted and complicate the election of '24.

If he'd stayed in Georgia, he'd have been dead long before '24.

IX. THE WRITTEN WORD

ABRAHAM LINCOLN SAT on a log on a sandbar in the Mississippi, near Alton, Illinois. He was holding a cavalry saber, and from time to time he swished it idly around in the air, slashing at branches, warming up while he waited.

Objecting to the tax policies of Illinois state auditor James Shields, he'd dashed off a fierce newspaper article calling Shields a fool and a liar and bad-smelling to boot. He signed the piece "Rebecca." Shields sent a friend marching into the newspaper office to threaten the editor, who hastily revealed the author's real name. Shields challenged Lincoln. Lincoln accepted.

Sources differ on the choice of weapons; some say Lincoln suggested they throw cow dung at each other. They settled on sabers, archaic but not a bad idea for Abe, considering his famously long arms. Everyone showed up as planned on the sandbar and waited around while the seconds conferred, trying to mend matters.

Presently a statement was agreed on, in which Lincoln is said to have said that he didn't mean anything exactly personal in the article; he was just complaining about the tax policies. It's not clear what Shields's smell had to do with taxes, but maybe he took that back too. Then everyone went home.

Before Gutenberg, you could insult a man only face-to-face or by rumors of gossip faithfully fetched or embellished or invented by his friends. Only the immediate bystanders heard what you thought of the scoundrel. Your opinions cried out for a wider audience. Then the printing press came to spread the word and for centuries, newspapers, pamphlets, handbills, and posted notices trumpeted insults and character assassination, accompanied by gross cartoons of your opponent losing control of his bowels during a duel, or his fat cronies stealing sacks of public funds. Anyone interested in public office needed a newspaper on his side. Newspapers decided elections the way television ads decide them today and they didn't cost nearly as much, even if you were printing your own.

It was a prime editorial duty to start a fight. Nothing boosted readership like violent libel. Say simply that X is a better man for the office than Y, and the audience drifts away bored. Call Y a "consummate traitor" and "contemptible scoundrel," and readers and advertisers flock to you like fleas. So, of course, do Y's followers, armed to the teeth and loaded for bear.

Here in the information age, the published word seems primitive. Dangerous, too, since editors could be bullied into naming the libeler who'd signed the letter "Primrose" or "A Citizen," and the author would find himself facing his subject at dawn. Now with the Internet at everyone's fingertips, free speech is finally free indeed. The new fountain of knowledge sprang up during the Clinton administration, and in a twinkling housewives in Nebraska, taxi drivers in Rome, and sheepherders in New Zealand learned all about the forty people Mr. and Mrs. Clinton were known to have murdered – forty-one, actually, counting Vincent Foster – and the details of Mrs. Clinton's tireless appetite for lesbian sex. Information, springing from nowhere, shorn of human agency, frolics and rampages freely over the globe. It's a whole new world.

Back in the previous world, print had sources. You knew where the newspaper office was and stalked into it with a challenge, or perhaps a cane or a horsewhip; those who considered newspaper editors too inferior socially for a proper duel simply beat them. William Coleman, editor of the *New-York Evening Post*, was paralyzed from the waist down from a caning. Joseph Charless of the *Missouri Gazette* was assaulted, spat at, and shot at, and had his office burned down; then the editor of the rival *Inquirer* waylaid him on the street and beat him severely with a cudgel.

Editors buckled on their pistols when they dressed in the morning and often kept a rifle propped up beside the press. One editor in San Francisco, pressed for time, posted a notice on his door: "Subscriptions received from 9 to 4, challenges from 11 to 12 only."

A dispute over whether or not to send aid to the snowbound Donner party moved General James Denver, secretary of state of California, to kill Edward Gilbert, editor of the *Alta California*. (Apparently this was a popular move; Denver went on to serve as congressman and territorial governor, and had a city in Colorado named in his honor.)

In New Orleans, Dr. Thomas Hunt shot and killed the editor of the *Crescent* for what he felt was a slighting reference to the Hunt family. In Vicksburg, Mississippi (pop. 3,500), three newspaper editors died in duels in 1843 and early '44.

From the 1830s on, slavery was the topic of the day, and hotheads on both sides regularly shot at each other. In the South, to call a man an abolitionist was the equivalent of "scoundrel" and required a duel. The controversy reached clear to California, a wide-open world where newspapers carried announcements of upcoming duels as if they were street fairs, and the former chief justice of the state supreme court, proslavery Judge David Terry, killed antislavery Senator David Broderick before a large crowd of fascinated spectators. In Kentucky, proslavery Charles Wickliffe killed the editor of the Lexington *Gazette* over an anonymous antislavery article. He was tried and acquitted, but the next editor disagreed with the verdict in print. Wickliffe challenged him and was killed at eight feet.

Journalism in Virginia was particularly perilous, and apparently its editors weren't chosen solely for their literary talents. Dr. George Bagby, a Virginia editor himself, wrote in the 1850s: "The Virginia editor is a young, unmarried, intemperate, pugnacious gambling gentleman. Between drink and dueling-pistols he is generally escorted to a premature grave. If he so far withstands the ravages of brandy and gunpowder as to reach the period of gray hairs and cautiousness, he is deposed to make room for a youth who hates his life with an utter hatred and who can't keep drunk for more than a week at a time."

The two brothers who edited the Richmond *Examiner* in the early nineteenth century both died in duels. Edgar Allan Poe challenged one of the paper's later editors, John Daniel, but showed up too drunk to shoot. Later Daniel disagreed with the editor of the *Whig* over the aesthetic merits of a particular public statue; they fired and missed.

"Rancorous" was the word for Daniel. A contemporary wrote, "His pen combines the qualities of the scimitar of Saladin and the battle-axe of Coeur de Leon." He believed that any sheet of paper not covered with abuse of high officials was a piece of paper wasted, and he enjoyed the repercussions. Wounded in the right arm, he had to fire with his left in subsequent duels.

He abused Northerners and Southerners impartially and called the Confederate treasurer a reckless gambler unfit for his office. The treasurer called him out and Daniel took a ball in his thigh. While he was recovering, the paper was in other hands and everyone missed his fiery touch.

Editors wielded their powers with a fine, free hand, restrained only by the possibility of getting shot at, if that was indeed a restraint; some seemed quite anxious to be targets at dawn. Perhaps duels boosted circulation. James Callender of the Richmond

Recorder, rejected for a postmaster's job by President Jefferson, printed a story claiming that Jefferson had had an affair with one of his slaves, Sally Hemings. He offered absolutely no evidence of any kind and seems to have invented it himself, but all the other Federalist papers whooped and leaped on the story. (Later Callender got so drunk he fell into the James River and drowned in three feet of water.) When asked, Jefferson, not the dueling type, said it was too silly to answer. Probably he hadn't read it. He only read Richmond's *Enquirer*.

The *Enquirer* was the voice of the Republicans, who then decided to call themselves Democrats instead, along about the time the Federalists decided to be Whigs, deepening the confusion for modern schoolchildren. One of the *Enquirer*'s editors, O. Jennings Wise, fought eight duels in less than two years. His problem was that his father was governor of Virginia – and no stranger to the field of honor himself, having fought at least one duel and served as a second in the fatal battle between Congressmen Cilley and Graves. The governor was subject to slander; his son defended his honor. The editor of the *Whig* wrote that the Democrats had changed their old policy of electing idiots and elected a lunatic instead. Wise had to go to the *Whig* office and beat the man severely with a rattan cane.

When Aylett of the *Examiner* sneered at the governor, Wise denounced him in print, and Aylett, though horribly nearsighted, challenged him. His shot went wild. Wise fired into the air, bowed, and said, "Sir, I present you to your wife and children."

It was the perfect thing to say. So gentlemanly, so unbearably patronizing that Aylett must have ground his teeth over it for the rest of his life.

Some Virginia editors were gentlemen, some were not.

Thomas Ritchie was the able and respected editor of the Republican/Democratic Richmond *Enquirer* for forty years, through the time when it was Thomas Jefferson's breakfast reading. He balanced on the delicate line of being against slavery but in favor of states" rights, almost a political oxymoron. Though he spoke out for various radical projects like educating women and the poor, he was never known to fight a duel, and he disapproved of insulting people's private lives and characters in print.

In 1845, President Polk begged him to come pull the party together by editing the *Globe*, so he went to Washington and left the *Enquirer* to his two sons. Editorially and temperamentally, they didn't take after their father.

At the helm of the Richmond *Whig* was John Hampton Pleasants. His father, like Wise's, was governor of Virginia. (We might suppose editing and politics were tangled together by close connections, and we might be right.) A convinced Whig, he came to Richmond and challenged the entrenched *Enquirer* by starting the *Whig*, with a hand press and two hundred seventy-five subscribers.

People said "his character was gentle and refined, attracting friend and foe alike." He was shy in public, but alone with his pen he could be rash and even reckless. He'd called Ritchie Sr. "an impotent dotard and driveller," though this was a compliment compared to what some editors called each other. Ritchie Sr. ignored him. The two men and their papers actually had a lot in common. Both were against slavery, for instance. (A good many Southerners, including plantation owners, were anxious to abolish slavery as soon as they could figure out what to do with all those freed slaves. They just didn't want the North to come barging down and do it for them, and when the war came along, they got their backs up and circled the wagons.)

After the Ritchie sons, William and Thomas Jr., took over the *Enquirer*, things got noisier. William was almost blind – even with his glasses on he could barely tell chairs from tables – but kept trying to start fights anyway. He challenged Pleasants over some words in the *Whig* and would have fought if Ritchie Sr. hadn't come along to stop it.

Thomas Jr.'s eyes were better and he was said to be "an experienced and enthusiastic duelist." Writing as "Macon," he accused Pleasants of planning to start an abolitionist journal. This was silly and quite untrue, and Pleasants said so. Thomas Jr. retorted by calling Pleasants, in print and in capital letters, "A COWARD."

Pleasants didn't know much about duels, but he knew when you couldn't dodge one. Using quite improper form, he wrote young Ritchie saying he'd see him at dawn the next day on the south side of the James, with pistols, ready to shoot on sight.

Ritchie sneered that this was all wrong – "savage, sanguinary, and revolting" – since it was the challenged party who got to pick the time, place, and weapons. Just the same, he accepted.

It wasn't according to code. Pleasants showed up with a revolver in his coat pocket, a pistol in each hand, a bowie knife in his vest, and a sword cane under his left arm. He didn't plan to use any of this artillery, but he must have wanted to put on a good show. Ritchie faced him with two pistols and a cutlass in his belt, a revolver in his pocket, and a pistol in each hand, and he did plan to use them. (Why? What did he have against Pleasants? Did he just want to shoot somebody? We don't seem to know.)

They started out some two hundred yards apart, and Pleasants walked slowly toward Ritchie. When they were within thirty yards of each other, Ritchie opened fire. Pleasants fired into the air but kept staggering toward Ritchie, taking three or four hits until he collapsed in his own blood. Going down, he slashed with the sword cane and cut Ritchie slightly on the face, and then fell. He was carried from the field and died two days later.

On his deathbed he said he had taken the ball out of his pistol the night before: "I didn't want to kill him; I went there to show him that I was not a coward." He was pleased to hear that Ritchie was alive and well, saying he was "a brave fellow" and shouldn't be blamed for anything, though he didn't say why not.

Everyone went to the funeral, mourning.

T. Ritchie Jr. was tried for murder. The jury, without bothering to leave the box, declared him not guilty and the whole courtroom burst into applause.

It wasn't that they didn't grieve for poor Pleasants, or blame Ritchie. They just liked to see a fine old tradition upheld.

X . HILL COUNTRY

I N THE NEW World as in the Old, the most punctilious gentlemen with the most delicately tuned sense of noblesse oblige had
good reasons for staying home. They held political offices and places
in society; they had family connections, land, plantations, property,
legal or medical practices, judgeships. They had a vested interest
in the settled civilization of the old colonial coastal and riverine
settlements. They played by the rules because they depended on
a ruly life, where gentlemen meeting each other in ballrooms and
courtrooms, on dueling grounds and the floor of the Senate, needed
a common code of behavior.

Other people moved to the hills.

An expanding population of younger sons and poor relations
of the landed gentry, failed farmers, unemployed soldiers, the

restless, the reckless, the disgraced, and those with nothing to lose went looking for land grabs, gold, poker games, freedom, elbow room, adventure, and trouble. Some were escaping from suffocating social restrictions. More than a few left gambling debts or dreary marriages behind. Virginians moved from the genteel Tidewater into what is now West Virginia or pushed south into the mountains of North Carolina and Tennessee; Georgians left old Savannah for the interior highlands. The wandering young of cultivated old New Orleans moved north to the open spaces in central Louisiana or the Ozarks of Arkansas.

They were not a decorous group, on the whole. They carried guns, not just when they planned to meet an adversary at dawn but everywhere, all the time. Sad to say, in their battles they sometimes neglected the niceties like seconds and a proper exchange of notes. Along the mountainous western edges of the South, the fighting had more in common with the tribal wars of the old Scottish Highlands than with the duels of old Savannah, and indeed Scotland sent us more than her share of fighters.

Inland political life was even rowdier than it was back home. After one fatal political duel in 1863, *Harper's Weekly* observed sadly from its safe perch on the coast, "There are parts of the United States where a politician must necessarily be prepared to fight duels . . . a politician who will not fight must stand aside, and cannot command the popular suffrage . . . Man is a carnivorous and bloody-minded creature. Civilization, even of the purest kind, only half tames him. Many of the best of men have a secret relish for blood, and slaughter, and horrors.

"Political duellists are the prize-fighters of their part of the country ... Jones and Smith, of Arkansas, may not like being shot at; but the people of Arkansas – like the rest of us – relish the excitement of a duel, and this is the price they set on their suffrages ... Candidates among them they require to be fighting men."

In Arkansas, Judge Andrew Scott of the superior court was a fierce little frontier gamecock from a numerous family, all of them fond of dueling. The judge had great respect for the ladies. A contemporary said, "He would not brook to listen to the faintest breath of scandal against the female sex, and his tender regard for the reputation of women was one of which any man might justly feel proud, but of which few can boast."

The hostess of the party at the post was pleased to entertain not one but both of the highest judges in Arkansas, along with the prettiest woman around. Judge Joseph Selden, also of the superior court, originally of Virginia, joined his fellow guests at cards. The pretty lady, at the climax of the game, cried, "Judge Selden, we have the tricks and honors on you!"

Selden, a mild-mannered chap, blinked and murmured, "That is not so."

The lady's feelings were hurt and her lips quivered. Apparently nobody bothered to check the cards and find out whether she was mistaken, but Judge Scott leaped up and cried, "Sir, you've insulted a lady, who is also my partner. You must apologize." Selden said, "I make no apology. What she said just isn't so."

Scott, in a most unjudicial manner, grabbed a candlestick and threw it in Selden's face.

The party broke up. Later, Selden thought it over and sent the lady an apology, which she accepted. However, frontier life depended heavily on gossip for entertainment, and the ladies of the post fell to talking. They picked over the incident backward and forward, perhaps disappointed that it ended so tamely, until finally Scott sent Selden a challenge, and the two highest judges in the Arkansas territory crossed over to Mississippi soil to try to kill each other.

They faced each other at the usual ten paces and fired. Selden clutched his chest and fell dead. Regardless of whether she was right or wrong about the cards, the lady's honor had been cleansed.

Rough country isolates kinship groups, hardens family ties, and deepens suspicion of the outsider: Clan feuds in Appalachia, as in Afghanistan, flourished well into the twentieth century. Some family feuds were carried out quite properly over the generations, with the opposing members fighting two by two. Some were more like long-running brawls. The Hatfields and McCoys passed into folklore.

They were among the earliest settlers in the Tug Valley, along the Tug Fork River on the border between Kentucky and West Virginia. Their patriarchs, William Anderson ("Devil Anse") Hatfield and Randolph ("Ran'l") McCoy, were both big-boned, shaggy, bearded giants. By local standards they were really quite prosperous, rich in timberlands and whiskey stills, but they didn't spend money on the cultivated life. They stayed shaggy and skulked in their scattered cabins, the McCoys on the Kentucky side of the river, the Hatfields in West Virginia. When family members wanted to send news to each other, they headed for high ground and warbled out code messages in birdcalls and animal cries.

With nothing else to do in the evenings, both families bred prolifically and raised whole regiments of hot-tempered sons.

Farther west, the ownership of horses was a sore point, but in the South, pigs started the fights, and the Hatfields and McCoys first fell out over a couple of razorback hogs. The court decided in favor of the Hatfields, so the McCoys stalked and ambushed a group of Hatfields out hunting, and then Staton Hatfield fired on Sam and Paris McCoy, injuring one of them before they fired back and killed him with a single shot to the head.

In the spring, the oldest Hatfield son, Johnse, moseyed over to Kentucky for the festivities of the Pike County elections and met Ran'l's daughter, Rose Anna McCoy. Like Romeo and Juliet, they fell in love, and unlike Juliet, Rose Anna moved into Johnse's cabin. Several months later she'd had enough and went home, a ruined woman. Ran'l seethed with rage.

At the next Pike County election, everyone had far too much corn liquor and Ellison Hatfield attacked Tolbert McCoy. Tolbert and one of his brothers drew knives and stabbed Ellison twenty-six times, and a third brother shot him. He died two days later, so the Hatfields tied the three brothers to pawpaw bushes on the Kentucky side of the river and pumped fifty rifle bullets into them.

Then Jeff McCoy attacked Cap Hatfield's cabin, and Cap went and found him and shot and killed him. Then Ran'l McCoy organized a raid into Hatfield country, seized a McCoy who had traitorously married a Hatfield, and brought him back to a Kentucky jail.

The Hatfields felt it best to kill off anyone who might testify against them in Kentucky courts. Nine Hatfields, armed to the teeth, stormed Ran'l's cabin, and after an hour's battle the place caught fire. A daughter, young Alifair McCoy, figured they wouldn't shoot a woman and stepped outside to douse the flames; they shot her in the stomach. When her mother tried to run to her, a Hatfield pistol-whipped her unconscious.

Now the states joined the feud, and the West Virginia governor refused the Kentucky governor's request to arrest Anse and some other Hatfields. Bands of McCoys, sometimes fifty or more, raided across the border until two more Hatfields were dead and eight were captured to stand trial for murder in Kentucky. Both governors called out the National Guard.

West Virginia claimed that the Hatfields had been kidnapped without due process. The case went to the United States Supreme Court, which ruled that the prisoners couldn't go home again and had to stand trial in Kentucky. Seven of them got life in prison and the eighth was publicly hanged for the murder of Alifair, an outrage to any court's sense of Southern honor. Thousands traveled long mountainous distances to watch; the area was short on public entertainment and a hanging was more fun than any election.

A shortage of personnel stalled the feud. The younger generation had sadly dwindled. The old folks, though, prospered peacefully. Ran'l operated a ferry in Pikeville until his death at nearly ninety, and Anse took up logging, got religion, and saw his nephew Henry become governor of West Virginia and later a United States senator. Henry's family background was apparently no political drawback and may have worked in his favor. On the frontier, real man trumped real gentleman any day.

The traditional prearranged duel still flourished, but nontraditional elements crept in. Back in Europe and the British Isles, gentlemen still popped away at each other with pistols, but in America, outside of the settled Eastern cities, rifles or shotguns were sometimes readier to hand, producing some alarming effects. They were joined by a peculiarly American institution on its way to conquer the West, the bowie knife.

As far as we know, it killed its first man in 1827, in a very strange duel, if duel is the right word. The fight involved just about every prominent man in Rapides, Louisiana, a parish in the central hills and piney woods far from elegant New Orleans. Rapides had split into two armed camps.

Originally there were just two principals, Dr. Maddox and Samuel Wells, and they agreed to fight, for reasons undisclosed, on a sandbar opposite Natchez. All their friends and relations came along, as seconds and audience, and most of them were far angrier than the initial combatants. Colonel Crane was Maddox's second. A few months earlier, he'd fought General Currey on Bayou Rapids and taken a crippling wound in the arm. Currey and his relatives were there on the sandbar, and so were Major Wright and the Blanchards and the Wellses and the Bowies, all furious.

The preliminaries duly arranged, Maddox and Wells each fired twice, missed, and agreed to call it a day. The bystanders disagreed. A local chronicler tried to explain what followed.

Bowie was just in the edge of the woods with Generals Wells and Currey, armed with pistols, Bowie carrying a huge knife. As the duelling party started to leave the grounds Bowie and his party advanced to meet them. The friends of Maddox and Crane on the opposite side of the sandbar, seeing this, and being furthest from the party, started to run to meet them as soon as they should reach the retiring combatants. General Currey was the first on the ground, closely followed by Bowie. Currey immediately advanced upon Colonel Crane and remarked, "Colonel Crane, this is a good time to settle our difficulty," and commenced drawing his pistol. Bowie did the same. Crane was armed with a brace of duelling pistols, and awaited the attack of Currey. At this point Currey was seized by his brother and begged to desist. Bowie and Crane fired at each other, it is said, without effect. There were those who said Bowie was wounded. The latter statement I think most probable, for Bowie stopped, felt his hip, and then, drawing his knife, limped towards Crane, who was watching General Currey. Released from the hold of his brother, Currey was advancing. At this moment Crane leaped across a small ravine ... and, resting his pistol upon his crippled arm, fired at Currey, wounding him fatally, from the effects of which he fell. Crane was now disarmed, and Bowie advanced cautiously upon him. Clubbing his pistol he struck Bowie over the head as he avoided his knife adroitly, and felled him to the ground. Crane retreated a step as his friend, Major Wright, advanced upon him, and with a long, slender spear, drawn from a walking-cane which he carried, attacked Bowie, who made a pass to parry the spear with his knife, in which he failed. The spear was of cold iron, and striking the breastbone bent and went round upon the rib. Bowie at this moment seized Wright and fell, pulling Wright down with and on top of him, and holding him strongly to his person. Wright was slender, and by no means a strong man, and was powerless in the hands of Bowie, who coolly said to him, "Now, Major, you die," and plunging the knife into his heart, killed him instantly. This knife was made by Resin P. Bowie out of a blacksmith's rasp or large file, and was the original of the famous bowie-knife. When James Bowie received it from his brother, he was told by him that it was "strong, and of admirable temper. It is more trustworthy in the hands of a strong man than a pistol, for it will not snap . . ."

There was no reconciliation between Crane and Bowie after the conflict, though Crane aided personally in carrying Bowie from the ground, and Bowie thanked him and said, "Colonel Crane, I do not think, under the circumstances, you ought to have shot me." Almost immediately after the attack of Currey upon Crane, the fight between their friends became general, in which there were fifteen wounded and at least six killed, among whom were Currey and Wright.

In time, we hope, the rains came, the river rose, and the sandbar returned to its original color.

Social life in Rapides, Louisiana, must have been thin indeed after the massacre. The chroniclers don't tell us why half the gentry of that parish wanted to kill the other half – one source says it had to do with land speculation – but the trusty bowie knife, born of a blacksmith's file, was now launched on its career.

News of the knife traveled all the way to England, where it confirmed what the British had long suspected: America had degenerated woefully since its independence and, without British guidance, its people had become what one writer calls a race of savages. The Scottish writer W. E. Aytoun wrote:

Why an independent patriot freely spits upon the floor,
Why he gouges when he pleases, why he whittles at the chairs,
Why for swift and deadly combat still the bowie-knife he bears ...

Jim Bowie, on his way to Texas, was met by three hired assassins and easily killed all three of them with his reinvented, all-American version of the sword.

Its manufacture was entrusted to an Arkansas blacksmith, John Black, who modified the prototype slightly by giving it a double edge, sharp top and bottom along the length of the curve from the point, so that most of the back was blunt for parrying but the end was double-edged for a backward slash. Black was a secretive man. The governor of Arkansas said, "I am convinced that Black possessed the Damascus secret ... He often told me that no one taught him his method of tempering steel, but that it came to him in a mysterious manner which he could not explain." Or would not. While tempering his blades, he hid behind a leather curtain, and not even his partners learned the secret.

Whatever he did, his blades didn't break, or bend like the spear from Major Wright's cane. Pioneers swore by them. They were "sharp enough to use as a razor, heavy enough to use as a hatchet, long enough to use as a sword, and broad enough to use as a paddle." What else did a man need? Well, pistols, of course, but nobody could chop wood or paddle a canoe with a pistol, and in a duel, at close quarters or after you'd emptied your gun, there was nothing like a supplementary bowie knife. It could slice off your nose so quickly and cleanly that you didn't notice until you looked down and recognized it, lying in the dust at your feet.

Jim Bowie was one of the nicest of fighters, a sort of Robin Hood of the western wilds. In 1832, he was on the steamer *Orleans* from Vicksburg to Natchez when he stopped a young man from throwing himself overboard in despair. The silly fellow, with his new wife, had been carrying over sixty thousand dollars entrusted to him by his fellow planters and managed to lose the lot to three professional gamblers plying their trade on board. Bowie turned the poor man over to his wife, told her everything would be all right, and went to join the card game. When he caught the dealer slipping a card to one of his friends, he grabbed him with one hand and whipped out his knife with the other. A witness tells the tale:

"The baffled gambler, livid with rage and disappointment, swore that the stranger should fight him, demanding, with an oath, to know who he was anyway. Quietly, and as if in the presence of ladies, the stranger answered 'James Bowie.' At the sound of that name two of the gamblers quailed, for they knew that the man who bore that name was a terror to even the bravest; but the third, who had never heard of 'James Bowie,' demanded a duel at once. This was acceded to at once by Bowie, with a smile; pistols – derringers – were the weapons selected, the hurricane-roof the place, and the time at once ... Ascending to the hurricane-roof, the principals were placed one upon the top of each wheel-house. This brought them about twelve yards apart, and each was exposed to the other from the knee up. The pistols were handed to them and the gambler's second gave the word, 'One, two, three, fire, stop,' uttered at intervals of one second each, and they were allowed to fire at any time between the utterance of the words one and stop. As 'one' rang out in the clear morning air both raised their weapons, as 'three' was heard the gambler's pistol rang out and before the sound had ceased and while the word 'fire' was being uttered, Bowie's pistol sounded, and simultaneous with this sound the gambler fell, and giving a convulsive struggle rolled off the wheel-house into the river."

Bowie blew the smoke out of his pistol and went below to reassure the newlyweds and divide up the pot. They were so grateful that Bowie, embarrassed, had to get off the boat at Rodney, while they "clung to him as though he was a father leaving them."

If people were reluctant to tangle with Bowie, they were downright terrified of Alexander Keith McClung of Kentucky, the Black Knight of the South. He offended a man – he was always offending someone – who handed him his card by way of a challenge. McClung gave him his own. The man read it, turned white, and stammered out, "Just let me have my card back, that's all I ask." McClung gave it back.

A handsome, dark-eyed redhead with a taste for poetry, whiskey, and eccentric clothes, he was the bad boy of a respectable family, a nephew of Chief Justice John Marshall and connected with the Breckinridges of Kentucky. His father, judge and legislator, died the year he was born, and he grew up wild. In *Gentlemen, Swords and Pistols*, Harnett Kane gives us the fullest account of him and says that he early showed "a marked, if moody, self-esteem," an understatement. He read Byron, cultivated an attitude, and did exactly as he pleased.

The concept of intelligence has become so socially irresponsible and politically incorrect that no nice person uses the word anymore, but in former times we might have said this was a bright boy who would have been happier and less violent if he'd been handled differently. Then as now, some single mothers were better at raising a wild boy than others. Sent to be schooled by his uncle, a famous classicist, he ran away and arrived back home carrying his clothes in his arms. In despair, his family got him into the navy, where he threw himself into the naval tradition of dueling until, in Rio, his exasperated commander decided he was a menace and asked him to resign. He left the ship with "his pay in silver dollars in a sock which did duty for a purse, and his clothes in a candlebox in lieu of a trunk," and went back to Kentucky.

He tried studying medicine, and then law, but study interfered with his freedom and his target practice. After a duel with a cousin of his, his poor mother begged him to give up fighting; he refused but conceded that he would never again issue a challenge. With his arrogant swagger, he didn't need to. Before his fame spread, plenty of challenges came his way.

He came into an inheritance at twenty-one, spent it before he was twenty-two, and when he was twenty-three his family decided everyone might be happier if he went somewhere else. In 1834, he set up a law practice in Vicksburg and Jackson, Mississippi, but spent more time on his hobby than his profession. Though he enjoyed the chance to make flowery speeches in court, he found law books too boring to read, after Byron and the duel-studded swashbucklers of Sir Walter Scott. A convinced romantic, he got a black horse and named it Rob Roy.

Mark Twain called this kind of thing the "Sir Walter Disease." It was rampant. He wrote that in our South, "the genuine and wholesome civilisation of the nineteenth century is curiously confused and commingled with the Walter Scott Middle-Age sham civilisation ... with the duel, the inflated speech, and the jejune romanticism of an absurd past."

McClung made friends with a popular politician, General Allen, and took his part in several disputes. He also liked the peppery Henry Foote and stood as his second during one of his various fights with S. S. Prentiss. Allen was there, and when McClung ordered the crowd to stand back farther, Allen stood still. McClung pushed him with his gun, saying, "Get back like everybody else." Allen cursed, but he moved. Afterward things weren't quite the same between the friends.

On the street, in front of a crowd of people, Allen called out that McClung was a "liar, scoundrel, and fool." McClung, remembering his promise to his mother, refrained from challenging but shouted back such a medley of Kentucky, Mississippi, and naval insults that Allen had to do the challenging himself.

This gave McClung the right to set terms, and they were odd. From eighty paces apart, each with four pistols and two bowie knives, they would walk toward each other shooting at will. If the last bullet was spent and both were still standing, the bowie knives would finish the matter.

They met in a bushy tract along the Pearl River. At the signal, they started forward, and Allen cried, "Now we'll see who's the coward!" and raised his first gun. "Yes, we will," said McClung, but he kept his own gun down. They were still over a hundred feet apart. Allen, nervous, fired and missed.

"Are you content?" called McClung.

"No!" cried Allen and pulled out his second pistol.

McClung replied, "Then I'll hit you in the teeth."

He fired almost casually, they say, but it was an amazing shot, considered an American distance record for a dueling pistol, and exactly in the teeth as he'd promised. The ball imbedded itself in the back of Allen's neck, and he died as he fell.

After that, McClung found it harder to scrape up a challenge. In a hotel, when he used his own knife to cut a piece of butter, another customer snapped his fingers and called, "Waiter, remove the butter; that man stuck his knife in it." McClung promptly seized up the butter plate and shoved it into the other's face and called, "Waiter, remove the butter; this man stuck his nose in it." The buttered man rose furiously to offer a challenge and then, recognizing the big redhead, turned pale and ran away.

With his excellent family connections, he was welcomed socially and visited among the plantations; with his dashing Byronic pose and outrageous reputation, he ravaged many a girlish heart.

Visiting around, he met and fell in love with Virginia Tunstall of Tuscaloosa, Alabama. She returned the sentiment. In her memoirs, she wrote, "The Colonel's devotion to me for many months was the talk of two states ... Many a winsome girl admired him, and my sweet cousin, Martha Fort, was wont to say the would 'rather marry Colonel McClung than any man alive.'"

Even she noticed, though, that as a husband he might prove rather a handful. "I loved him madly while with him, but feared him when away from him; for he was a man of fitful, uncertain moods and given to periods of deepest melancholy."

Sometimes he rode out to the cemetery and flung himself down on a grave and stared wildly up at the sky for hours. According to some sources, he was afflicted with a vision of a line of grayish figures, the ghosts of men he had killed, that appeared at nightfall, wherever he was, filing endlessly past him in silence. This may be purely apocryphal, but obviously he was subject to fits of rage and fits of despair.

With Miss Tunstall, he went too far. As her story goes, he took her out for a drive along the river, and when they reached the bank, he said that if she didn't promise to marry him, he would drive the carriage into the water and drown them both. She hastily assented, but the next time he came to call, she said, "No. You behaved like a coward. Good day." Instead, she married a rising Alabama legislator who was almost certainly easier to live with than the Black Knight.

There are no rumors of any further romances, and it's said that young women in several states remained spinsters forever, having vowed that if they couldn't have McClung, they would never compromise with a lesser being.

Back in Vicksburg, he struck up a friendship with John Menifee, or Menefee, a Virginia-born planter and merchant. By this time you'd think wise men would steer clear of McClung's volatile friendship, but Menifee was the leader of the Vicksburg Rifles and known as "the gamecock of the river," so he probably felt invincible. Two such manly egos could hardly stay friends for long, and presently they clashed.

They were swimming in a creek one hot day when a group of boys happened by and hid the clothes they'd left on the bank, a popular pastime of the day. Menifee grabbed one of them and thrashed him, McClung objected, and the two struggled until McClung knocked the planter down. They parted enemies.

A week later Menifee found McClung sitting in a billiard parlor drinking, and words were exchanged. Menifee hit McClung with a billiard cue, knocking him dizzy, and as he staggered out, aimed a kick at him. A kick was unforgivable, overriding any promises you'd made to your mother: McClung challenged him.

The weapons were Mississippi rifles at twenty paces. They met on a sandy island near Vicksburg, and the whole town turned out to watch, including all of Menifee's Vicksburg Rifles in full uniform, joined by throngs from Natchez, Port Gibson, and Memphis. The island was jam-packed. Menifee was the popular favorite and the betting was heavy.

Menifee fired and missed McClung's face by an inch. McClung stared wildly at his own rifle, tried to break it, and then swore and threw it twenty feet away in a rage. It had hung fire. The seconds dug it out of the sand, cleaned it, and handed it back for the second exchange. The betting grew hotter. Both men fired. Menifee staggered.

McClung did not behave like a gentleman. He stood on tiptoe to peer through the smoke, and when Menifee slowly dropped, he rejoiced. He knelt down and kissed his rifle, thanking God for its accuracy. Menifee's friends scowled.

The doctors probed the dead man's forehead and found only half a bullet. It looked like fraudulent loading, some sort of trick. The crowd shouted angrily and threatened violence; McClung's second hustled him away to safety. Threats of lynching rang through the town. Then the doctor's report came in: The bullet had broken when it struck the cock of Menifee's gun, and half of it flew into his forehead. Various fragments were found, adding up to only one bullet.

Just the same, bad feeling lingered, and according to reports, McClung had to fight various members of Menifee's family. One source says he fought and killed seven of his brothers, but local legends have a way of improving on themselves.

After some unsuccessful forays into politics, he went off to fight in the Mexican War, serving as lieutenant colonel under Jefferson Davis, lost two fingers, and of course his temper, over and over. He took a musket shot through both legs and came home, limping, a hero, and more romantic and gloomier than ever. He told people he was sorry he hadn't been killed in Mexico. He took to drinking seriously.

He slept badly, and the gray ghost figures kept filing past. He was broke and in debt, and sat in the Jackson Hotel staring out the window, reading and drinking.

Then he called in a carpenter to make him a new back for his chair, with a deep V slashed into its top. As soon as it was nailed into place and the carpenter had left, he bathed, shaved, combed his hair, and sat down with his neck fitted into the top of the V. When he shot himself in the temple with one of his dueling pistols, his head was held back so the blood didn't run down and stain his clean white shirt or the handwritten poem he'd pinned on it.

The poem owed a lot to Shelley, but he'd touched it up a bit. The last lines were

> O, vainly the mariner sighs for the rest
> Of the peaceful haven,
> The pilgrim saint for the homes of the blest
> And the calm of heaven,
> The galley slave for the night wind's breath
> At burning noon,
> But more gladly I'll spring to thy arms, O death;
> Come soon! Come soon!

XI. MOVING WEST

T HE WESTWARD PUSH continued across the Mississippi. Beyond the big river was a rough neighborhood, where probably many men went from cradle to grave without firing a gun at a fellow citizen, but certainly many others didn't.

McClung of Kentucky could still point east to his distinguished relations, but west of the river no man established his status and identity by family, education, or the boxwood hedges on the old plantation. Plain, raw courage was your ticket – you literally fought your way up the social ladder, showcasing your bravery and marksmanship rather than your pedigree or your political principles. A new image of Americans emerged from the gunsmoke: tough, two-fisted, independent of social constraints.

Where politics was the issue, the duel's goal might be simply to kill your opponent: As Missourian Peter Burnett, later California's first governor, put it, "It becomes desirable to kill off certain aspirants, to get them out of the way." A local minister who'd watched many a bloody combat said, "No new man can ascend to eminence without displacing someone who is already there ... All that fell were men in office, of standing and character." (This wasn't strictly true; lesser folk fought and fell too, but they attracted less notice.)

After one fatal duel, the *Missouri Gazette* harrumphed that murder was "the most abominable crime," but in Missouri it was now "an honorable profession, a gentlemanly accomplishment," and the duelist was "the favorite of the fair" and admired by all.

The East had grown a relatively stable substructure to hold society in place, but in Missouri all was shifting ground. After the Louisiana Purchase made it a territory, people came in from all over. Hardy mountain men from Kentucky and Tennessee, touchy Southerners with slaves, and ambitious Yankees joined Spaniards and French Creoles left over from previous administrations, along with assorted Indians who walked the streets in feathers and carried tomahawks.

Those planning to push on farther west milled restlessly around the Santa Fe and Oregon-California trailheads in Independence. Judges and lawyers came to court fully armed, and sometimes casualties ensued. Land speculation led to battles both judicial and personal.

Settling disputes by combat was generally considered an essential encouragement to the testosterone needed by a pioneering people. Some even believed that the formalities of the duel were decadent

European frippery, and proper Americans should simply slug out their differences on the spot. Many thoughtful citizens, however, welcomed the duel as a sign that proper, controlled, ceremonious procedures were taking over from unregulated brawling and casual assaults. Dueling was a step forward for civilization, and high-class too.

Other voices crying in the wilderness considered it a kind of disease, a character flaw, an animal instinct, a social vice, or evidence of Original Sin. Back East, the Reverend Lyman Beecher, father of Henry Ward and Harriet, cried, "We are murderers, a nation of murderers!"

Missouri's Thomas Hart Benton got off the riverboat in St. Louis in 1815, out of North Carolina by way of Tennessee, a lawyer in search of new worlds to conquer. Like McClung, he grew up fatherless – his had died when he was ten – but his mother managed to get him into the University of North Carolina. Three months after he got there he was expelled for stealing. Indignantly he insisted that, too proud to ask for a loan, he had secretly borrowed some money from fellow students but planned to replace it before it was missed. He offered to duel anyone who questioned him, but the university expelled him anyway and it rankled all his life. His wounded honor pulsed just under the surface like a gumboil.

He defended Missouri's Creole élite in their claims on Spanish land grants and, as editor of the *St. Louis Enquirer*, defended their position in print.

At the same time, Charles Lucas came from faraway Pennsylvania to join his father, a judge in St. Louis. Aristocratically, father and son looked down on rough-cut local lawyers who didn't even have proper classical educations, and they sneered at the Creoles who cared about nothing but their land claims instead of the good of the republic. In short, they were a bit smug, perhaps unbearably so. Young Charles started a law practice, aligning himself against Benton and the Creoles.

Both were men on the rise. Both were intensely political. Statehood hovered on the horizon: Who would control the new state? Who would go to the United States Senate?

Benton thought Lucas was an effeminate snob; Lucas thought Benton was a barbarian. They clashed in court over a point of evidence. The argument got personal. Each felt himself absolutely right. The jury saw it Lucas's way. Benton brooded: In a sense, by disagreeing with him, Lucas had called him a liar. He sent a challenge, and Lucas wrote back loftily, "I will not for supporting the truth be in any way bound to give the redress or satisfaction you ask for, or to any person who may feel wounded by such an exposure of the truth." No apology, only the terse note, implying that Benton was hardly worth arguing with on equal terms and that Lucas's superior status made his honor self-evident.

It was a clash between the old Europeanized East and the new American West, between the cockiness of education and breeding and the cockiness of personal valor.

Lucas, however well-bred, wasn't above a nasty trick. The territorial elections came up, and voting was restricted to property owners. Three slaves were Benton's only taxable property, and Lucas suspected that they hadn't been registered in time for Benton to vote. Publicly, at the polls, he challenged the landless

Benton's ballot. Stung, Benton told the poll watchers, "Gentlemen, if you have any questions to ask, I am prepared to answer, but I do not propose to answer charges made by any puppy who may happen to run across my path."

Lucas sent his second, Joshua Barton, to invite Benton to meet him, on account of his "vehement, abusive and ungentlemanly language." "Puppy" was a fighting word. Besides, the political power struggle was coming to a boil.

The challenge had been carefully timed to catch Benton exhausted; he'd sat up all night with the family of a friend who'd just died, and the note came as he was changing clothes for the funeral. He agreed to fight as soon as it was over.

At first fire, Benton took a wound in the knee, but his shot caught Lucas in the throat, perilously close to the jugular vein. Lucas's surgeon said he couldn't stand for a second shot, but Benton was reluctant to quit without arranging for another meeting.

This was a breach of code etiquette, but six weeks later Lucas had quite recovered and they met again, egged on by friends and family. Judge Lucas told everyone that his son would surely have killed Benton if his bullet hadn't been weakened by defective powder; others claimed that after the first fire, Lucas had wanted to shorten the distance but the cowardly Benton refused. Rumors ran through town like rats. The judge, people said, urged his son to fight again in the name of the family honor, because conciliation was shameful. Everyone took sides. The second fight could scarcely be avoided.

Half of St. Louis lined the shore to watch the little group set out for Bloody Island. The September day was hot and sticky and breathless. Benton took off his coat and rolled up his sleeves and, to historians" enduring horror, showed his red flannel underwear. It blazed like the banner of barbarians approaching the civilized gates. Gentlemen didn't wear red flannel underwear, and if they did they wouldn't expose it, most particularly not for a duel, for which the dress code was strict and formal. (Why, on a steaming hot day, he was wearing long underwear at all is a mystery.)

The distance was ten feet, murderously short, and the count went awry. One of Lucas's seconds was supposed to say "fire – one, two, three," with nobody to shoot before "one" or after "three." Flustered, the man forgot to say "fire" before the count, and for a moment both parties hesitated. Then they both fired at once and Lucas fell, hit through the side; the impact at such close range had knocked his own shot wild.

Benton was dismayed. Later he wrote of the "pang which went through his heart when he saw the young man fall, and would have given the world to see him restored to life." (He always wrote about himself in the third person.)

It's curious, the number of sensible men who steeled themselves to the risk of the duel, came to terms with the possibility of death, hoped to die bravely and well, wrote their wills and a few last letters to their families, said their prayers, and went forth to the meeting, and then were stricken with horror to find themselves still standing and their adversary dead. They'd readied themselves to die but not to kill. The other man lying there bleeding to death caught them by surprise.

Sometimes, like McClung in his unseemly rejoicing over Menifee, they reacted with glee at the moment, and then slowly the awful reality of killing crept over them and the ghosts gathered.

The duel, though, had established Benton's credentials in spite of his red underwear. He was widely known and either respected or vilified as a duelist now, and he didn't need to fight again. The dead man's father, Judge Lucas, among many others, challenged him, but he politely declined. He did, as previously noted, liven up the dueling scene in the nation's capital during his many years as senator, urging other men on to fight and standing by them as a second, but as far as we know Lucas remained his only kill. One can be enough.

Even on the American frontier, duels weren't an absolute prerequisite for public office, but judging from the record, they certainly helped. Look at Sam Houston, congressman from Tennessee, governor of Tennessee, president of Texas, senator from Texas, and governor of Texas. Of course he was a war hero too, carried home from the War of 1812 on a stretcher with an arrow wound in his thigh, two bullets in his shoulder, and a nasty case of measles, not to mention later capturing Santa Anna at the San Jacinto, but the duel cemented his position.

War was all very well, but a man had plenty of help and company in a war. In a duel, you stood there all by yourself looking into the end of a gun that was pointed at you alone. In a war, you had the heat of battle to carry you along; in a duel, you needed cool instead of heat. As a test of character, duels rounded out the curriculum vitae. (In 1819, the newly anointed state of Illinois actually hanged the survivor of a duel, but it was fought with rifles at the uncomfortable distance of twenty-five paces. The jury must have felt this was unsporting; juries liked their duels more decorous than murderous.)

It made no difference at all whether the cause of the fight was noble and worthy, or even whether the principals had anything to do with the original problem. However elaborate the preliminary skirmishing, however complicated the relations of the various people mixed up in it, the fight itself was an isolated moment. It happened in a sealed bubble, cut off from before and after, immune to reason.

When Sam Houston was in Congress, he mailed the folks back home in Tennessee some packets of vegetable seeds to plant. (He doesn't seem like the vegetable-gardening type, but he must have had a domestic side.) For some reason they were never delivered, and Houston called Nashville's postmaster Curry a scoundrel and said he would settle the matter when he got home. Curry sent his second, General White, with a challenge, but Houston said he wouldn't stoop to fight with such a lowlife as Curry. White offered himself instead.

The trouble with contemporary reports is their sheer complication. Too many people get involved, and the chronicler assumes we know who they are and can keep the minor players straight. In the Houston fray, one Colonel Willoughby Williams explains it all:

"The matter was public, and great excitement existed among the friends of both parties, and rumors were afloat that a duel would follow. Col. John T. SMITH, a noted duelist in Missouri, arrived in the city, and it was understood that he would be the bearer of the challenge to HOUSTON. It was believed that Col. McGREGOR, who was General HOUSTON's second, would refuse to accept the challenge through the hands of Col. SMITH, for reasons which he explained. This caused some excitement among the friends of General HOUSTON, as they expected a difficulty to occur between Mr. McGREGOR and Col. SMITH, because of the refusal to accept the challenge if borne by SMITH, he being well known as a desperate man."

In Missouri, Smith was called John Smith T, no doubt to distinguish him from lesser John Smiths. In his day he was Missouri's most famous fighter, with fifteen kills to his credit. As for being desperate, his attorney insisted he was "as mild a mannered man as ever put a bullet into a human body."

Williams goes on: "It was anticipated that the challenge would be delivered at the Nashville Inn, where Gen. HOUSTON was stopping that afternoon, and all were on the lookout for the movements of SMITH. He was soon seen, about where now [1878] stands the Hicks china store, walking in the direction of the Nashville Inn, and the friends of both parties hurried to the Inn, where the meeting was to take place. Maj. Philip CAMPBELL, a gallant soldier in the Creek war and a warm personal friend of Gen. HOUSTON, with ten or fifteen other HOUSTON men made their appearance at the Inn, prepared to take part, as it was expected there would be a fight when McGREGOR refused to accept the challenge borne by SMITH. The challenge was presented by SMITH to McGREGOR in front of the Nashville Inn, with these words: 'I have a communication with Col. IRWIN to Gen. HOUSTON, which I now hand to you, sir,' extending his hand with the challenge. McGREGOR replied: 'I can receive no communication through your hands from Col. IRWIN,' and the paper dropped on the pavement before them. Col. SMITH then returned to his quarters, walking down the Public Square ..."

And out of the story. It seems odd for a man of such fire-breathing reputation to stroll away from such an insult; perhaps he simply wasn't much interested in the whole affair, or the errant vegetable seeds. Who "Col. Irwin" is and what he was doing there, we know not, nor why the entire population seems composed of senior military officers.

"The crowd rushed into the hall of the Inn where Gen. HOUSTON was standing, greatly relieved that there was no fight between McGREGOR and SMITH. Gen. Wm. WHITE, a brave and chivalrous gentleman, remarked that he did not 'think the proper courtesy had been extended to Col. SMITH.' HOUSTON heard the remark, and said: 'If you, sir, have any grievances, I will give you any satisfaction you may demand.' Gen. WHITE replied: 'I have nothing to do with your dif-ficulty, but I presume to know what is due from one gentle-man to another.' This ended the conversation. The next day it was rumored on the streets that Gen. HOUSTON had 'back down' Gen. WHITE. When it reached the ear of the gallant WHITE, through some evil-minded person, he resented the imputation by sending a challenge to Gen. HOUSTON, who readily accepted."

At this point a local busybody, referred to as a "preserver of the peace," came to town, heard about the upcoming fracas, and got the sheriff to issue a warrant to arrest both parties. Our chronicler hurries off to alert Houston, but he's already slipped out of town. Apparently White did too. The next day, Houston sent word to

White that he'd meet him in Kentucky to "offer him any redress he might desire."

Houston knew the area. A spot near Bowling Green, Kentucky, had somehow escaped the surveyor's eye and wasn't quite either Kentucky or Tennessee. The confused jurisdiction made it a popular spot for illegal sports.

"WHITE met him according to appointment, and they fought a duel at sun rise ... On the evening of the fight a large crowd was assembled at the Inn to hear news of the duel, among them Gen. JACKSON ... [A] personal friend of Gen. HOUSTON and a noted character, John G. ANDERSON, who had gone up to witness the fight was seen coming at full speed over the bridge, and soon announced that HOUSTON was safe and WHITE mortally wounded."

He wasn't. He'd been shot through the groin at fifteen feet, but he eventually recovered, perhaps wondering what he could have been thinking of. He had had absolutely nothing to do with the quarrel, or the seeds, or the postmaster; he'd just been hanging around at the inn and mentioned that he thought McGregor was rude to Smith, which he was. He knew "what was due from one gentleman to another," though, and very nearly died of it.

Houston was indicted in Kentucky, but the governor of Tennessee refused to extradite him, and a year later, before the jurisdictions got sorted out, he himself was the new governor of Tennessee and didn't extradite himself either. Whether the packets of vegetable seeds ever turned up in the back room of the post office, and where Curry the postmaster was hiding during the excitement, history doesn't tell us, but Houston went on to fame and fortune, with a city and a space program named for him, and perhaps, in the future, whole galaxies.

Missouri's favorite son, Mark Twain, wrote in his autobiography that he was "inflexibly opposed to the dreadful custom" of dueling, in spite of or maybe because of his own brush with one.

By 1864, the frontier had been pushed far to the west and Twain was in Virginia City, Nevada, dabbling in silver mines, drinking heavily, and writing irascible columns in the *Territorial Enterprise*. As always when territories hovered on the edge of statehood, stakes were high and tempers ran short.

With his trademark uncombed hair and ratty clothes, Twain was outrageous even by local standards; his colleagues called him "The Incorrigible" and his foully smoldering pipe "The Remains." His editorial opinions were witty and insulting and occasionally wild. One insulted fellow threatened to kick him clear across Nevada. Twain replied, "Well, if you think you've got enough money to put me over all these toll roads, just start in!"

The projected duel originated in a fund-raising scheme that began as a wager, and then a hoax, and then went legitimate, proceeds to benefit the United States Sanitary Fund, ancestor of the American Red Cross. Twain wrote in the *Enterprise* that the rival *Virginia City Union* had reneged on its pledge. The piece was badly timed, since the *Union* had paid up before the paper hit the streets. James Laird, the *Union*'s publisher, protested so vehemently that Twain challenged him to a duel.

His second, Steve Gillis, led him off to brush up on his marksmanship with a target nailed to a barn door, but Twain couldn't even hit the door, or maybe even the barn, though he fired over and over again. Perhaps he wasn't entirely sober. Nearby he could hear Laird, also practicing, probably more effectively. His courage leaked out and he collapsed.

Laird and his friends were approaching. Quickly Gillis snatched the gun, shot the head off a small bird, and stood there openly admiring its corpse.

"Who did that?" asked Laird's second. Gillis said that Twain had done it, and furthermore, he could do it over and over, decapitating small birds whenever he wanted, and added, "You don't want to fight that man. It's just like suicide. You'd better settle this thing, now."

This is the accepted version, as detailed in Andrew Hoffman's scholarly *Inventing Mark Twain*, so we have to believe it, but it sounds a great deal like something Tom Sawyer would have thought up. It may have lost nothing in the telling. At any rate, they settled.

Twain wrote, "I have never had anything do with duels since. I consider them unwise and I know they are dangerous. Also, sinful. If a man should challenge me now I would go to that man and take him kindly and forgivingly by the hand and lead him to a quiet spot and kill him. Still, I have always taken a great interest in other people's duels. One always feels an abiding interest in any heroic thing which has entered into his own experience."

Unwise, dangerous, sinful – but just the same, heroic. Not an uncommon opinion.

Twain, never a man to shun the printed word, had published the challenge and correspondence in the paper. Dueling in Nevada was nominally illegal and the authorities took notice. Depending on your version, either Twain calmly decided on a change of air and got on the next stagecoach or, according to himself, was run out of the territory with "four horse-whippings and two duels" still owed to him. In either case, he headed for San Francisco, by this time the dueling capital of the country.

In 1848, the *San Francisco Californian* reported, rather piously, "The whole country resounds with the sordid cry of 'gold! Gold!! GOLD!!!' while the field is left half planted, the house half built, and everything neglected but the manufacturer of shovels and pickaxes." A carpenter working at a California sawmill had found some gold flakes in a stream and America poured westward to look for more.

By sea, it was fifteen thousand miles around Cape Horn, and when the ships put in at San Francisco, their crews jumped ashore and headed for the gold fields without looking back. Some thirty thousand more prospective prospectors came trudging overland, joined by adventurous types from all over the world. Cooler heads stayed in the towns selling overpriced supplies and services to the hopeful miners; they were more likely to get rich than the lone men out sloshing the creek bottom back and forth and peering into the pans. Lawyers, sensing disputed land and mineral claims, swarmed in like locusts.

The new Californians were overwhelmingly male. It was no sort of place for a lady and, of the handful of women, few were ladies. The freshly arrived, rootless population of ambitious men, thrown together in a strange land, crowded into boardinghouses, veering from hope to despair to hope again, jumping each other's claims, competing for women, did just what you'd expect them to do. Fights were so common that nobody paused to watch. They fought with pistols, rifles, fists, and bowie knives. They fought over card games and gambling debts and flecks of gold. They fought for any reason or no reason at all. Sometimes the more respectable among them even calmed down long enough to organize a proper duel.

With the influx of gold diggers into the territory, California would soon be eligible for statehood, and the burning question was whether it would be a slave state and vote with the South or a free state and vote with the North. As settlement had pushed west and new states crowded in, the delicate balance of North and South trembled, Washington's chambers and corridors rumbled, and blood was shed. Both sides felt strongly on the matter.

David Broderick was a former New York saloon keeper and Tammany Hall politico. He came, he made money speculating in claims and real estate, and he bought the San Francisco *Herald*. He spoke out against slavery and his paper made him enemies left and right.

The Southerner William Smith, whose father had been governor of Virginia, called him out, and they fought on the shore of San Francisco Bay at ten paces. They used revolvers, the lightweight naval .36 six-shooters, which gave you much less chance of missing than the old single-shots. Broderick managed to miss Smith with all six bullets, but one of Smith's hit him in the chest and was stopped short by his heavy watch case. (Strictly speaking, your second was supposed to relieve you in advance of coins, watch cases, Bibles, and similar body armor.)

California was admitted to the Union. The slave/free debate grew warmer.

Broderick of the *Herald* went to Washington as a senator of the new state. A nice one, apparently; one writer said, "The purity of his life and his scrupulous honesty, associated with pride, energy, and ambition, commanded respect from men of both sections and all parties." Back home in California, though, he had his enemies.

David Terry was a Southerner and proud of it, though since he was born in Tennessee, the Old Guard of Charleston and New Orleans would have considered him a hillbilly. In California, he practiced law and spoke out in favor of slavery, became a judge and then chief justice of California's new supreme court.

Terry's proslavery faction was rampant, and tempers ran high. When Broderick left Washington to go home and campaign, he said to the clerk of the House, "I feel, my dear friend, that we shall never meet again. I go home to die. I shall be challenged, I shall fight, and I shall be killed." (At least, that's how the clerk remembered it, though he may have retouched it a bit after the fact.)

The campaign was fractious, with Terry in the thick of the opposition. Broderick forgot his usual gentility and cast aspersions on Terry's honesty. According to one reporter, "Between the 1st of July and the 7th of September, the political campaign was accompanied by the bitterest personalities, and Broderick in his speeches did not spare the name of Terry. The latter was ultra-Southern in his morality as well as his politics. On the morning of the 8th, the day after election, before breakfast, while

Broderick was still in the height of his rage on the first news of the overwhelming defeat of his party, he received a polite little note from Terry ..."

They met on the beach south of San Francisco at six in the morning, but somehow half the city had found out and trooped down to watch. Some rowdies got arrested, and the principals postponed it till the following day, in a quieter place, a valley near Merced Lake. They drew lots for the choice of weapons, and Terry won, opting for the delicate hair trigger. He knew all about hair triggers. Broderick didn't, and the one he drew was so sensitive that it fired if you breathed on it. The distance was ten paces. Both men were dressed in black, with slouch hats. Broderick seemed nervous.

A local correspondent tells it. "'Gentleman,' said Mr. Colton, in a clear voice, 'are you ready?' Both replied, but Broderick delayed a few seconds. He then said, 'I am ready.' 'Fire! One –' There was a report from the Senator's pistol. It was answered in a second by Terry's weapon. Broderick's pistol was discharged before he brought it to a level. This was probably caused by the fineness of the hair-trigger and his want of familiarity with that particular weapon. The bullet buried itself in the ground, two-thirds of the distance between himself and his antagonist. It was a splendid line-shot, fallen short of its mark. Broderick had the reputation of being an expert with the pistol, and this result surprised those who knew his skill. With the crack of Terry's weapon Broderick winced, turned half round, and then made an effort to recover himself. 'Hard hit,' his friends murmured. These words were proved by his unavailing efforts to maintain an upright position. He drooped until finally he fell prone on the ground, with his pale face toward the sky. He was hard hit."

It was a big, jagged chest wound. He lingered in pain for several days and spoke only with a great effort, but he managed to say, "They have killed me, because I was opposed to slavery and a corrupt administration." (The "they" was well considered; according to gossip, Terry was only the first of three who'd agreed to challenge him serially, with murder in mind.)

Ten thousand people came to the funeral.

It was only one of countless warmup slavery duels, trial runs for the greatest honor duel of them all.

The big one began back east, of course, at slavery central. It was arranged quite classically and properly, with an exchange of increasingly stiff notes in Charleston, South Carolina.

The Union's Fort Sumter sat in the harbor, right in the face of the first state to secede from the Union. Militarily, it wasn't terribly useful, and various Northerners, including the doughty General Winfield Scott, hero of the Mexican War, thought it might be wise just to abandon the place and stop provoking the touchy Carolinians, but the North could be every bit as gentlemanly as the South in these matters: Only a cowardly poltroon would back down.

Nobody in South Carolina would sell any groceries to the fort, so Major Anderson, the man in charge there, appealed to the federal government to send him supplies, as they were running out of bacon, and some more men to help reinforce the place.

South Carolina's governor sent Anderson a note saying, "Let your

President attempt to reinforce Sumter, and the tocsin of war will be sounded from every hilltop and valley in the South."

Naturally the North couldn't take that lying down and sent a supply ship.

General Beauregard sent his seconds out to the fort with a challenge to Major Anderson, telling him to evacuate the place and leave, or else. (The two principals already knew each other, as all proper duelists should. Anderson had been Beauregard's artillery instructor at West Point.)

Anderson wrote back saying he couldn't really do that yet, but he'd leave as soon as he ran out of food.

Beauregard replied that if he'd name an exact time for his surrender, he wouldn't bombard the fort.

Anderson wrote back saying he'd leave at noon on April 15. It was only April 11.

The Confederate secretary of war told Beauregard that reinforcements were on their way to Sumter, so he'd better start loading the cannons.

Beauregard wrote to Anderson saying he had the honor of notifying him that he was going to start shelling the place in exactly one hour, and an hour later, at four-thirty in the morning, he did.

Both sides had behaved impeccably. They had both defended their honors and continued to defend them for a long, long time. As with so many duels, honor was really all there was to fight about. Politically, slavery made a fine football, but morally and economically it was a dinosaur staggering toward extinction, just as it had staggered bloodlessly in other countries, and the North's determination to preserve the Union by force, over the objections of some of its members, seems a theoretical reason for war.

It was a question of honor.

If, instead, Abraham Lincoln and Jefferson Davis had faced each other with pistols at Bladensburg, there's half a million lives saved right there, maybe minus one, and quite a lot of money.

XII. ELSEWHERE

E NGLAND WAS GOVERNED by the customary arrangement: Duels were illegal but nobody got convicted. Important duels were routinely reported in the newspapers, like any other sporting event; in the last three months of 1835 alone, the *Times* of London found fourteen of them notable enough to mention. Wimbledon Common was the favorite venue.

Among upper-class English civilians, though, fatalities were dropping. In 1822, when the duke of Bedford fought the duke of Buckingham over a question of parliamentary reform, Bedford fired into the air and Buckingham didn't fire at all. No ducal blood was spilled. Honor had been satisfied. Showing up was the point.

Charles, Lord Tennyson, uncle of poet Alfred, called out Lord Thomas Cecil, who'd complained after losing an election to him.

223

They met at Wormwood Scrubs and fired and missed and went back home.

Some people found it undignified when the duke of Wellington met the tenth earl of Winchelsea, who'd objected to Wellington's support of Catholic emancipation. Wellington was prime minister at the time, and sixty years old, and as the conqueror of Napoleon at Waterloo had little left to prove in manly prowess. At this point in his career he didn't even own a pair of dueling pistols, and his second had to borrow them from the attending doctor.

They met in Battersea Fields, with the earl of Falmouth acting as Winchelsea's second. Wellington fired intentionally wide; Winchelsea fired into the air. Falmouth then whipped out a letter of explanation, which the duke refused to receive until it was rewritten to include the word "apology."

When someone objected to the incident, Wellington said, "You speak as a moralist, and I assure you that I am no advocate of duelling under ordinary circumstances; but my difference with Lord Winchelsea, considering the cause in which it originated, and the critical position of affairs at the moment, can scarcely be regarded as a private quarrel ... His attack upon me was part of a plan to render the conduct of public affairs impossible to the King's servants."

Matters of state came first. Dueling was part of a prime minister's job: Wellington's predecessors Lord Bath, Lord Shelburne, Pitt, Fox, and Canning had obeyed the code of honor, and afterward Peel carried on the tradition. The aspiring classes took note, and Disraeli, who was Jewish and anxious to improve his social position on his own road to prime minister, challenged the Irish leader

Daniel O'Connell, who had killed Captain D'Esterre in a duel. O'Connell declined, but Disraeli got credit for trying.

If dueling was growing less dangerous among politicians, the military was another matter. In his history of the British army, J. W. Fortescue reported that the young officers were mainly interested in "sport, horseflesh, and women" but "varied the monotony by quarreling and fighting duels, generally after some foolish controversy over their cups."

Europe sent its sons abroad to run its empires, as soldiers and settlers and civil servants. Most of them didn't take much thoughtful interest in the exotic countries where they found themselves; they sulked, drank, and fought within their own claustrophobic groups. Ocean voyages to and from the colonies were long and monotonous, and the passengers quarreled and, as soon as they touched dry land, fought.

The West Indies were as turbulent as Ireland. In Cuba, the Spanish plantation owners, idle and hot, fought each other whenever the need arose; one senator shot another dead on the Senate floor but, being rich and blue-blooded, escaped censure.

Tortola boasted of a "beautiful little fighting ground . . . always kept in a state of preparation, for many a Tortolan had kissed the daisies on that emerald turf."

In Barbados, round-the-clock cockfighting whiled away the days, accompanied by heavy betting and drinking that frequently led to the dueling ground.

In Jamaica, according to a historian, quarrels between friends, no doubt enhanced by the local rum, usually ended in duels.

In Martinique, a sensitive young writer was upset by a bad

review of his novel; he called out the journalist and got himself killed. No record survives of the novel, or whether its good name was worth dying for. Martinique was also the refuge of choice for French-Canadian duelists who ran afoul of the stricter Canadian rules; sometimes, back home, they were tried in absentia and then hanged in effigy while they lounged in the beachfront cafés.

In India, the jewel in Britain's crown, dueling was commonest in the military. Officers who were not quite socially top-drawer back home grew self-important from their new status as sahibs and reinforced it by fighting each other and sometimes even lesser mortals. One J. H. Stocqueler had been a mere soldier, a lowly other-ranks, but he took up editing a newspaper. When his editorial criticized the management of the army's orphan school in Calcutta, a staff captain, furious at his presumption, called him out. They rowed across the Hooghly River that night in separate boats. Stocqueler fired at the moon, the captain fired at the ground. Then, said Stocqueler, "the good little man made me a graceful bow; he was quite satisfied – so was I – and we were always better friends afterwards."

Long-standing Old World feuds spread into the Empire. In 1842, at Poona, a young Ensign Sarsfield from an Irish Catholic family found himself in a regiment where all the other officers were Protestants. They sent him to Coventry, shunning him so mercilessly that finally, at the mess table, he lost his temper and threw a wineglass in the face of a brother officer. The duel took place by moonlight. Sarsfield's death was attributed to cholera and no questions were asked.

After the opening of the Suez Canal in 1869, a flood of

eligible British women known as "the fishing fleet" swept over the subcontinent and calmed down the freewheeling bachelor expatriates with marriage and muffins. As an alternate outlet, the military took up blood sports instead, killing an amazing quantity of animals; you could prove your manly courage just as well by stalking a tiger as by shooting your fellow officers.

Some few, even in the face of the strict new laws, managed to fight anyway. In India in 1894, two British colonial officers, Captain Phillips and Lieutenant Shepherd, suffered a falling-out and contrived an exotic local variation on the duel. They locked a deadly venomous snake, probably a cobra, into a dark room, waited an hour, and then entered the room from opposite doorways, groping their way blindly around the furniture. After ten minutes, Lieutenant Shepherd screamed. Phillips, they say, rushed out of the room with his hair turned instantly white; Shepherd died gruesomely a few hours later.

The French and the English emigrated to Canada. Aside from the occasional separatist movement in Quebec, Canada today seems a placid place. Americans think of it as bland and law-abiding and a bit self-righteous; Europeans, when they think of it at all, feel it must be something like Australia, only colder. Still, it did have its duels, though it was never a world-class player.

It saw its first fatal duel back in 1669, when it was still "New France," between two soldiers garrisoned at Trois Rivières. The French colonial laws were surprisingly strict at the time, and the survivor was tried, sentenced to hang, and hanged later the same day. Things must have eased off after that, because in 1684,

François-Marie Perrot, governor of Montreal for fifteen years, fought a public duel with a belligerent local fellow; both were wounded, but no repercussions were recorded.

French soldiers came to New France to fight the Iroquois and get ready to fight the English colonies to the south. Like idled military everywhere, they drank and fought each other, sometimes in casual brawls, sometimes with proper duels. As usual – "different spanks for different ranks" – the fighting officers were ignored and the fighting enlisted men punished. General Montcalm, for his part, quite approved of officers dueling; it kept their spirits up.

In 1760, when the French surrendered their sovereignty and the British took over, swords were replaced by pistols. The Canadian historian Aegidius Fauteux wrote that "Gallic ardour" was suited to the grace and agility of swordplay, while "the phlegmatic British found more satisfaction in pistol duels in which two adversaries were placed face to face, at a distance, in an attitude as cold as it was correct, the advantage being that one could be killed without having one's uniform or attire even rumpled." (Note that his name was Fauteux, not Jones.)

In a typical garrison duel in 1797, Lieutenant Evans of the Twenty-fourth Foot was chatting with Lieutenant Ogilvy of the Twenty-sixth, in Ogilvy's room, after he'd gone to bed. They compared the respective merits of their respective regiments, and Evans mentioned that he thought the quality of the spruce beer served in the messes was about the same in both. Ogilvy, stung, retorted that the Twenty-sixth's beer was infinitely better. Evans said that must mean Ogilvy was calling him a liar. Ogilvy retorted that he was indeed "a damned lying scoundrel." The next day Evans sent asking Ogilvy to apologize. Ogilvy refused and went around saying that Evans was no gentleman.

After the first round of shots, Evans again asked for an apology, Ogilvy again refused, and they broke out another case of pistols. After this round, Evans again suggested they come to terms, Ogilvy refused, and Evans this time took careful aim and shot the scoundrel dead. The Court of the King's Bench, Chief Justice Osgoode presiding, acquitted, and regimental honor and the equal merits of the beer were vindicated.

This same Justice Osgoode was quite in favor of dueling as long as it was done properly, though once he couldn't persuade the jury and it convicted; he was forced to fine the survivor thirteen shillings and fourpence. This was the only Canadian duelist convicted under British rule, from 1761 until 1888.

Bloodshed was averted in a less typical garrison duel when one Broadstreet, an officer in the same Twenty-fourth Foot, said that one Mr. Nesbit was actually a woman. Nesbit challenged Broadstreet. Broadstreet's second, who had his own suspicions, went to the governor, and the governor ordered Nesbit to be examined by the garrison doctor to settle the matter. Nesbit protested violently, and then broke down and admitted she was indeed a Miss Nevile and shortly afterward left the country.

Dueling is an outdoor activity and the Canadian weather was foul a good deal of the time. When it wasn't raining it was snowing, and even in April the combatants rode to the dueling ground in sleighs or tramped across the ice to islands.

From the diary of an Ontario magistrate: "February 11, 1839. A very snowy morning. Rose at 5 & accompanied by Capt. Rudyerd to the place of meeting. We arrived there half an hour before the Enemy. Very cold. Mr. W. R. Wood was attended by Lt. Cameron & I by Rudyerd. Distance 12 paces. At the first fire my Pistol missed fire. On the 2nd shot I hit Mr. Wood in the Jaw & the ball lodged there. He missed me both shots. Home by 8 to breakfast. I sent him home in my sleigh, & Rudyerd and I walked all the way."

In eastern Canada the mix of French and English, Catholic and Protestant, caused fights. A distinguished Protestant surgeon and public figure fought and almost killed a distinguished Catholic legislator over whether the Catholic hospital in Montreal should be supplemented by a publicly funded Protestant hospital. With unusual determination, they each fired five rounds.

In the inner reaches of the country, Irish and English clashed. Called in to consult over a childbirth, two eminent physicians, one English-born, one Irish, disagreed on the procedure and the words "liar, scoundrel and coward" and "liar, villain, scoundrel and fool" were exchanged, apparently across the prostrate form of the laboring lady. At the appointed place, in the best New Orleans tradition, they each fired two shots and missed. The condition of mother and child is not recorded.

Back home on the old sod, Ireland continued blazing away according to custom. Stendhal wrote that the country was still "in that curious state . . . when people who are breakfasting cheerfully with one another may meet two hours later on the field of battle." Or, as Sir Jonah Barrington put it, "the strongest friendships were sometimes formed, and frequently regenerated, on the field of battle." Another writer complained that the land was full of small-time country gentry, squireens, "who hunt in the day, get drunk in the evening, and fight the next morning."

In such manly countries, Italy was still held up to ridicule. All fuss and feathers, posing and posturing, but where was the blood? By the end of the nineteenth century, even pretending to duel was fading out, except in Naples, where it died harder. A London journal conducted a study of Italian duels in the ten years between 1879 and 1889 and found records and statistics for only a paltry 2,759, though it admitted that many others weren't on the records.

Originators of swordplay, Italians clung to their rapiers; ninety-three percent of the time they fought with blades. Nearly four thousand wounds resulted, 1,066 listed as serious and fifty as fatal. Of the causes of combat, thirty percent were political, nineteen percent cards and other games, ten percent religious discussions, and only eight percent insults. Five times as many happened in summer as in winter, either because of the inflammatory nature of warm sunshine or because nobody wanted to go outdoors and fight in the cold rains of January. Almost none were fought during Lent; perhaps dueling was a popular indulgence to renounce for the season. Of a hundred principals singled out for inspection, thirty were military and twenty-nine were journalists, along with twelve lawyers, four students, three professors, three engineers, and three members of parliament.

Most damning of all in some eyes, only two percent of the combatants died, making the Italian duel not much more dangerous than football. Since facing possible death was central to the whole mystique, why bother to fight at all with odds like that?

*   *   *

France fought on. After their revolution, the duel provided a perfect union of the glamorous old aristocratic past with the new world of *liberté*, *égalité*, and *fraternité*; butchers and bakers and enlisted men now dueled like gentlemen to their hearts" content. In 1836, the comte de Chateauvillard published his *Essai sur le duel*, with a complete list of insults and options, and it was promptly translated for an eager public in England and Germany. The civil upheavals of the midcentury provided fine fodder for disagreements all over Europe, with the middle classes happily joining the aristocracy on the field of honor.

By the end of the nineteenth century, duels were the national French pastime.

Unlike the Italians, the French preferred to fight in winter and spring; perhaps then as now they all went off on vacation for the month of August. French labor leaders fought aristocrats, conservatives fought republicans. Novelists fought each other over stylistic points and other literary matters. Alexandre Dumas fought the playwright Gaillerdet over the authorship of a drama. Edouard Manet challenged, fought, and wounded an art critic who, in his review of a group show, mentioned Manet's work only once. In 1896 Marcel Proust, remembered as a reclusive invalid, fought a critic who had slammed his first book and called him "one of those pretty little society boys who have managed to get themselves pregnant with literature." A brace of literary critics fired four shots at each other to determine the relative merits of the classical and the romantic schools of fiction. Guy de Maupassant had an eye for the ladies that led him to various duels; he was a fine marksman, though, and walked away after all of them. (In the end he paid the piper with syphilis.)

Clemenceau, the pre-eminent French statesman of World War I, was an expert with both sword and pistol and survived, they say, twenty-two duels, though by this time they were easier to survive.

In Paris, the *salles des armes* were lavishly decorated like nightclubs, or perhaps like bordellos, and their fencing masters swaggered around putting on airs. In 1900 a member of the Assembly did shoot and kill a municipal counselor in a pistol duel, but in general France still preferred the elegant épée to the plebeian gun, for maximum grace and flair with minimum bloodshed. Carefully wielded, it did very little damage, and its flourishments looked more like ballet than battle and lasted longer, providing more fun for the spectators, whose opinion was growing important. In one Parisian duel in 1904, two rival fencing masters fought each other for three hours without shedding blood. The reporters loved it.

At the end of the nineteenth century, the American satirist Ambrose Bierce defined the French duel as "A formal ceremony preliminary to the reconciliation of two enemies. Great skill is necessary to its satisfactory observance; if awkwardly performed the most unexpected and deplorable consequences sometimes ensue. A long time ago a man lost his life in a duel."

Reporters and the general public usually turned out in force, and presently photographers showed up too. One journalist suggested that French duels would wither away overnight if the newspapers quit writing about them: "In ninety-one out of ninety-two cases, one duels for the gallery. Suppress the gallery and you exterminate the duel."

Journalists, like those of their calling everywhere, were asked to do a lot of dueling themselves, and *Le Figaro* and *Le Gaulois* set up their own fencing salons to keep their reporters in shape.

Parties were held. After a successful – that is, conclusive but virtually painless – duel, caviar and champagne were served to all in a celebratory breakfast. Mark Twain said he'd rather be the hero of a Parisian duel than a crowned and sceptered monarch. In 1906, while the minister of war and General de Negrier fought a pistol duel in the garden of a prince's Parisian mansion, aproned waiters served food and drinks to the reporters waiting out in the street.

In 1908, the Bourbon infante of Spain, Don Alfonso, complained that he wasn't making any progress in his struggles for an international no-dueling agreement, and France was the problem. France had savaged the plan.

The French and the English have rarely seen eye to eye, and as dueling declined in England, the English could point smugly at their own superior civilization, compared to the barbarians across the channel who were still brandishing blades. In England in 1890, *The Cornhill Magazine* printed "The Duello in France," attributed to Arthur Conan Doyle of Sherlock Holmes fame. "In spite of the incessant wars which make up the history of France, the record of private combat and bloodshed is an unbroken one, stretching back in a long red stream through the ages, sometimes narrow, sometimes broad, occasionally reaching such a flood as can only be ascribed to a passing fit of homicidal mania. Recent events have shown that this national tendency is still as strong as ever, and that there is every prospect that the duello, when driven from every other European country, may still find a home among a gallant people, whose solicitude for their honour makes them occasionally a trifle neglectful of their intelligence ..."

In past duels between French and English soldiers, he reflects proudly, "The French ... were incomparably the better swordsmen, but the young Englishmen, relying on their superior bodily strength, would throw themselves upon their antagonists with such a supreme disregard for the science of the thing that they not unfrequently succeeded in cutting down their bewildered opponents."

As the nineteenth century draws to a close, "An Englishman can scarcely be censorious when he speaks of the duels of the past, for his own chronicles are too often stained by encounters as desperate as any across the Channel. The time at last has come, however, when the duel is as much an anachronism in our own country, and in the settled states of the Union, as judicial torture or the burning of witches. Only when France has attained the same position can she claim to be on a par with the Anglo-Saxon nations in the quality of her civilisation."

The French paid no attention. They were having too much fun.

XIII. RUSSIAN SOUL

T HE RUSSIANS ARE credited with inventing Russian roulette, a parlor game in which two men take turns loading a single cartridge into a revolver, spinning the cylinder, and firing it at either his own or the other man's head. If played only once, each player has a five-to-one chance of surviving, or about the same as in a proper Irish duel, but if the players are extremely depressed, they can keep on until one of them scores a hit. Like the so-called American duel of drawing straws, this is more a sociable form of suicide than an encounter and it's hard to see how honor would be vindicated. As entertainment, though, I suppose it helped to pass the long winter evenings.

The Slavic soul is a dark and moody place, lit by flashes of marsh gas, and has given us great splendid, brooding novels and operas. Vodka may be a factor.

Alexander Pushkin not only gave Russia its first truly native literature but, some say, created the Russian soul, the Russian identity. His life, his work, his duels, and his death cast their long dark shadow forward across the nineteenth century. Many Russians still, when they think of Russia, see it as Pushkin. When he started writing, Russians and Russian literature yearned to be French, elegant, mannered, European. Pushkin lifted the national inferiority complex and made it all right, even noble, to be Slavic.

He was their nationally adored poet. The idea of a living poet whose works are revered, memorized, and recited by everyone from the empress down to the farmhands now seems so archaic as to be almost perverse. It was a nineteenth-century phenomenon, maybe some wildcat genetic fluke that turned out to be evolutionarily useless and faded from our genes. America had Whitman and Longfellow, England had Byron and Tennyson. Russia had Pushkin, and still has.

Well-brought-up Americans and Europeans are expected to have read, in translation, *War and Peace*, *Crime and Punishment*, *Anna Karenina*, *Fathers and Sons*, *The Brothers Karamazov*, Uncle Vanya, and *The Cherry Orchard*, or at least the Cliffs Notes, but we who don't read Russian have to take Russia's word for Pushkin. His poetry was rhymed and metrical, and everything about his language was so profoundly Russian that, translated, the spirit evaporates.

Opera fans know his *Boris Godunov* and *Eugene Onegin* but judge them in terms of the tenor rather than the poet. We could read them in English in translation by the likes of Vladimir Nabokov, but we don't. Peter Shaffer borrowed his Tony- and Oscar-winning play and movie *Amadeus* from Pushkin's *Mozart and Salieri*, but who noticed? Pushkin's groundbreaking prose novel is still in print in translation and his biographer, Henri Troyat, claims that if he hadn't written *The Captain's Daughter*, with its grand historical events filtered through the witness of ordinary Russians, Tolstoy could never have written *War and Peace*. Somehow it never made it into our canon.

In Russia in 1800, life was pleasant for the upper classes. Serfs were plentiful and cheap; a purebred hound dog cost four times as much as a healthy male peasant with useful skills. Even minor civil servants owned a dozen or so serfs just for the house, and back home on his country estate a gentleman had thousands.

St. Petersburg was the center of government and Moscow was the center of culture. The gentry partied and danced and gossiped all winter, and in summer took themselves and a few dozen select house serfs to their rustic summer cabins, where they admired nature and entertained parties of guests. Imported French champagne flowed in rivers.

Alexander Pushkin was born in 1799. His mother was the granddaughter of the Abyssinian Abraham Hannibal, who'd been a favorite of Peter the Great. Son of a prince, or so they say, he'd been captured by the Turks and sent to Constantinople as a hostage. Peter wanted a little blackamoor child – they were all the rage and every proper European court had one. He negotiated for this one, fetched him back, stood godfather to him, and had him educated in Paris.

Hannibal was a turbulent fellow. He married a pretty girl very much against her will, then tortured her, dangled her from the dungeon walls with thongs around her wrists and, while she was dangling, married his mistress. This secondary wife called him a "black devil" who "begets on me black children" – eleven of them. Still the pet of the czar, Hannibal became a major general and acquired a considerable estate, and his children married well.

On the other side of the family, Pushkin's father came of ancient, famous, and equally unpredictable stock. A great-grandfather flew into a fit of rage and cut his pregnant wife's throat. His son, Pushkin's grandfather, decided his wife was having an affair with their son's French tutor; he locked her in his private dungeon, where she either starved or froze to death, and hanged the tutor in his courtyard. It seems every proper household came with its own dungeon and gallows.

Generations of Westerners grew up marveling at the fertile imaginations of Russian writers: How could they make up all those dark and stormy deeds? Apparently they didn't need to.

Pushkin's father was lazy and silly and entertained Moscow's literati, wasting more money than he could afford. (Aristocrats everywhere were flinging away their patrimony gambling and buying up baubles, but the Russians had a positive genius for it. Show a Russian count an estate or a sack full of gold and his first thought was how fast he could lose it.) Pushkin's mother had a talent for sulking and for thinking up bizarre punishments when her children displeased her.

The infant poet displeased her from the start. He was a throwback to Hannibal, with dark skin, thick lips, and crinkly black hair; she said he looked like a badly bleached African. His father didn't think much of him either. A serf of his grandmother's raised him, a farm woman who told him Russian folktales, at a time when the best Russian families spoke French and pretended not to understand Russian at all, and he loved her dearly.

An ever-changing parade of tutors from all over Europe did their best to teach him, but he was lazy and disobedient and just wanted to be left alone to read and write verses; like others in his family, he could rattle the rafters when he lost his temper. At twelve, he was sent to the Imperial Lyceum at Tsarskoye Selo, in the lap and under the wing of Alexander I in St. Petersburg.

This was a splendid stroke of luck. Any English boarding-school boy would have thought he'd gone to heaven. The teachers were inspiring, many of them shockingly liberal, and allowed to teach whatever they wanted. The headmaster was gentle and friendly, the schedule was easygoing, and even the food was good. The famous imperial gardens were open to play in, and Wednesdays and Saturdays were devoted entirely to dancing and fencing lessons.

In spite of the amiable atmosphere, young Pushkin continued lazy and careless, and his report cards featured comments like "violently hot tempered" and "fits of violent rage." (Perhaps there was a genetic component. And perhaps all the great Russian writers would have benefited from modern psychoactive drugs, though whether anyone on Prozac would even *want* to write *Crime and Punishment*, we know not.)

What saved him were his fellow students. They wrote poetry.

Hard as it is to imagine today, half a dozen randomly enrolled twelve- to fourteen-year-old boys hung around together to write poetry, read it aloud, and critique each other. They published a school newspaper of their work and wrote and recited slanderous doggerel about the school and their teachers. Pushkin was distinctly an oddball, with his African looks and a temperament by turns listless, hyperactive, and raging, but he must have had winning ways. Then as later, he made good friends who stood by him loyally in spite of himself.

His poetry helped. It was good. When he was fourteen, the highly respectable *European Herald* published his "To a Poet-Friend"; at fifteen he had a poem in the *Russian Museum* and he was famous. Unlike most beginners, he didn't maunder on about the scenery and seasons but bit off great chunks of public matters, Napoleon's invasion, the burning of Moscow, Napoleon's retreat. Important people came to the school to meet him. The empress sent him a gold watch and chain.

He wrote love poems too. All his life, starting at age seven, he fell in love with every pretty woman he met and some he'd just glimpsed in passing. At school he made improper advances, in the flesh as well as in verse, to the wrong women and got in trouble. (Sometimes they were the right women, and he didn't.) Troyat says he was "small, lean, and nervous; his dusky skin, thick lips, strong white cannibal teeth and, above all, his eyes – his eyes sparkling with glee – could not fail to impress the undemanding young women of Tsarskoye Selo." He was a novelty. He was also a terrific swordsman and horseman.

In his last year at school, he took to slipping out-of-bounds and carousing with the regiment of hussars stationed nearby, drinking and wenching. (Unlikely as it seems, the hussars read poetry too.) He graduated so far down in his class that the only post he was offered was as tenth undersecretary in the foreign ministry.

He lived with his parents in St. Petersburg and paid no attention to his nominal job. He went to every ball and every play, hung out in fashionable drawing rooms, drank, gambled, and suffered from assorted venereal diseases, which didn't slow down his romantic activities. He kept a life list of his lady loves, in two columns, one for those he'd bedded and one for those who'd spurned him. And he cultivated his outlandish image. He let his fingernails grow outrageously long and groomed and tended them and wore a golden sheath on the longest to keep it from breaking. (In later life he was once arrested, out in the boondocks, on suspicion of being the Antichrist, because "he had claws instead of nails.")

And of course he fought duels whenever he could scratch one up. They were an essential part of social life. When he was twenty, a society woman wrote, "Pushkin fights a duel every day; thank God they are not fatal, and the adversaries come back unscathed."

A fortune-teller told him that he'd live a long life if he escaped a certain danger in the year he was thirty-seven.

All these entertainments kept him from writing except when he was confined to bed with a hangover or the unpleasant medical treatments for gonorrhea. Luckily these problems came up often. He wrote a rousing long poem about a legendary prince and princess, *Russlan and Ludmila*, full of enchanted maidens, magicians, sorcerers, and kidnappers; it sounds like a mixture of Sir Walter Scott, *Beowulf*, *The Lord of the Rings*, and *Snow White and the Seven Dwarfs*. Some people loved it, but others found its plain language and roots in Russian folklore a bit vulgar.

In the meantime, his school friends were getting together in secret political meetings and talking about liberalizing some of the emperor's more autocratic ideas. They didn't invite Pushkin, since everyone knew he couldn't keep a secret, but he found out anyway. He decided to reform the emperor his own way, with words, and wrote assorted scurrilous verses and odes to liberty and witty epigrams that circulated secretly all through the social, military, and intellectual worlds.

Naturally the emperor found out and thought about sending him to Siberia, but decided instead to pack him off to a job in southern Russia, ten days" journey from the capital.

Pushkin professed to be weary of fame and dissipation and glad to get out of town. In the south, he never went near his office and fell in love with most of the women in town; his favorite conquest was a woman said to have slept with Byron, his hero. His bosses treated him like a son, fed him, and let him go on long journeys to visit friends. Sometimes a boss would place him under house arrest to stop him from fighting the more dangerous duels, or take away his boots to keep him safe at home.

He got bored. He drank, gambled, and quarreled with those he found insufficiently respectful. As he wrote to a friend, "In this country, writers belong to the upper nobility and have both the pride of the aristocrat and the artist's sensitivity," and he himself was "a gentleman whose lineage goes back six hundred years."

To liven up the "accursed town," he dressed in preposterous costumes, and everywhere he went he carried a brace of pistols and a heavy iron-clad cudgel. For years, nobody ever saw him without the cudgel. He said it was to strengthen his wrist for duels, of which he fought at least a dozen during his southern stay, to break the monotony.

Once he accused an officer named Zubov of cheating at baccarat. Zubov challenged him, and Pushkin showed up at the dueling ground carrying a bag of cherries. These he ate, spitting the pits in Zubov's direction, while the latter aimed, fired, and missed. "Are you satisfied now?" he asked, and strolled away, still eating cherries and so pleased with himself that he used the episode later in a story.

In another duel, in a blinding snowstorm, he and his opponent kept firing and missing and shortening the distance until they could almost touch each other but still couldn't see to shoot. They had to call it off.

As at least nominally a civil servant, he never had to work but he did have to fast and pray during Easter week, which annoyed him so much that he wrote *The Gabriliad*, in which the Virgin Mary is serially seduced by Satan, the Archangel Gabriel, and God dressed as a white pigeon. This was circulated privately and got him into trouble later.

Stuck in the provinces, he began to write *Eugene Onegin*, the novel in verse that was going to take him over seven years.

Pushkin was the first Russian writer to insist on getting paid for

245

his work. Money had always been considered beneath a writer's notice; writing wasn't expected to be a means of support. He sneered, "The poet is not to think of his living . . . he must write in the hope of wresting one small smile from the lips of the fair damsels." He was famous enough to insist, and stood his ground, and to everyone's surprise *The Fountain of Bakhchisarai* was actually a commercial success. He made three thousand rubles and paid off his debts. His reputation was growing too, and other poets were calling him "nightingale" and "the Jesus Christ of Russian poetry."

Then Count Vorontsov, a high official, suspected Pushkin of sleeping with his wife – which he was. To separate them, he told Pushkin to go off to inspect a plague of locusts infesting the steppe. After seven years on what seems to have been a wildly inflated government payroll, he was suddenly given some work to do, and he was furious and insulted. He wrote saying he was a *writer*, not some errand boy, and what he was paid wasn't really a salary, just compensation for his exile. He resigned, hoping to keep hanging around town anyway enjoying Mrs. Vorontsov, with whom he was deeply in love.

Unfortunately the emperor, who had plenty of spies, heard that he'd been writing about atheism and was probably dangerous. He sent him off to house arrest, under surveillance by family, church, and state, at his parents" farm in a dreary little village in the middle of nowhere. His friends were horrified. He'd be buried alive. He'd never survive the solitude.

Off he went, a curious figure in a flowing red Moldavian cape and full red pantaloons, with golden slippers and a Turkish fez topping his shoulder-length wiry curls, cudgel in hand.

After his parents went to St. Petersburg, he was left alone on the farm, with only his valet and his aged nanny for company. Nothing to do but write, drink, ride, read, bed the servant girls, practice his marksmanship. Sometimes he visited the neighbors and wreaked havoc among their assorted daughters and cousins, falling deeply in love with several.

He got one of the servant girls pregnant. Time passed. Alternately, depending on the seasons, he complained bitterly about his exile and rhapsodized about country life and the simple country folk. He finished *Eugene Onegin*, in which the hero shoots and kills his dear friend in a duel and suffers bitter remorse; duels figured often in his works. Though written in an elaborate rhyme scheme, it uses plain language about commonplace contemporary matters, altogether too Russian for the critics, who preferred pretty metaphors, but the public liked it.

From there, he dug into sixteenth-century history for *Boris Godunov*. He wanted to revitalize the Russian theater, at this point all pseudo-French, but he never managed to get the play produced; it was five years before he could even get it printed.

The emperor Alexander I died. There was some confusion about the succession, and Pushkin's old radical friends took advantage of it to rise up in the Decembrist revolt. It was a disaster. Almost to a man, they were executed or exiled to the Siberian salt mines.

Rummaging through their effects, the authorities found that they all carried copies of Pushkin's *Ode to Liberty*, their inspiration.

The new emperor, Nicholas, sent guards to bring him to Moscow to explain himself. Asked if he would have joined his friends in the rebellion if he'd been in town, he bravely answered yes, he would;

they were his friends. He was gambling that Nicholas would be impressed by his honesty, and he was. Nicholas lifted the exile order and made him promise not to write any more subversion against the government. On condition that he send all his works to Nicholas to check before publication, Pushkin was free.

St. Petersburg welcomed him back rejoicing, followed him in the streets, cheered him whenever he gave a reading, and invited him to all their parties. The Rimsky-Korsakovs invited him over and he tried to seduce their daughter. He lost a bundle gambling, fought a few duels. The close police surveillance didn't hamper his social life; by the end of a month he'd fallen deeply in love with half a dozen young ladies. He began to think about marriage, romanticizing a simple life of hearth and home and children.

He decided on the sixteen-year-old Natalya Goncharov, though she wasn't at all interested. Her mother didn't like the idea either; she was hoping for somebody richer; the family was in dire straits. After a fall from a horse, Mr. Goncharov had turned into a dangerous madman, and his wife mismanaged the estate so badly that she'd had to sell off two thousand of the serfs.

Natalya was said to be cold and timid and not very bright. She disliked poetry, though perhaps she'd never tried it. She didn't like her suitor's looks either, his exotic African features, long curled fingernails, and long crinkly sideburns. The adored and lionized poet, for whom women all over Russia pined and sighed, had chosen one who simply didn't understand what it was all about. Perhaps this was part of her charm. Everyone likes a challenge.

Her mother insisted that he wait a while for a decision and kept hoping for something better. Waiting, he seduced some other society beauties and fell in love with Katarina Ushakov, but he was determined on Natalya. Her indifference drove him to a frenzy of love; he wrote poems calling her a "haughty maid" and a "regal virgin."

She was a recognized beauty, and nobody pretended that women were loved for anything but their looks. Pushkin had always promised himself the most beautiful woman in Russia, and that was Natalya, with her high, narrow forehead, long, dark eyes, and fashionably weak chin. Though perhaps a bit languid looking for modern tastes, she was the epitome of elegance. A friend of his wrote, "You, as our foremost romantic poet, owe it to yourself to wed the foremost romantic beauty of our generation." He thought so too.

He waited for an answer, agonizing. He wrote, "The dreams of the night before a duel are nothing by comparison." Finally her mother despaired of bettering the offer and Natalya accepted: She "holds out a cold limp hand." Apparently there was no question of kissing her.

Perhaps the agony had been part of the point. Accepted, he seems to have suffered misgivings and wrote wrenching poems of regret to many of his past loves. Instead of celebrating the New Year with his betrothed, he went out and got drunk with some gypsies. Still, he was thirty, tired of being "a scholar of debauchery," and surely marriage would bring him peace at least.

It didn't. Even before the wedding, his future mother-in-law demanded a king's ransom so that she and her two other daughters, as well as the bride, could be dressed like empresses, and the bride herself needed an entire new wardrobe suitable to the foremost romantic beauty. He wrote frantically, sold his poems line by line, and mortgaged the family property.

At the wedding, during the exchange of rings, he dropped one, and when he bent to pick it up he knocked over the crucifix and put out his candle. He was fiercely superstitious, and these were the worst possible omens.

Still, he turned into such a dutiful husband that some said he was more like a pet monkey. She was dutiful too. In bed, he wrote, she was "So ashamed and cold, Scarcely responding," and none of his experienced attentions warmed her up for a minute. From not caring about poetry, she progressed to quite hating it. There's a story that one night he woke up inspired, lit the bedside lamp, and scribbled some lines. Excited, he woke her and read them to her. "Don't you ever do that to me again!" she snapped.

When the emperor Nicholas met her, he was so enchanted that he offered Pushkin five thousand rubles a year to write a history of Peter the Great and stay around and bring his wife to the balls. The empress was delighted with her too.

Mrs. Pushkin was going to need a lot more clothes. He tried to win the necessary money by playing cards, with the usual results. Pregnant, she was still lacing in her corsets tightly and dancing and flirting all night, and he worried himself sick over her health. Half St. Petersburg was in love with her. She flirted with them all equally.

Their first child, a daughter, was born, but unfortunately looked more like him than her. Hannibal's genes were potent stuff. The second child was a boy.

The emperor asked why Natalya didn't show up at all his

parties, and Pushkin explained that, without a court title, he couldn't bring her to imperial receptions. Nicholas promptly gave him a title: gentleman of the chamber. This was an insult. It was rather the equivalent of pageboy and usually conferred on eighteen-year-olds; on a man in his thirties, the jaunty adolescent uniform looked absurd. Probably he wasn't allowed to carry his cudgel with it.

Now there was no reason to stay home, ever, and often there were two balls a night. Pushkin hated it and lurked around sulking. Witty conversation with admiring friends was his idea of fun, but Natalya would rather dance. After a particularly brisk mazurka one night she had a miscarriage, but that didn't distract her from her calling. Her schedule didn't allow much time for the children; she danced till morning, then slept until time to dress for the next ball. As foils for her beauty, she brought her two sisters, who weren't nearly as pretty, to town to live with them, buy expensive dresses, and go to the dances.

Pushkin was now trying to support himself and his wife, two children, two sisters-in-law, and his parents. In her portrait, Natalya's hat alone, with its cascade of marabou, looks worth a year's worth of verses. Broke, he had to sell some of the serfs on the family estate, and he owed money to everyone, including his chambermaids, cook, and coachman. Then they had a third child, and a fourth. He pawned a lot of the household goods and mortgaged two hundred more serfs.

In 1837, he published *The Captain's Daughter*, a historical romance. The worshipful Gogol wrote that its "purity and restraint reach such heights that reality itself seems artificial . . ." It was too

Russian for the literati, though, who still yearned for French elegance.

In the same year, Natalya finally fell in love. He was Baron Georges-Charles D'Anthes, a Frenchman who'd arrived under the wing of the Dutch ambassador, Baron Heckeren. D'Anthes spoke no Russian, but he'd come highly recommended and was made an officer in the horse guards; the empress herself paid for his outfit. People said he was "one of the most handsome men in the horse guards, and one of the most fashionable men in society," tall, blond, and a terrific dancer. He and Natalya saw their lovely selves reflected in each other's eyes and fell in love.

It seems she'd finally realized, after all those dutiful chilly nights with Pushkin, what passion was all about, but there's no evidence that they did anything about it beyond lighting up like Christmas trees when they met at the parties. Troyat has unearthed some unpublished letters: D'Anthes begs her; she writes back saying that her heart belongs to him but the rest of her, by right and duty, is her husband's. History makes her a villain, but it seems that all the poor woman did was fall in love.

The real villain was D'Anthes's patron, Baron Heckeren. He'd formally adopted D'Anthes, though the lad was fully twenty-five years old, and there was talk. Heckeren was a compulsive trouble-maker. Pushkin got a letter, as did at least ten other people, written as a certificate formally announcing Pushkin's appointment to the Society of Cuckolds. Heckeren was behind it.

The letter gave Pushkin no choice but to challenge D'Anthes. D'Anthes was out of town with his regiment, but Heckeren accepted for him and then tried desperately to get his protégé out of danger. He ran around telling everyone that it wasn't Natalya but her older sister, Katerina, D'Anthes was in love with. When the young man got back to town, he learned that he had either to fight Pushkin or court Katerina. He decided prudently on the latter course and took up flirting with the delighted lady.

Pushkin agreed to withdraw the challenge in return for a promise of marriage. But his agreement was only verbal. With nothing in writing, it would look to the public as if D'Anthes had weaseled out of the duel. Through his second, Vicomte D'Archiac, he wrote to Pushkin rather loftily, ". . . now that you say you have no further reason to desire a duel, I must know, before allowing you to take back your word, what has induced you to change your mind . . . Explanations must be given on either side, for the sake of our mutual respect hereafter."

Pushkin was furious. At a dinner party that night, he sat next to his second, Count Sollogub – the same count he'd challenged the year before – and in the midst of the witty chitchat he whispered fiercely, "Go to D'Archiac tomorrow. Settle the details of the duel. The bloodier the better. Do not consent to any explanations." Then he went back to chatting.

Poor Sollogub was wretched. He could just imagine what his countrymen would think of him if the worst happened. "No Russian could have raised a hand against Pushkin," he wrote. "But a Frenchman had no cause to spare a Russian glory."

Then D'Anthes agreed to marry Katerina and the duel was dodged. They were married in January. For a while, in public, he managed to seem attentive to his wife, but he had no luck with his new in-laws; Pushkin refused to receive him or read his letters and publicly insulted Heckeren. D'Anthes went back to his old ways with Natalya, dancing with her too often and whispering in her ear. St. Petersburg's gossips were having a delightful winter.

Pushkin seethed. Young Ivan Turgenev, future author of *Fathers and Sons, A Month in the Country*, and other required reading, saw him at a party and wrote that he was "staring disgustedly at the crowd ... his small, swarthy face, his African lips, the gleam of his strong white teeth, his drooping side-whiskers, his deep eyes muddied with liverish yellow, his high forehead and almost invisible eyebrows, and his bush of frizzled hair ... he seemed to be in a bad mood." He was in a bad mood all winter. A society woman wrote that he "gnashes his teeth and scowls like a wildcat" whenever he sees the dashing D'Anthes.

Then a wicked lady invited Natalya to her house and surprised her with another guest. She slipped out and left the two alone. D'Anthes fell on his knees and begged her to run away with him; he whipped out a pistol and threatened to shoot himself. Natalya cried that she would never submit to blackmail, and at the noise, the hostess's daughter rushed into the room and Natalya escaped.

The same day, Pushkin got a letter crowing that he was now officially cuckolded. Natalya wept and explained everything. The poet still believed in her innocence; he thought D'Anthes was a young fool and rightly blamed Heckeren. He wrote furiously to the ambassador, calling him a pimp for his adopted son and demanding that the flirtation be stopped "if you wish to avoid another scandal from which I, you may be sure, shall not draw back."

Heckeren was too old for duels. D'Anthes would have to fight for him. Dutifully, the young dandy sent D'Archiac with a challenge, which Pushkin promptly accepted.

He chose an old schoolmate, Danzas, as his second. The terms were twenty paces, each man standing five paces behind his barrier, the barriers ten paces apart. Once a shot had been fired, both were to stay where they were, and he who fired first had to wait for the other man to take his turn.

It was January 27 and the time was set for five o'clock in the afternoon. Pushkin washed and dressed in, Troyat says, a strangely lighthearted mood. Perhaps he thought of his own *Eugene Onegin*, and the duel in which Onegin the dandy kills Lensky the poet; perhaps he remembered the fortune-teller's warning of a danger, now, in his thirty-seventh year. The tension and waiting, however, were over, and it was hardly his first encounter. He met Danzas in a sweetshop, where each downed a lemonade and then set forth.

The seconds" coats were thrown down for the barriers. It was getting dark; they had to hurry. The pistols were loaded, the adversaries placed on their marks. Danzas waved his hat as the signal. Pushkin walked up toward his barrier and raised his pistol to aim, but D'Anthes, probably nervous, jerked up his own and fired before he came to the mark. Pushkin fell onto the barrier coat, and the seconds rushed up. He looked terrible. "I think my thigh is shattered," he said.

D'Anthes turned to go, but Pushkin cried, "Wait! I feel strong enough to take my shot!" D'Anthes stopped and turned sideways, with his arm protecting his heart. Pushkin had dropped his pistol into the deep snow, but Danzas handed him the other one. Raised up on one arm, he took the full two minutes allowed to a fallen man, aiming carefully, and fired. The bullet passed through D'Anthes's right arm and broke two ribs, nothing serious, but he fell from the impact. "Bravo!" Pushkin cried, and then, "Did I kill him?"

D'Archiac said no, but he was hit. Pushkin said, "It doesn't matter, once we have recovered we shall have to start all over again."

Gut shot, he was bleeding heavily. The seconds managed to get him into the sleigh. The road was rutted and the sleigh lurched, but he kept struggling to talk, warning them not to alarm Natalya, remembering other duels, trying not to vomit.

His valet carried him into the house. Natalya screamed and fainted. Doctors came. Friends came. Pushkin, his early atheism long forgotten, sent for a priest. In hideous pain, he worried that innocent Natalya would be blamed and shunned. Danzas swore he would avenge him by challenging D'Anthes, but Pushkin said, "No, no! Peace, peace."

It was a long night. Nothing could be done for the pain. His hip was shattered and his intestine ripped apart. He howled and convulsed. The house was full of anxious friends. Then the next day passed, and the next night, and he was still alive. At a quarter of three the next afternoon he finally died, more peaceful toward the end.

Everyone came. Not the upper classes, who still thought of him as a dangerous liberal, but simple men in sheepskin coats, old women in head scarves, poetic young girls, all filing past the coffin in tears. A review framed its page in black and wrote, "The sun of our poetry is set. Pushkin is dead, dead in his prime, in the prime of his magnificent career! ... Every Russian heart knows the meaning of this irremediable loss, every Russian heart is rent by it. Pushkin! Our poet, our joy, the glory of our people!"

Alarmed about the effect on the masses, the authorities gave orders to publish only brief, bland obituaries. He was a symbol for the political malcontents, though in the flesh he'd never really been much of a radical and he'd long ago lost interest. His early calls to liberty had been more emotional and poetical than political, and probably his central grievance was government literary censorship: The authorities had no right to tamper with his work. Russians cherish his memory now as an insurgent on the barricades, but when offered the chance he'd compromised cheerfully with the emperor. He never really opposed the monarchy; he just wanted it toned down. Just the same the radicals raged, and rumors flew that the duel was a put-up job, that the emperor wanted him dead, that the emperor was himself in love with Natalya.

The authorities decided that a cathedral funeral would attract too dangerous a crowd, so a contingent of police went to the house to collect the coffin and carry it secretly off by night to an obscure little church. The funeral was conducted under armed guard and only his aristocratic enemies were allowed in.

Out beyond the locked church, all Mother Russia mourned. In recent memory, Kennedy's assassination comes closest. Even Europeans paid attention. From Italy, Gogol wrote, "No worse news could have come to me from Russia."

A sixteen-year-old boy named Dostoevsky went into full mourning, as for a beloved father.

The brilliant young poet Lermontov wrote a passionate poem on Pushkin's death, blaming the government, and got jailed and exiled for it. Four years later, carrying on the dramatic tradition, he himself was killed in a duel.

Tolstoy, though he got religion and repented later, fought famously murderous duels.

Late in the history of dueling, in 1891, Chekhov wrote "The Duel," and his protagonist thinks, "Whether he killed Von Koren the next day or left him alive, it would be just the same, equally useless and uninteresting ... Laevsky played, drank wine, and thought that duelling was stupid and useless, as it did not decide the question but only complicated it, but that it was sometimes impossible to get on without it." They shoot, and miss, and both men are strangely improved by the experience.

In Iceland, far back in mythic times, the deaths of two beloved poets had caused the whole country to forswear dueling, but Pushkin's death seems to have had the opposite effect and, at least in literary circles, sanctified it. Pistols became a Russian literary symbol as essential as the pen.

Beautiful Natalya had no trouble marrying again. Because of the public outcry, D'Anthes was busted to private and sent home. Heckeren was recalled from his post. And the tormented giant of nineteenth-century Russian literature uncoiled in its cave and came forth, vast and brooding and preoccupied with death.

XIV. THE GERMAN VERSION

E ACH NATION'S SPIRIT found its signature expression in the duel. The French took a festive and larky view and served champagne; the Russians unbosomed their tortured souls; the Irish punched each other out; the English calibrated the social castes and sportsmanship involved; the Americans played bare-knuckle politics. The Germans treated it as basic training for war.

Germany added some Teutonic touches to the ancient rite and worked it into the university curriculum as a kind of bellicose gymnastics. When the philologist Max Müller was a student at Leipzig in the 1840s, four hundred duels were fought there in a single year, though with only two deaths. The curved sabers they used weren't designed as piercing weapons, so they rarely killed on the spot, though you could bleed to death later. Good swordsmen complained that by eliminating the thrust, as in épée dueling, you'd eliminated half the skill involved and given the contest to the stronger and heavier man.

Theology students, Müller reported, preferred to use pistols, so as not to have to explain their scars to the congregation later in life. For everyone else, the scars were part of the point; Müller himself sported a collection from three fights. Without scars you were nobody. You could scarcely even prove you'd been to university at all.

Only one young man is recorded as privately carving his own face with his own clean razor to avoid the mêlée. German rules, being German, did require that saber blades be rinsed with a carbolic solution prior to fighting, to reduce the risk of infection, but infections happened anyway. Some of them may have been self-induced; the wounded often encouraged their wounds, reopening them, rubbing wine into them, anything to keep them from healing too neatly. The ladies loved them, though missing or badly reattached noses were less alluring. The student *Mensur* was a variant of the duel, a practice warmup, involving groups of students slashing away at each other, two at a time, while others waited in line for their turns. Sometimes the combatants had grudges to settle, mostly contrived; the clubs would meet and mingle the evening before and cruise around with stein in hand looking for someone in a rival club to insult. Sometimes they were just relieving hormonal stress. Winning or losing was beside the point; what counted was standing up stoically and paying no attention when your face was slashed open.

Apparently the combatants mostly wanted to mark their opponents" faces as a sign of their prowess and to have their faces marked in turn as a sign of participation. A *Renommierschmiss*, it was called, or "bragging scar," and it took you a long way in government and the professions; it was rare to meet an unmarked man of any importance. Of course, it was better to leave more scars on the other man than he left on you. The great statesman Otto von Bismarck, veteran of many a *Mensur* – though after graduation he preferred pistols – went through life with only one small decorative mark on his cheekbone. His opponents were patched together like Frankenstein's monster.

Some earnest young Catholic students formed antidueling societies of their own and then, after graduating, got turned down for army commissions. Jews, shut out by the élite dueling clubs, set up their own dueling fraternities, described as "ferocious."

Soccer and tennis and such frivolous collegiate sports were officially sneered at as un-German and "lacking in any higher ideals such as service to the *Vaterland*." Duels were good training for cannon fodder.

The manly custom spread around central Europe and proved amazingly durable. In 1988, Kevin McAleer, researching his book *Dueling: The Cult of Honor in Fin-de-Siècle Germany*, was taken to a private celebration of the *Mensur* and, during the evening's final bout, got his temple grazed by a flying fragment of a blade that had snapped in the heat of the moment.

Alumni of student dueling clubs called themselves *Alte Herren*, old men, superior men. After graduation, though, most abandoned these childish games and used pistols instead.

*   *   *

Army life was especially hazardous: Duels were compulsory. They were under the auspices of their own courts of honor, established in 1808 by Friedrich Wilhelm III to keep an eye on "the good reputation of the entire officer corps as the joint share of each." Who insults an officer insults the whole army and, by extension, since the army was the country's soul, the whole country.

In Saxony, at midcentury, an officer who refused a fight was automatically dismissed. In the 1870s, Wilhelm I proclaimed that his officers should abstain from drunkenness, gambling, and dabbling in the stock market; surely dueling was all the recreation they needed? He added, ominously, "I will just as little tolerate an officer in my army who is capable of wantonly injuring the honor of a comrade as I will an officer who does not know how to defend his honor."

From 1871 until 1914, other European armies had exciting colonial battles to fight, but the German army stood idle, and what status has an army without battles? Dueling took up the slack. In Austria in 1900, Lieutenant the Marquis Tacoli was stripped of his rank for not bothering to resent an insult.

In Prussia, the army mattered. Civilians admired it. There was a lot of it, including the reserves, the militia, and the former officers who were still allowed to strut around in uniform, complete with sword. Prussia thought of itself as a nation of warriors, and what the army did, everyone wanted to do. Marshal Helmuth von Moltke wrote that war "is an element of the world established by God. In war the noblest virtues of men unfold, courage and renunciation, duty and self-abnegation with the sacrifice of one's life. Without war the world would sink into materialism." What mere civilian could resist a piece of the glory?

A friend, contemplating a duel, asked Karl Marx for advice. Marx consulted with Engels and sent a long letter advising against fighting to avenge a mere street insult. He called dueling "irrational and the relic of a past stage of culture" but "as an exceptional emergency resort may be adopted in exceptional circumstances." In general, though, "Our party must set its face resolutely against these ceremonials of rank ... the times are far too serious now to allow one to become involved in such childishness."

Several years later the friend ignored his advice and was killed in a duel over a woman. Marx was sorry about it but felt that the fellow had sacrificed himself to an aristocratic pose.

He was wrong. Dueling in Germany was neither aristocratic nor the "relic of a past stage of culture." It spread democratically through society; in 1898 a mere first lieutenant fought a duel with His Highness Prince Philipp von Sachsen-Coburg. Those officially eligible to duel, besides officers, included doctors, judges, engineers, architects, civil servants, university graduates, wealthy businessmen, industrialists, bankers, and entrepreneurs generally, a sizable group. Even the literati weren't excluded; Goethe and Heine had both been bloodied dueling. The Zionist philosopher Theodor Herzl wrote, wistfully, that "a half-dozen duels would very much raise the social position of the Jews."

And far from being a past stage, it was just then going into high gear, becoming a national pastime from the 1880s until the First World War and never entirely dying out.

The word *Standesehre* meant the honor of one's social class and the duel was fought to maintain it and its honorable entitlements. It was a kind of civic duty, which made the German duel a heavy-handed affair compared to the debonair flourish of Italy or the cheerful gusto of the Americans.

It was dangerous too. It had to be. Good Germans didn't do girlish things like stopping the fight at first blood or firing into the air; indeed, squeamishly firing wide was a violation of the code and the seconds made you start over again and shoot straight, not to make a mockery of serious matters. Death, in the German duel, wore the same exalted aura as personal honor in the French. Hurting and being hurt were essential to national pride, and the mortality rate in German duels became the highest in the world.

In France at the tail end of the nineteenth century, out of four or five hundred duels a year, deaths never exceeded a dozen and sometimes dropped as low as two. In 1901, Berlin's *Das Kleine Journal* sneered that "the whole world knows that French duels, be they with pistols or swords, present not the slightest danger to their participants," with a pinprick on the finger considered enough to end the matter. In Germany, through the nineteenth century and up until 1914, roughly a quarter of the postgraduate duels were fatal.

Dueling in England by then was a dead issue. One German historian said, with open contempt, that there "the duel fell into disuse and disappeared completely; the riding whip ousted sword and pistol, and this victory of brutality was celebrated as a triumph of Enlightenment." Actually, it was boxing, not whips, that had taken over in England, and this too was considered pretty vulgar: Brute strength was inferior to brute courage. A black eye was not as good as a scar. Besides, few participants got killed, and what kind of sport was that?

As to America, the Germans told each other stories of the rowdy and foolish customs there; a man might fight "to appear original and monstrous so as to publicize himself"; combatants threw sticks of TNT at each other, they said, or slashed blindly away with daggers in a pitch-dark room. (It's a mystery where Europeans got their news of the United States.) They also picked up the ubiquitous legend of the "American duel," with the combatants drawing straws and the loser shooting himself. This they liked – it had a kind of stern simplicity about it – and took it up themselves, so enthusiastically that a bill against it was introduced in the Reichstag.

A German saw himself as first and foremost a warrior knight; McAleer calls it the Round Table mentality. He was loyal to his caste, his group, like the Japanese samurai. A contemporary wrote in 1893, "The duel is for the sake of the individual only insofar as he is a member of an entire caste, his honor being identified with caste honor ..." It must have been comforting, in a way. Setting forth at dawn to be shot at, a man could feel the invisible support and comradeship of the rest of his kind at his side.

They told each other that the duel was a purely German custom. People trying to stamp out the practice pointed to its origins in effeminate nations like France and Italy, but the Junkers would have none of this: They were upholding their ancient, warlike Nordic *Kultur*, product of a superior people.

Taking over the existing European dueling codes, they adjusted some loopholes, like the precise qualifications for seconds and the minimum and maximum elapsed times between insult and challenge, challenge and response, response and battle. Germans like timetables.

The time-limit rules accepted no excuses and it was hard to postpone a duel for any reason. In 1901, in Insterburg, an artillery lieutenant got into a quarrel on the eve of his wedding, at his bachelor party, where everyone was pretty well oiled. The quarrelers met at the appointed place at dawn. The bridegroom took a bullet through his spinal cord and was buried instead of married.

There were assorted laws against dueling, rarely invoked, as even the lawmakers admitted, dueling being one of the "necessities of life" and basically inevitable. The legislators, lawyers, judges, and attendant bureaucrats were usually *Alte Herren* themselves and inclined to see the defendant's side. Sometimes brief sentences were imposed, served in comfortable, well-appointed jails, and in some the prisoners were let out in the evenings to carouse in the local bars. McAleer reports that one inmate lost his pub-crawling privileges only after shooting the warden's cat.

A jail term for dueling conferred a kind of postgraduate degree. The only recorded case of a really stiff sentence was in 1903, when a man seduced a married woman and then shot and killed the poor cuckold. He was sentenced to six years. It had not been an *alte* way to act.

The kaiser himself usually pardoned any duelist serving more than a few months. He too was sympathetic to the cause; a man had to do what he had to do. Germany actually had the strictest formal laws against slander and insults and even rude stares, but they were seldom used: Appealing to the court for redress was an open admission of cowardice. A real man extracted his vengeance in person, taking a real man's risk in the process.

In 1907 the Prussian minister of justice, addressing parliament, declared, "It is not to be mistaken that our duel rests not only on injured honor but also indirectly on the fact that the masculinity of the injured is attacked and that the offended seeks restoration of his questioned masculinity in the duel. It is impossible to find punishment wherein it would be expressed that the impugned masculinity is once again recognized."

In short, if a man insults you, he's saying that he doesn't think you're man enough to fight him. Blood was the only answer to a slur like that.

Marx's Socialists gave up struggling with the custom and told each other that if things went on like this, the upper classes would kill each other off and vanish from the face of the earth – and a good thing too.

As in other lands and times, the duel's semi-illegality gave it an extra fillip of drama. Seconds scouted the chosen sites the day before. If the authorities interrupted it anyway, they simply moved, from the Grunewald or the Tegeler Forest to Hasenhaide to the Tiergarten. (One saber duel in the Hasenhaide was interrupted when the fathers of the two young combatants burst out of the bushes and soundly caned their offspring on the spot, an insult to their manhood that must have rankled for life.)

Unlike the French and Italians, Germans fought duels with equal determination in all seasons of the year, since taking notice of freezing fog or blowing snow – or any weather – would have been unmanly. (In a snowstorm, it was a good idea to take off your dark coat and stand there camouflaged in your white shirt against the white snow.)

The proper smoothbore, single-shot dueling pistol, accurate to within maybe three inches at fifteen paces, was becoming a quaint antique in an era of semiautomatic Lugers and double-action revolvers. Sometimes, among normally peaceable men, there were no old classics to be found, and then the rules could be relaxed and allow something more sophisticated, increasing your chances of death. The rifled barrel sent a much more accurate bullet and sent it fast enough to go clear through you, damaging a variety of organs on the way, instead of lodging clumsily in the outer flesh. If you had to use revolvers, though, only one chamber was to be loaded, providing for the dignified pause between shots.

In England, where sportsmanship was dear to upper-class hearts, it had been considered nice to shoot casually, offhandedly, as if brushing away a fly, and no proper gentleman would be seen to take careful, murderous aim. In Germany, the opposite view prevailed, and they invented a style called *Zielduell*, or aiming duel, with each man given a full minute to steady his hand and pinpoint his target. The effect on his waiting opponent can only be imagined.

The German Anti-Dueling League held a congress and a petition was introduced forbidding the members to fight, which seems like a reasonable idea for such a club, but it was furiously rejected. In principle the members opposed the duel, but in practice they might be obliged to challenge. Most particularly, if some cad seduced their wives, daughters, or sisters.

Seducing one's womenfolk was a third-level insult, comparable to cheating or stealing, because it implied that the husband, father, or brother wasn't to be feared. It sneered at his courage. Nobody suggested that the woman in the case might have welcomed or even encouraged the seduction. Nobody imagined that seducer and seducee might be blinded by love or even inflamed with lust. It was taken as given that the seducer seduced only as an act of aggressive contempt, purely and simply to thumb his nose at the woman's rightful owner, who was obliged to resent it.

As in Spain, women were the totally passive vessels of their menfolks" honor, not the beer but only the mug that holds it. As Schopenhauer put it, women existed at all "solely for the propagation of the race." Nietzsche disagreed; he felt they were solely for the recreation of warriors. In either case they were morally inert and as blameless as a stolen candlestick or the glove a man throws in your face. And nobody supposed that the duel fought over a woman's seduction had anything to do with love or the alienation of affections. German duels, for whatever cause, were flavored and colored military.

In 1933, shortly after Hitler was appointed chancellor, the Prussian minister of justice sent forth an edict officially celebrating the *Mensur*. Its joy, he said, "springs from the fighting spirit, which should be strengthened, not inhibited, in the academic youth ... Only an insult washed away with blood counted as expiated in the code of honor of the old Germany, and this idea must be granted full recognition for it also promotes the ability and preparedness of young Germans to defend themselves."

When the day of glory arrived and the fight turned real, the officers of the *Wehrmacht* had been in training since their happy college days.

XV. WINDING DOWN

E XCEPT FOR THE saber-wielding Germans and the occasional
French legislator, European dueling cooled off after 1918.
Optimistic chroniclers believe this was due to an increase in
civilized Christian forbearance; pessimists attribute it to fiercer
law enforcement. A cynic might argue that after four years in
combat, the survivors had had ample chance to satisfy the urge
to shoot at people and were sated therewith.

A simpler explanation might be that France, home of the happiest
combatants, had lost fully a quarter of the impulsive generation
between eighteen and thirty years old, a million and a half young
men, leaving only a few elder statesmen to settle their grudges in
the time-honored way.

The same would apply to the American South earlier, in the late

1860s. Some claim that the spectacle of carnage during the Civil War instantly wiped out Southern dueling – in the North, it had long been waning – but it didn't happen overnight.

The young men who did come home from the war could decide they had nothing left to prove; they'd faced their enemy, upheld their honor, and could show you a missing arm or a wooden leg to prove it. And they had other problems. They grappled with punitive Reconstruction and poverty and carpetbaggers and rebuilding their houses; with freed slaves, slaughtered livestock, and ruined fields.

Some, though, who still had some leisure and the money to enjoy it, went on defending their honor in the old way. In Savannah, in 1870, Aiken and Cohen fought over a sailboat race. Richardson Aiken, a sixty-year-old rice planter, was popular among sporting gentleman and owned a fast sailboat of which he was inordinately proud. Ludlow Cohen, age thirty or so, was a partner in a firm of fertilizer dealers, a sociable fellow with hosts of friends, and equally proud of his own boat.

Life in the postbellum South was not all mourning and hardship. A group of sporting gentlemen got together at Beaulieu, a stately home out on the point, and, taking note of the stiff breeze, decided it would be a good day for a match race between the two.

Aiken's son was put in charge of the stake boat, to be stationed a mile or so from the starting point; the contestants would sail out to it, around it, and back. Cohen's boat easily beat Aiken's out to the stake point, but then the breeze died and both crept ignominiously home.

Back at Beaulieu, a man named Ferrill, a friend of Aiken's, suggested that since Aiken's boat had seemed to be gaining on

Cohen's before they lost the wind, they ought to settle it with a rematch.

Cohen said, "I will not race with Aiken again. He is not a gentleman."

"What do you mean by that?" asked Ferrill.

"I mean what I said. His son moved the stake boat forward in order to give his father an advantage of shorter distance. I will not race with a man who would profit by such a move as that."

Ferrill said if he didn't take it back, he'd go tell Aiken. Cohen said he had nothing to retract. Ferrill went straight to Aiken, Aiken dictated the challenge note to him, and he carried it back to Cohen.

Cohen's friends tried to discourage him – Aiken was a famously good shot – but he refused to apologize. They met on the Brampton plantation outside the city.

Savannah historian Thomas Gamble tells us, "It was the freshness of the early dawn. The dew was still on the grass and shrubbery, the birds were singing their matins, butterflies fluttered about them, the varied insect life of the woods and fields was astir, nature was just awakening from its night's rest." The weapons were old-style smoothbore pistols loaded with quarter-ounce ball.

The seconds drew for positions and the choice fell to Cohen. Where you were standing mattered in a pistol duel, especially in sunrise or sunset encounters, and Cohen chose to stand with his back to the rising sun, leaving Aiken squinting into it.

The seconds don't seem to have made much effort to reconcile the parties; perhaps they could tell it was useless. Cohen was positive that Aiken and his son had cheated; Aiken was positive that Cohen had called him a cheat in front of his friends. Both were, even for duelists, unusually angry: Four shots were exchanged, though none hit home. Seconds were supposed to stop the proceedings and argue for closure after each exchange, but they didn't. One or two shots were usually quite enough to satisfy honor, but here the pistols were loaded for a fifth firing.

At the word "Fire!" Cohen fired and missed again. Aiken fired and hit Cohen through the abdomen and intestines. He died that same afternoon.

The case actually came before a coroner's jury. The verdict was: "We find that the deceased came to his death from a gunshot wound received at the hands of Richard F. Aiken, whilst fighting a duel, contrary to the laws of Georgia." Aiken posted a twenty-thousand-dollar bond and the case was supposed to go to a grand jury. The newspapers made much of it, but nothing further happened except that everyone missed the amiable young Cohen.

He was buried back home in Charleston, where the *Courier* said, "The deceased was well known here as a young gentleman of high tone and character."

Even in the heart of the chivalric South, people began to feel that duels were a needless waste of friends and merry companions. No amount of laws and courts and threatened punishments had ever made a dent in the practice, but people of the dueling classes could decide for themselves to quit. They might even serve on juries and vote to convict.

Back before the Civil War, Southern courage had always been socially important, the mark of the natural superiority of the landowning classes, just as it was for seventeenth-century French aristocrats. Fathers had always impressed their sons with the need to prove their manhood and the permanent taint that cowardice would cast over the whole family. Boys as young as fourteen fought duels, cheered on by enthusiastic fathers, their possible deaths a mere nothing compared to their honor.

A prominent citizen in Mississippi was rumored to have acted cravenly. He was burned in effigy and posted in the local newspaper with a verse:

> Alas! Let this hereafter be
> A warning to the rest
> We love a brave and valiant man
> A coward we detest.

Penalties for dueling were all but nonexistent; penalties for not dueling were severe. A man who refused a challenge, one Southern writer said, "would never again be permitted to join gentlemen even in a fox hunt. He's utterly out of it."

After the War, the once-despised Courts of Honor began to acquire more prestige; angry, insulted men could submit their grievances for consideration and, without disgrace, yield to the court's arbitration and decision. Battle-scarred veterans of established courage, like General Joe Johnston in Savannah, sat on the courts and knew whereof they spake. If the court told the gentlemen to apologize and forget it, the gentlemen could bow to their decision, and the court would publish its deliberations to clear their names of cowardice.

At the same time, the society that crawled out from under the war's wreckage was a different world. The land-based aristocracy that treasured its honor had never discussed money, never thought of it; money was the gentle background music of their lives, the nameless fountain of culture and ease and self-confidence. After the war, everything changed. Land, with no one to work it, was useless. Money was the new social grace, source of power and prestige and even honor. Not his courage but the depth of a man's pockets was the measure of his manhood.

Dueling for dollars replaced the pistol. Carpetbaggers came South. Industries replaced cotton. Some of the old aristocracy scrambled, like Scarlett O'Hara, up the new ladder, tooth and claw, while others, like Ashley Wilkes, collapsed in helpless nostalgia for a gentler world.

Money could make a man indifferent to his image. A cash mentality seems to thicken the skin and pad the sensitivities in a way that noble birth and thousands of acres, reputation or distinguished careers or political position never did. Money became the calling card, the genealogy, the good name and the body armor, and having made it, you were impervious to calumny unless actual jail was at stake, in which case you hired the best lawyer money could buy.

If you still longed for the adrenaline rush of risk, you found it in the financial risks of venture capital, with your most precious possession trembling on the tightrope of the stock market.

It was a new social order, and a simpler one, and needed no hand-to-hand defense.

Once public opinion began to sway, the dueling laws stiffened.

Under Georgia's State Code of 1873, sending or accepting a challenge brought you a fine of five hundred dollars and a six-month spell in the county jail or, if the jury thought fit, a year or two of hard labor in the penitentiary. The seconds served time along with the principals and it got harder to find a friend to serve as your second.

Sometimes the laws were even enforced. In 1872 James Southall, editor of the Richmond *Enquirer*, and Alexander Moseley, editor of the Richmond *Whig*, went through the usual exchange of notes and challenge and were promptly arrested, posted heavy bail, and decided against the fight. In 1880, Colonel E. B. C. Cash of South Carolina fought and killed one William Shannon in a duel. He was arrested and tried for murder. He got off on a technicality, but the word "murder" stuck to him and he was shunned, spending the rest of his life writing plaintive justifications of what he'd done.

By 1883, even the battling newsmen of Virginia were calming down. Their swan song was sung by Richard Bierne, owner and editor of the *State*, and William Elam, editor of the *Whig*, who'd been insulting each other's politics in print for ages. Of the Whigs, Beirne editorialized that "a more vicious, corrupt, and degraded group never followed any adventurer." The next morning Elam wrote an equally insulting editorial and questioned Beirne's courage, winding up, "We laugh at the *State*'s vituperation and vaporing, and beg to remark that not only does the *State* lie, but its editor and owner lies and the poor creature who may have actually written the article in question also lies – all jointly and severally, deliberately, knowingly, maliciously, and with the inevitable cowardice that is always connected with insolent bravado." (Journalism may have been more dangerous in the olden days, but it was certainly more fun.)

The mayor of Richmond, reading the paper, concluded that this was a challenge and ordered the men arrested. They evaded the law, however, and Beirne's friends challenged Elam. Navy six-shooters at eight paces were chosen.

The other newspapers chose up sides and cheered the combatants on, proclaiming that Elam had the advantage, since he weighed only a hundred and forty pounds, while Beirne at two twenty-five made a solider target. What with all the publicity, the mayor sent police to the dueling ground in the nick of time; they arrested Beirne, but Elam escaped and holed up in Richmond.

Then Beirne escaped too and caught a westbound train for Lewisburg. Either law enforcement in Virginia was in a primitive stage, or the hearts of the enforcers weren't fully dedicated to the cause. The Washington *Evening Star* wrote, "Nothing has yet been heard from the Virginia duelists. A gentleman from Richmond, who knows both men, but who has no connection whatever with this affair, said today the belief in Richmond is that a fight will eventually take place, but that it will not occur in this vicinity. The impression is that the men will meet somewhere in West Virginia."

With all the publicity, things had gone too far to back down. They set the meeting for a patch of ground called the Devil's Punch Bowl, near Waynesboro, halfway between Richmond and Lewisburg. (The *Richmond Times* printed this information, along with the secret password, "Number One.")

It poured rain. The wagon Beirne was riding in got swept down a mountain stream in full flood, and Elam had to have a friend with a lantern walk in front of his horse. With duels under the new legal scrutiny, they were more and more uncomfortable to fight; simply getting to the field of honor could be life-threatening. Both men crept up on the site by back roads, in the dark, meeting just at sunrise.

Beirne's first shot missed, but Elam's cut through his coat and grazed him slightly. At the second fire, Elam was hit in the thigh and his own bullet went over Beirne's head. According to a later article in the *Richmond Times-Dispatch*, "Beirne and his second came forward; Beirne tipped his hat to his opponent; and he and his party left the field. Elam's wound was not too serious, and he returned to his home in Louisa in about ten days and was back in Richmond a short time later. Beirne returned to Richmond before Elam and offered to surrender to the police. But his offer was not accepted. Neither editor was ever prosecuted."

The following year it was John S. Wise, then serving in Congress and hoping to be governor of Virginia, who put the cap on the whole practice. Nobody was better qualified. The Wises, governors, editors, and legislators, had long been known as the "duelingest family in Virginia," and John S. had upheld the family reputation with the best of them.

Page McCarty, of the battling McCartys, was editor of the *Richmond Campaign*, in which he called the gubernatorial candidate a jackal and apologized to jackals for the comparison.

Wise refused to fight. Only a few years before it would have been his political death, but now he published a long, caustic reply to the insult and said he was determined never to fight another duel, whatever the provocation; he would rather be called a coward than commit murder. The public response to this was called "glacial," but coming from a Wise, it carried weight.

With cash money established as a kind of ultimate virtue, libel suits, once shameful and cowardly, were suddenly respectable: Don't shoot the editor, sue him. If you win, then you'll have more money and he'll have less, establishing your honor as clearly as if you'd killed him.

Newspapers grew more polite and less entertaining.

If a gentleman insulted you, you could blackball him at the club or cut him dead in the street.

At least in the settled areas of the Old South, the Code Duello was dead. Perhaps our Founding Fathers would applaud this advance in civilization. Or perhaps they would find us degenerated into a nation of greedy cravens.

West of the coastal plain, the hills still rang with gunfire, though often informally. Carrying a gun around as routinely as a Londoner carries an umbrella makes a man feel taller and braver. It makes him faster to take offense than if he had to go up to the attic for the dueling pistols.

The name "Bleeding Kansas" was well and truly earned, and Missouri, before, during, and after the Civil War, reeked of gunpowder. Slavery was the flashpoint. It would have been madness for an abolitionist to raise his voice in Charleston or a slavery enthusiast to mount the soapbox in Boston, but people had crossed the Mississippi from all over and brought their differing viewpoints, and aired them, and shot at each other. During the Civil War they even managed to muster two opposing armies and stage a self-contained war of their own, burning down towns in the process.

Violence was endemic. Calamity Jane and Belle Starr the Bandit Queen grew up in Missouri before they struck out for the wilder West. Confederate General John S. Marmaduke of Missouri shot and killed Confederate General Lucien Marsh Walker in a duel with Colt navy revolvers at fifteen paces, and later became governor of Missouri. In 1865, General Joe Shelby's Missouri legion introduced what came to be known as the Missouri duel. After the new fashion for simplicity, the combatants, each with a nine-inch bowie knife, stripped to the waist and each held a corner of a bandanna in his teeth. The first man to let go of the bandanna lost. According to the *Kansas City Times*, "It is not of record that any man ever released the bandanna alive, and not infrequently both adversaries died."

The trans-Mississippians who still followed the code and dueled by proper arrangement saw themselves as the cupbearers of higher civilization. They came late to the territories, preceded by the hunters, trappers, military scouts, and small farmers; they were the land speculators and lawyers with political ambitions. After the war, officers from the Northern and Southern armies fought each other over the courage and war records of their respective allegiances. They did things properly, though often murderously, using their military revolvers instead of the old smoothbore single-shots. And they were outnumbered and presently replaced by the new informality.

Wild Bill Hickok played poker with David Tutt, a former friend with whom he'd fallen out over a lady. He lost his shirt. Either

Hickok put up his watch for collateral or Tutt was afraid he'd renege on the fifty dollars he owed him – we don't know – but Tutt seized the watch and held on to it. Hickok said if he wore it, he'd kill him.

The next day at high noon, Tutt walked down the main street in Springfield wearing the watch. Hickok met him there. At seventy-five yards they both drew and fired. Tutt fell dead.

It was the duel of the future, the noonday shoot-out replacing the ritual at dawn and now familiar to moviegoers everywhere. *Harper's New Monthly Magazine* called it a "Date with Destiny" and published all the details. Hickok was the first of the famous wild westerners. Mere duels came to seem stuffy, old-fashioned and, with their roots in the mannered ways of Europe, élitist. Undemocratic. Also not nearly as dashing. When a duel was over, surviving duelists went back to being lawyers or congressmen, wearing three-piece suits, while after a shoot-out the James brothers galloped across a rugged plain and holed up in the mountains, wearing chaps and spurs. For public appeal, it was no contest. They gave the country a new image of itself, rugged, independent, a law unto itself.

The once-legendary duelists of heroic story were overlaid by the new myth. Their names – Smith T, McClung, the Wise family – were replaced by Wyatt Earp and the Younger brothers, and the punctilio of Bladensburg and Bloody Island gave way to the OK Corral. The oppressed working classes in the drab industrial cities wanted to hear about these new working-class heroes and their daring deeds. Hollywood has given their ambuscades moral clarity and divided the combatants into good guys and bad, lawman and outlaw, but for the general public it didn't make much difference, and in actual fact the sheriff and the desperado might change places or take turns; they were brothers under the skin and their skills were interchangeable.

In *Duels and the Roots of Violence in Missouri*, Dick Steward writes, "The ranch became the embodiment of the plantation minus the slaves as the cowboy version of democracy merged with the Southern gentleman's penchant for honor."

As the formalities faded, the general level of mayhem rose: "Democracy" might mean burning a man's house down at midnight rather than sending a cartel in the morning. With an eye to the community's social tone, though, newspapers went on referring to any brawl as a "duel," whether fought with pistols or pitchforks, by two or by twenty, and of course if someone was killed and a case came to trial, it was helpful to call it a duel, with the word's lingering overtones of respectability.

Meanwhile, back in the centers of power, the new century nationalized the duel, broadened its scope, put its principals in uniform, and made it legal – and compulsory.

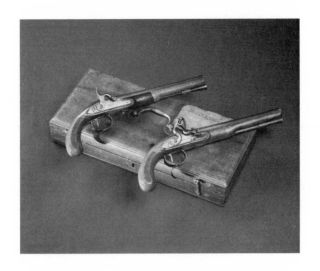

XVI. AFTERWARD

ALTHOUGH CURRENTLY OVER ten thousand people in America die every year by firearms, we can congratulate ourselves that none of these deaths are in duels, formally arranged with seconds and a doctor standing by. Most of the deaths are spur-of-the-moment, and this is considered progress. We've turned the rules upside down.

By the standards of the old codes, the cooling-off period, with its exchange of notes, was essential to the dignity of the affair: A gentleman didn't bluster and threaten, but strolled away to find a friend to carry his written complaint. By modern standards, this was gruesomely cold-blooded. First-degree murder, premeditated murder with malice aforethought. Our laws recognize that a man who, furious, seizes the nearest heavy object and bashes someone to death in the heat of the moment is less guilty than the one who thought it over first. We're civilized; we would never plan ahead of time to shoot at someone. We're embarrassed by the historical fact of dueling and thrust it away into the clouds of myth and fiction and melodrama.

White-collar people are expected to commit white-collar crimes – lying to Congress, misleading stockholders, eluding taxes, fudging accounts. Violence is the province of the poor, the deranged, underprivileged teenagers, and the mentally substandard. The otherwise respectable man who shows signs of temper is sent to anger management classes, where he learns to count to ten before hitting people.

We've tamed the male animal. In just a century or so, we've harnessed the impulses built into him, as they've been built into male mammals and birds since the dawn of time. What Teddy Roosevelt praised as America's "manliness and vigor" has been cosseted down into family values. San Francisco is now famous for its coffeehouses and its flourishing gay community, not its pistol-packing editors. Our politicians, once the most tireless duelists, now bloodlessly insult one another in competing television commercials. Watching his sons play soccer, the primal male may burst through, bellowing threats and sometimes smiting the father of another soccer player, but this is only the sturdy American competitive spirit that made us great.

More than half of Americans own guns, and treasure them, and march in rallies and stage protests for the right to own as many as they like, but outside of deer season they're just to gaze at, perhaps a bit wistfully.

They stand for something.

Men spring from the womb needing to prove that they're men. Women don't need to prove they're women; they simply are, they were born that way, and for much of history it was nothing to brag about anyway. On the expressway, when a more powerful car cuts in front of her, a woman usually feels, if she notices, that the driver must be in a hurry; perhaps his wife is in labor. Men feel insulted. Personally insulted. A Mercedes has left his Honda in the dust and its driver feels himself superior. It rankles all day and leaves a toxic residue which, when he gets to the office, he tries to work off on his colleagues or, when he gets home, on his wife. On weekends, he gets together with friends and they shoot each other with pellets of paint, or dress up as Civil War soldiers and march back and forth with bayonets fixed to their muskets.

Men struggle to dominate. Parents separate and scold the battling brothers; teachers separate the battling ten-year-olds; legislation is currently under discussion making it illegal for little boys to insult each other – the parents of the insulted child can sue the school. All to no permanent avail.

Back in the forest, the stag finds another stag and locks antlers with him. Biologists tell us this is purely competition for mates, but "mates" is shorthand for proving yourself the better, stronger stag, whose genes shall prevail while the other's perish. The defeated stag retreats, humiliated, resolved on vengeance. Next year, when his antlers have grown more points, he will prevail.

"A wounded spirit who can bear?"

*   *   *

Since the ancient urge demands an outlet, in the twentieth century we've channeled much of it into wars. Wars have always been with us, but in the past they were mostly fought on battlefields by professionals. Armies provided steady work for the lower orders and a chance to get away from the farm and see the world, and for what the British called "the officer class," they offered prestige and a lark and a uniform that collected pretty girls like candy. Now civilians fight wars, either drafted for combat or incinerated as bystanders, and national honor, avenged by shooting at strangers while under orders, has replaced private honor, avenged by deciding for yourself whom to shoot at and when.

We're taught since childhood to identify with the nation-state instead of caste, class, clan, or family. Any nation – or even a handful of stateless terrorists – that insults our country has insulted us, and we go forth more or less willingly to expunge the stain. The Geneva Convention, replacing the Code Duello, lends an almost courtly, duel-like air to the proceedings: Gentlemen don't torture prisoners or rape civilians – except, of course, when they do, but no code is perfect.

Unfortunately, like the impersonal pistol replacing the personal sword, the weapons involved have moved a long way from the human hand. Pushing a button to launch a missile into the unseen can never give you the visceral satisfaction of impaling your enemy yourself. It lacks even the physical rush of a cavalry charge. In war now as everywhere, money rules, and victory rests not on the courage of fighting men but on the budgets of nations: The richest country builds the best bombs and planes, and wins.

Few soldiers come home from the wars now swaggering and

288

bragging and pelted with flowers. Wars aren't the outlet that they used to be.

Battle now is not only too mechanized, it's also too big. Thousands of people can be killed at a clip, in the blink of an eye. Since Hiroshima, the idea of making elaborate arrangements to try to kill a single man seems ludicrous; surely one enemy's death is hardly worth the trouble of unsheathing a sword.

Or perhaps it is.

Perhaps a chance for personal vengeance would defuse some of the tension in the world. Perhaps, properly regulated, a return to the duel would serve a social purpose. Not the blunt and brutal pistol duel, which to modern eyes looks too much like inner-city mayhem, but the aerobic and elegant duel with blades. Under supervision, it need cause no more bloodshed than such battles in twentieth-century France, or considerably fewer than we inflict on each other with road rage.

Only a handful of people today can wield a rapier, but with fencing promoted as sport, exercise, and manly preparedness, their numbers would swell. The duel would recover its old-time glamour as the newspapers sent reporters to cover the conflicts and celebrity ensued. Politicians would save untold sums of money by facing each other at the appointed place instead of buying television time to trade insults.

Millions of Americans toil daily on boring treadmills and rowing machines in the name of fitness. Fencing is surely more fun than lifting weights, promoting grace and balance as well as muscle; let the gyms install fencing instructors. A population properly versed in the skill might find fresh outlets for hostility and new uses for the stubbornly lingering testosterone.

In October of 2002, when America's relations with Iraq were sliding quickly toward war, the Iraqi vice president suggested settling the conflict with a double duel: "A president against a president and vice-president against vice-president, and a duel takes place, if they are serious, and in this way we are saving the American and the Iraqi people."

He seemed to be in earnest, and there were those who thought it might be a humane and inexpensive solution, but neither of the challenged Americans replied.

Still, it was a thought.

BIBLIOGRAPHY

Baldrick, Robert. *The Duel: A History of Duelling.* City: Spring Books, 1965.

Billacois, François. *The Duel: Its Rise and Fall in Early Modern France.* Trans. Trista Selous. New Haven: Yale University Press, 1990.

Burton, Captain Sir Richard F. *Book of the Sword, The.* New York: Dover, 1989.

———. *The Sentiment of the Sword.* London, 1911.

Carpenter, Frank G. *Carp's Washington.* New York: McGraw-Hill, 1960.

Cocran, Hamilton. *Noted American Duels and Hostile Encounters*. Philadelphia: Chilton Books, 1963.

Dabney, Virginius. *Pistols and Pointed Pens: The Dueling Affairs of Old Virginia*. Chapel Hill, NC: Algonquin Books, 1987.

Eaton, Clement. *Jefferson Davis*. New York: Free Press, 1977.

Freeman, Joanne B. *Affairs of Honor: National Politics in the New Republic*. New Haven: Yale University Press, 2002.

————. "Dueling as Politics: Reinterpreting the Burr-Hamilton Duel." *William and Mary Quarterly*, April 1996.

Funcken, Liliane and Fred. *The Age of Chivalry*. Upper Saddle River, NJ: Prentice Hall, 1983.

Gamble, Thomas. *Savannah Duels & Duellists, 1733–1897*. Savannah, Georgia: Oglethorpe Press, 1997 [1923].

Greenberg, Kenneth S. *Honor & Slavery*. Princeton: Princeton University Press, 1996.

Halliday, Hugh A. *Murder Among Gentlemen: A History of Duelling in Canada*. Toronto: Robin Brass Studio, 1999.

Hoffman, Andrew. *Inventing Mark Twain: The Lives of Samuel Langhorne Clemens*. New York: William Morrow, 1997.

Holland, Barbara. "Bang Bang You're Dead." *Smithsonian*, October 1997.

Kane, Harnett T. *Gentlemen, Swords and Pistols*. New York: William Morrow, 1951.

Kelly, James. *"That Damn'd Thing Called Honour": Duelling in Ireland, 1570–1860*. Cork, Ireland: Cork University Press, 1995.

Kelvin, Martin. *Collecting Antique Firearms*. London: Stanley Paul, 1987.

Kiernan, V. G. *The Duel in European History: Honour and the Reign of Aristocracy*. Oxford: Oxford University Press, 1986.

Martinez, Raymond J., and Jack D. L. Holmes. *New Orleans Facts and Legends*. New Orleans: Hope Publications, n.d.

McAleer, Kevin. *Dueling: The Cult of Honor in Fin-de-Siècle Germany*. Princeton: Princeton University Press, 1994.

McCarty, Clara S. *Duels in Virginia and Nearby Bladensburg*. Richmond, VA: Dietz Press, 1976.

Melville, Lewis, and Reginald Hargreaves. *Famous Duels and Assassinations*. New York: J. H. Sears, 1974 [1929].

Saxon, Lyle. *Fabulous New Orleans*. Gretna, LA: Pelican, 1988 [1928].

Scott, Sir Walter. *Manners, Customs, and History of the Highlanders of Scotland*. New York: Barnes & Noble, 1993.

Seitz, Don C. *Famous American Duels*. Freeport, NY: Books for Libraries, 1966 [1929].

Stater, Victor. *Duke Hamilton Is Dead! A Story of Aristocratic Life and Death in Stuart Britain*. New York: Hill and Wang, 1999.

Steward, Dick. *Duels and the Roots of Violence in Missouri*. Columbia: University of Missouri Press, 2000.

Troyat, Henri. *Pushkin*. Trans. Nancy Amphoux. Garden City, NY: Doubleday, 1970.

Williams, Jack K. *Dueling in the Old South: Vignettes of Social History*. College Station: Texas A & M University Press, 1980.

INDEX

A NOTE ON THE AUTHOR

Barbara Holland is the author of thirteen books, most recently
Hail to the Chiefs—a BookSense pick—and *They Went Whistling.*
She lives in Virginia's Blue Ridge Mountains.

A NOTE ON THE TYPE

This old-style face is named after the Frenchman Robert Granjon, a sixteenth-century letter cutter whose italic types have often been used with the romans of Claude Garamond. The origins of this face, like those of Garamond, lie in the late-fifteenth-century types used by Aldus Manutius in Italy.